Writing Postindustrial Places

Exploring the relationship between postindustrial writing and developments in energy production, manufacturing, and agriculture, Michael J. Salvo shows how technological and industrial innovation relies on communicative and organizational suppleness. Through representative case studies, Salvo demonstrates the ways in which technical communicators formulate opportunities that link resources with need. His book is a supple articulation of the opportunities and pitfalls that come with great change.

Michael J. Salvo is Associate Professor of English and director of Professional Writing at Purdue University.

Routledge Studies in Technical Communication,
Rhetoric, and Culture
Series Editors: Miles A. Kimball and Charles H. Sides

For a full list of titles in this series, please visit www.routledge.com.

This series promotes innovative, interdisciplinary research in the theory and practice of technical communication, broadly conceived as including business, scientific, and health communication. Technical communication has an extensive impact on our world and our lives, yet the venues for long-format research in the field are few. This series serves as an outlet for scholars engaged with the theoretical, practical, rhetorical, and cultural implications of this burgeoning field. The editor welcomes proposals for book-length studies and edited collections involving qualitative and quantitative research and theoretical inquiry into technical communication and associated fields and topics, including user-centered design; information design; intercultural communication; risk communication; new media; social media; visual communication and rhetoric; disability/accessibility issues; communication ethics; health communication; applied rhetoric; and the history and current practice of technical, business, and scientific communication.

Writing Postindustrial Places
Technoculture amid the Cornfields

Michael J. Salvo

Routledge
Taylor & Francis Group

LONDON AND NEW YORK

First published 2018 by Routledge

2 Park Square, Milton Park, Abingdon, Oxfordshire OX14 4RN

52 Vanderbilt Avenue, New York, NY 10017

Routledge is an imprint of the Taylor & Francis Group, an informa business

First issued in paperback 2019

British Library Cataloguing-in-Publication Data
A catalogue record for this book is available from the British Library

Library of Congress Cataloging-in-Publication Data
CIP data has been applied for.

ISBN: 978-1-4724-1048-1 (hbk)
ISBN: 978-0-367-88235-8 (pbk)

Typeset in Sabon
by codeMantra

For Matthew Won Salvo
11 minutes
August 31, 2012

Contents

Acknowledgments

I am always amazed when I ask for peoples' time and they give it to me. This book simply would not exist if not for the willing participation of people and the institutions for which they work and which they constitute: Denise Coogan and Mike Mattingly of Subaru of Indiana Automotive; Sophia Fisher, Josh Van Deylen, Prof. Alvin Compaan, and Carl Salupo; Dennis McKee; Chris Krohn and the Braun Corporation; Pat Sheehan and Chuck Carrel, Fort Wayne Metals; and Jason Hodde and Perry Guine at Cook BioTech in West Lafayette, as well as all those people who asked to remain anonymous. Our economy, our workplaces, and our futures are in good hands.

Miles Kimball wove important ideas into this new book series. I am grateful to him first for his vision, as well as for his encouragement and support. Felisa Salvago-Keyes was patient and supportive; Assunta Petrone sharp-eyed and generous. Ann Donahue was understanding and encouraging. Writing in Digital Environments hosted my visit to Michigan State University, and Michael Knievel hosted a generative meeting at the University of Wyoming.

I am grateful for my Purdue colleagues: Patricia Sullivan who reminded me of the importance of making stuff, Jenny Bay, Thomas Rickert, and Samantha Blackmon. I also am grateful for the support of the English Department's Faculty Research fund that supported trips to Michigan and Ohio.

My newest colleagues helped me knit ideas together: Charlotte Hyde, Adam Strantz, Ehren Pflugfelder, Jeff Bacha, Adam Pope. Fernando Sanchez, Don Unger, Caitlan Spronk, Mark Hannah, Julie Staggers, Enrique Reynoso, and Joy Santee always listened. Jeffrey Gerding, John Sherrill, Devon Cook, Michelle McMullin, and Allegra Smith are the newest nodes in my network.

Finally, to my partner Tammy Conard-Salvo, who lived with these ideas long before they were on paper, and then read them in different versions, always making them better. Thank you for so much more.

Much of the value in these words emerges from all these thoughtful people. The mistakes, missteps, and problems are of my making.

Introduction

What does it mean to write a postindustrial place?

This book supports those interested in technical communication and rhetoric to take advantage of the opportunities inherent in the postindustrial world. Advanced materials, next-generation manufacturing, clean energy, agricultural production—all require rhetorical as well as technological interventions. Numerous opportunities change the image of the rustbelt of the industrial Midwestern United States into the postindustrial heartland, and I have had the privilege of learning about workplaces and organizations leading the revitalization of manufacturing and of tracing global connections that bring prospects for meaningful high-technology work. But as the next chapters assert, this impression is not assured. While many exciting, groundbreaking, and truly world-class organizations that rely upon long-lasting traditions have made this region strong in the past, and these organizations are the raw materials from which a bright future can be forged, that future must still be made. Imagination and creativity can reconfigure what exists in nascent form into what is needed. The source of that innovation drives this study. It comes from everywhere in an organization and the context surrounding it. The challenge is creating an institution made to absorb and improve as it transforms.

This project began in Boston many years ago. I had left West Texas with what was then a brand-new degree at Texas Tech, Technical Communication and Rhetoric, and I had been working in Boston, Massachusetts, for three years. The economic downturn that followed the terrorist attacks on New York and Washington, DC, had shuttered a number of the high-technology industries where I had made research contacts along Route 128 west of downtown Boston in the so-called "silicon suburbs." In the economic downturn following 9/11, not only did I lose my contacts, but many of the firms I had been working with simply disappeared. Because of the nature of these firms, I sometimes had inaccurate phone numbers or email contacts that no longer worked, perhaps where contacts had moved on to other positions. Perhaps a contact had been laid off; perhaps they had doubled their salary through promotion. Or perhaps they had cashed in their newly vested stock options and, as in one case, moved to Norway.

More than one call ended with a machine-generated operator's voice telling me that not only the extension but also the entire firm's phone number bank had been disconnected. Entire organizations were being eliminated and no trace remained. There were many "for rent" signs visible from the highway along Route 128, and those signs represented a true desperation as an entire economic sector of the economy sputtered. Doug Henwood (2003) narrates the aftermath of this boom-and-bust cycle admirably, and I will leave that story to him to tell. For my story, this bust meant that many of my digital-economy contacts and research sites were gone, and I was starting from scratch.

Having come of age during the dawn of the internet, I thought I understood the high-tech creative economy, and I enjoyed mentoring students who were getting snapped up as professionals in emerging fields of information design, user experience engineering, usability, and information architecture. The technology, and the jobs supporting high-technology industry, morphed too quickly to build specific programs to address their swiftly shifting needs, and education was under considerable pressure to accommodate new digital technologies and the pace they bring. Now, graduates of the professional writing program I direct are joining gaming firms as storyline consistency experts and user research experts, working as social media experts for national and international journalism companies, and as communication logistics analysts: job titles I could not and would not have guessed when they began their studies. It is exciting and unnerving both to know that the future is both liquid and somewhat unpredictable yet built on historical patterns and planning. Neal Stephenson famously said, at the dawn of the internet age, "The future is already here—it's just not very evenly distributed." My findings presented in this book are consistent with this observation, but I go further to argue that educators can (and *should*, indeed, *must*) reconfigure ourselves to help our students prepare not for existing jobs but to recognize the elements of what my colleague Patricia Sullivan asserted is "the constant of change" in which not just jobs but work itself is being redefined. In this postindustrial age, technical and professional writers become increasingly valued and valuable, as technorhetorial work achieves so many promises of the postindustrial age.

As I moved from one research and development heart in Boston to another in Lafayette, Indiana, I was at first shocked by the differences, but Indiana is no less high-technology or future-oriented than Boston's silicon suburbs. It's just interested in the future of different technologies, such as manufacturing processes and materials, in automation, in robotics, in technologies of flight and of space exploration, as well as in the future of agriculture and farming technology. I now live in a research and development cluster centered at Purdue University which, as a land-, sea-, and space-grant institution, has varied interests and seeks to cross-pollinate fields by transferring ideas from one realm of knowledge into others. It is a world that was unknown to me. And after working so long with ephemeral digits and virtual worlds, with people building online and web-based services, the turn to studying the making of tangible *stuff*[1] was refreshing, even intoxicating. What has become clear to me is that every industry now is a high-technology company. Every workplace needs experts in communicating and connecting—designing—communication and knowledge-making practices both inside and outside the organization. While there may be a high-technology sector to the overall economy, there simply is not much sense to discussing separate digital and manufacturing economies. The boundaries have become fuzzy. Indeed, these sectors have much to learn from each other.

Early in this transition to studying manufacturing, I was invited to visit the Braun Corporation in Winamac, Indiana, where I was struck by this small company's unique place in auto manufacturing and accessibility. Unlike companies that have built from-scratch products to assist people with mobility constraints, Braun customizes after-market minivans and SUVs to meet user-specific needs of differently abled bodies. An entire study can be done at the site of accessibility and design; Graham Pullin's *Design Meets Disability* (2011) is an excellent introduction that interconnects an activist position with industrial design, as Dolmage (2016) traces the language of disability and differently abled bodies.

By using another industrial product and relying on partnerships with other manufacturers and institutions, Braun exemplifies the postindustrial. According to Bell's (1973) forecasting, there are three major components to a postindustrial society, all of which have come true to a greater or lesser extent and can be seen, to some extent, in Braun: one, a shift from manufacturing to services; two, the centrality of new science-based industries; and three, the rise of new technical elites and the advent of a new principle of stratification. It seems beside the point to debate whether these changes are good or bad. They are disruptive and have been ongoing for quite a long time.

Unlike companies that have built from-scratch products to assist people with mobility constraints, Braun specializes by customizing after-market minivans that meet user-specific needs of differently abled bodies. At the assembly facility in Winamac, I first articulated the phrase *Technoculture Amid the Cornfields*.[2] This production facility, a high-tech factory set in rural farmland, seemed an unlikely location for a globally competitive firm. Yet I recognized my own bias in assuming that the setting would somehow preclude high-technology work. Braun lifts and vehicles were being prepared for shipment to Asia, Africa, Europe, South America, and Australia from this shipping dock at a small manufacturing facility in Winamac, Indiana. As I would find out, Braun resides at the edge of the automotive cluster of institutions centered in Detroit as well as on the edge of the medical cluster centered in Indianapolis—perfectly placed to participate in global economic trade. Enrico Moretti's *The New Geography of Jobs* (2012) articulates this notion of clustering and allows the first glimpse of the importance of place in the network, of gathering related industries together around research and development hubs, around which interwoven organizations intersect skills, expertise, and best practices in sustainable and mutually supporting relationships. Out in the cornfields, I was just beginning to recognize the networks in which Braun was participating, dispelling my own assumption that industrial meant urban.

In 1971, David Ward in *Cities and Immigrants* called the four-state region the East-Midwest. He included four states, Michigan, Illinois, Indiana, Ohio, in this area synonymous in the mid-20th century with industrial production from steel to automobiles and from glass to rubber. Pursuing an understanding of new and emergent work and writing practices, I have restricted my focus to Ward's East-Midwest, and traveled to sites as far north as Ludington, Michigan, west to Decatur, Illinois, east to automobile assembly plants in Youngstown and glass research in Toledo, Ohio. I have traveled all around the state of Indiana, learning about competitive manufacturing concerns, witnessing and narrating processes of globalization situated amid the cornfields.

Indiana's economy, often assumed to be about corn and soybeans, leads the United States in employment in manufacturing. The Economic Policy Institute (EPI) is a self-described "non-partisan think tank created in 1986 to include the needs of low-and middle-income workers in economic policy decisions."[3] The EPI report of 2013[4] asserts that Indiana leads the nation with 491,900 jobs followed by Wisconsin, Iowa, and Michigan. Even after decades of declining employment in manufacturing and production, the EPI report asserts that the sector continues to account for 12 million workers in the United States, or 8.8% of total employment. California employs over 1.2 million of its citizens in manufacturing jobs, while Texas, Ohio, Illinois, Pennsylvania, and Michigan all employ more than half a million Americans in the direct production of manufactured goods. Indiana is seventh overall, and the focus of this book includes 4 of the top 10 manufacturing states. Postindustrial manufacturing testifies that while industrial *production* has not left the United States, it is industrial *employment* that has decreased.

The knowledge-based information sector continues to grow as a percentage of overall economic production, yet has not yet demonstrated the ability to employ the same numbers of workers as the industrial economy. Nowhere is this more evident than in the production of automobiles, which drove American economic development through the mid-20th century, and all the design, materials research, and manufacturing expertise necessary to create automobiles has not disappeared, nor have the clusters of knowledge supporting these communities dissipated.

Automobile know-how from design to manufacturing to insurance to highway design still clusters around Detroit. Another smaller cluster of specialized medical implants and prosthetics gathers around Warsaw, Indiana. The cluster of medical device firms in Warsaw is itself part of a larger constellation of medical research and development centered in Indianapolis, Indiana, and the historically significant firm of Eli Lilly and Company. Braun, like other firms described later in this text, is placed on the edge of two highly specialized clusters, and circumscribe access to local assets. The Braun assembly plant—its factory—is also within an hour's drive of both Purdue University and Notre Dame University. With easy access to train and truck transportation, and to shipping channels through the Great Lakes, there is nearby access to regional and global transportation. One challenge Braun has is attracting well-educated engineers and effective line workers to its rural site. The industrial corridor of Indiana is only an hour north, yet workers from Elkhart, Indiana, are unwilling to look outside their immediate vicinity. Skilled workers are tantalizingly close yet unwilling to commute or relocate for work.

Designing and creating a facility for building and inventing procedures for assembly for customers without legs capable of reaching the gas and brake pedals in an automobile; rearticulating a van with a new steering interface for a customer without the arm strength capable of turning a steering wheel; reassembling a minibus as an accessibility vehicle; even figuring the logistics of transporting any or all of those vehicles from Portage, Indiana, to Doha, Qatar: these technical and design challenges are *tamed*. However, the challenge of convincing a 22-year-old engineer from Purdue or a skilled welder from Elkhart to move to Winamac presents a different kind of problem—one that is layered, complex, and *wicked*.

This concept of wicked and tame problems comes from the 1973 essay titled "Dilemmas in a General Theory of Planning" in which Rittel and Weber distinguish the two. At the time, they asserted there was little available to them for working through layered and complicated social problems. Since then, a broad range of disciplines including rhetoric and technical communication have developed theories to address messy situations. Iterative design, new hybridities, deep recycling, quasi-objects, and respect for local innovations and practices address wicked challenges. These emergent ways of thinking represent innovations first realized in digital workplaces designed to support new ways of working and of seeing the world. For postindustrial manufacturing, these themes recur in the ways in which firms solve problems. Tame problems become routine and present minimal challenge. They require work but do not pose threats to the existence or identity of the organizations taking them on. Wicked problems present existential threats, such as whether manufacturing remains viable and sustainable in a first-world context like the American Midwest. Such problems pose serious challenges to routine work and require resources in research and development.

From workers' perspectives, the impacts of postindustrialization have been increased instability, loss of employment, and general loss of opportunities to work. The ground-level impact has been literal elimination of human labor from the factory floor replaced by automation, robotics, and labor-saving devices of many kinds, all of which remove human beings from the site of work. While Braun's practice may not precisely match Bell's decades-old prognostications, the forecast is potently accurate in other ways. Old orders of worker power and influence in the workplace have changed, resulting in "new principles of stratification" in the form of new management philosophies as well as a more active back office where engineers and design professionals get paid more than assembly line workers. The Winamac plant uses finished products—automobiles—as the raw ingredients for building its highly specialized products. These customized vans have a worldwide market based on service in the form of accessible design. Industrial production has not disappeared from the postindustrial, but rather human labor has been removed from industrial processes, mimicking the 19th-century removal of labor from agricultural processes.

Nowhere is this shift more evident than the steel mills of northwest Indiana, northwest of Winamac. Gary, Indiana, produces similar amounts of steel as it produced in the 1960s, and the steel produced is of a higher quality. However, it employs 10% of the workers it once had in direct manufacturing. According to Bureau of Labor statistics, "Over the past 25–30 years, steel producers have, in some cases, reduced the number of work-hours required to produce a ton of steel by 90%."[5] Employment shrinkage has been occurring consistently in "material moving and production" while other industrial occupations are decreasingly more slowly, maintaining numbers, or modestly increasing: millwrights, industrial machinery mechanics, electricians, and computer controls for machine tools.[6] Meanwhile, new employment for engineers, chemists, computer specialists, metallurgical engineers, industrial engineers, mechanical engineers, environmental engineers, accountants, sales agents, various managers, and administrative and clerical workers are all projected to continue to increase in number in steel production in the United States for the foreseeable future.

The *Occupational Handbook* of the Federal Government's Bureau of Labor Statistics continues to forecast strong growth for technical writers and communicators through 2022 and beyond representing "above average" job growth.[7] Yet the Society for Technical Communication (STC) reports significant decreases in paid membership, dropping from "20,000 to 14,000 members" from "2000 to 2007"[8] and currently reports "over 6,000" members, a 60% decrease from its high.[9] Why are paid professional memberships dropping in a healthy job market? Tom Johnson, author of the *I'd Rather be Writing* blog, attributes it to a number of factors, among them a lack of excitement and passion practitioners feel for the profession, "After work, they want to relax, enjoy life, escape the drudgery of click-this, select-that, and so on. Technical communication is not a passion; it's a paycheck." However much I wish to disagree that the work does not or cannot sustain passionate engagement, there does seem a disconnect between what the work of Technical and Professional Communication (TPC) has been and what careers are possible with preparation in rhetoric and technology. STC appears to represent a population of workers nervous about their status as professionals, particularly after the Great Recession of 2008, who are unsure about their role as documentation specialists and who wish for the return of accustomed roles and levels of remuneration. In other words, they face "The Ubiquity Paradox," where digital technologies are no longer disruptive but have become mundane. Robert Johnson's argument supports discussion of a range of potential redefinitions of the field. Of particular interest is the portability practices developed for an historical moment when software and hardware documentation was the main employment generator in the sector. What might documentation look like in an advanced manufacturing facility like Braun? Do minimalist documentation practices transfer from software to clean energy production? Are there applications for agile practices appropriate for next-generation automobile manufacturing? Smaller task teams, outsourcing businesses, and articulating new and emergent opportunities represent a possible future. Silicon Valley makes its biggest contributions to innovation and seeks to move beyond internet businesses—the Valley is creating innovations broadly applicable to business practices that increase company profitability, job satisfaction, and the redefinition of meaningful work.

After three decades of digital artifact invention and creating new practices and technologies, workplace communication practices are coalescing around new digital standards and technologies. In industries as varied as insurance, education, transportation, mining, and medicine, work is being mediated through nearly identical interfaces. While the work accomplished varies widely, the tools of these sites are largely mediated by the same digital communication technologies. The Macintosh/PC wars are relics of the 20th century, replaced by liquid boundaries where users flit between interfaces to accomplish their work, embedded in technological environments in which attention shifts to the interfaces where things are getting done.

Full-time jobs creating routine documentation in large organizations no longer define technical communication work. The field has been articulating new and emerging opportunities in symbolic-analytical work, requiring a corresponding shift away from a narrow understanding of technical communication as scribal work in support of digital computing technology. Instead, user experience designers, broadly trained in user-centered theory and iterative design, guide the professional communication of subject matter experts. It is simultaneously a shift away from an industrial age definition and a return toward rhetorical action—professional, technical, and scientific communication in the postindustrial high-technology workplace. The meaning of work remains transitional.

As I found when visiting the plant in Winamac, Braun's management philosophy is decidedly industrial in structure and practice.[10] The assembly lines remain dominated by workers who brought with them an older sense of what it means to work: sweat and toil leading to physical exhaustion at the end of an honest day. While the engineering and design workstations had high-end computers and high-speed internet, digital communication—lifeblood of the networked economy—was discouraged. The label postindustrial fits Braun yet so many aspects of industrial-age work organizations and relationships continue to accurately describe the organization. While Braun epitomizes the postindustrial in many ways it remains industrial, almost traditional, in others, further exemplifying the transitional definition of work and the redefinition of activities that merit reward.

Chapter overviews

I have had the privilege to visit dozens of workplaces that fit the definition of emergent postindustrial hybrids that meld the innovations of the high-technology digital workplace with the knowledge of industrial manufacturing. Some of these places represent completely new ways of working, revealing innovations in need of new ways of creating and then sustaining institutions. Others remix existing practices in novel ways that challenge the people who inhabit these workplaces to create new relationships and definitions for their work and, ultimately, their identities. For this study, I have chosen the most revealing and most interesting for readers who share an interest in what Robert Johnson calls the techno-rhetor. I also use TPC as shorthand for Technical and Professional Communicator. Johnson's techno-rhetor is a more generalist title, used for anyone displaying rhetorical awareness in a variety of high-technology environments, where TPCs are more self-aware and often have formal preparation and/or education. I use these monikers in this study not to confuse but to illustrate core competencies William Hart-Davidson linked together in his important article from 2001, as well as to draw attention to rhetorical capabilities that may be more common elements of what Kimball (2016) asserts is a "golden age" of widespread technical communication in culture.

This chapter introduces the Braun Corporation in Winamac, Indiana, placing it within networks of automotive manufacturing, medical devices, and advanced materials research. This chapter presents Braun as a multifaceted site, mapping the firm geographically as well as culturally (see Sullivan and Porter, 1997), while also constructing the firm as a representative example of a postindustrial site. Because Braun has implemented some new practices, yet not others, it remains transitional and inhabits the space between the theoretical endpoints of industrial and postindustrial. This oscillation between how the site both is and is not postindustrial is what makes it a valuable representative anecdote, related to but different from a case (see Burke, 1941; Damousi et al., 2015).

These examples of people embedded in their working context cannot pretend to offer a comprehensive vision of the future of work. Rather, I strive to offer compelling and powerful examples of technorhetorical work as a future and emergent form of technical communication. Manufacturing work may directly employ fewer people than at the height of the industrial age, but building things, producing cleaner energy for home and business use, and creating new agricultural/industrial hybrids will continue to drive economic activity in the "East-Midwest." This region that David Ward ascribed as a central industrial region of the United States is dense with legacy networks of goods and skills that, with strategic nurturing and re-investment, become the postindustrial Midwest. But I return to the industrial inheritance as a unique strength that animates the region's future as much as it populates its past. Indiana, Ohio, Michigan, and Illinois are bound together by history as well as geography. My focus is clearly my own specialty of technical and professional communication, but engineers, managers, and entrepreneurs can leverage the insights of the analysis and understand both the advantages and challenges the industrial legacy provides the region. Each site reveals its postindustrial nature in its reliance on design to move from older practices to meet new challenges, wedding innovations developed in Silicon Valley and other centers of innovation, to homegrown invention. Existing relationships are rearticulated in the network to reveal deeper, recyclable skillsets.

Awareness of and response to the impacts of these global networks define sustainability of work. It is no longer enough to specialize, do a task, and do it well. Rather, the task needs to be contextualized—articulated—within the organization's networked relationships. Here, at each site, something new and valuable happens. Iterative and user-centered design, zero landfill, re-articulated and unbound agriculture, deep skillset recycling, pumped storage and cleaner energy, and recognizing the power of local innovation: each chapter emerges from specific places with histories of manufacturing, and each offers disruptive and attendant technologies to offer global networks of the postindustrial economy. These sites were chosen specifically because they represent innovation that requires effective articulation for them to become viable elsewhere—for their value to be seen beyond their local context of development and be both understood and valued—in larger networks. They require technorhetorical intervention to be viable. These are not routine documentation and manual writing jobs, which I describe as 20th-century jobs, not because they are not important, but because their context of reward and value is fading. Worksites value emergent Technical and Professional Communication (TPC) work where breakthrough products and services develop, and they require rhetorical intervention to make their contribution widely understood.

Set at the Subaru of Indiana plant in Lafayette, Indiana, Chapter 2 narrates Subaru's commitment to recycling, zero landfill impact, and plans for carbon neutrality. The concept of Kaizen, only mentioned here in the introduction, is described in detail, with extended comparison of the current situation of manufacturing and automation in the automobile industry. Through Kaizen,[11] Subaru profits from its organization structure that welcomes constructive criticism and invites alternative ideas for improving its practices from all areas of its workforce. Not without its controversial elements, this integration of constant improvement is an institutionalization of iterative design. The chapter draws a clear distinction between design used for its own sake, a disruptive application of problematic genius design, insisting instead on the cyclical application of iterations of design. Iterative design distinguishes Subaru from its American automotive manufacturing peers. From its location in Lafayette, Indiana, the manufacturer ships automobiles around the globe, and the new seven-seater design will only be built at this plant and shipped globally.

Chapter 3 moves the study's focus west to the ADM plant at Decatur, Illinois. The agricultural foundation of the Midwest cannot be ignored, and part of the innovation represented in Decatur blurs boundaries between agricultural and industrial products. So much know-how produces the next generation of farm-sourced raw materials that will make their way into both agricultural and industrial products. The artifact, the greenhouse, at the center of Chapter 3 is not possible without the hybrid knowledge of materials manufacturing coming together with technologies and practices of next-generation agricultural production. ADM is practicing industrial-agricultural hybrid manufacturing that represents a prominent economic engine driving central Illinois, from which agricultural products are distributed around the world.

Chapter 4 describes an emergent cluster of photovoltaic glass technology centered on the research and development hub of Toledo, Ohio. Beginning in the middle 20th century, Toledo became an important participant in the Detroit-centered American automobile manufacturing industry. Sometimes referred to as Glass City, Toledo's specialty has been etched into its identity first as a supplier of tempered automobile glass and then later as a production and research hub for fiberglass. That specialty has given glass-related research a special place at the University of Toledo's Launchpad Incubation space that houses the Northwest Ohio Solar Hub (the Hub), the Wright Center for Photovoltaics Innovation and Commercialization, and Clean Energy Alliance of Ohio. Automotive glass defined Toledo's mid-20th-century rise to industrial prominence, with fiberglass for both insulation and lightweight construction defining its late 20th-century identity. The early 21st century is already defined as high-technology glass research and manufacturing. Glass research and commercialization drive Toledo today, with particular emphasis on photovoltaic glass used in solar electricity technology as well as specialized toughened glass used in handheld computing and telecommunications devices. Today, Toledo is driven by research in solar energy and smartphone manufacturing. As important as glass products have been to Toledo's growth, today, the processes of mass manufacture are perfected and communicated worldwide as information products: shipping not the photovoltaic cells but the knowledge necessary to manufacture solar panels reliably and inexpensively around the globe.

Chapter 5 focuses on a small town that hosts a large energy storage site. Ludington, Michigan, is an old mining and lumber town that rose to prominence around its harbor through which raw materials were shipped to factories in larger southern cities around the Great Lakes. Detroit, on the southeast coast of Michigan and bordering Lake Erie, defines the eastern edge of the central population center of the state, west to Ann Arbor and north to Dearborn and Flint, Lansing, Battle Creek, and Kalamazoo, northwest to Grand Rapids and Holland, northward to Cadillac. This is Michigan's automotive manufacturing belt. Today, the challenge is supplying reasonably priced, plentiful electricity to millions of people. Ludington is part of the energy production network, located farther north than the population centers on the northwest coast of the state. Its pumped storage station is undergoing a billion-dollar maintenance, upgrade, and rehabilitation investment, and it remains a symbol of the never-realized potential for production of nuclear energy in the postindustrial Midwest. Ludington's pumped storage plant is described as a Latourian quasi-object in Chapter 5 that supports discussion not just of the design of the physical plant and its pump generators, but also of the larger cultural networks in which these electricity generation technologies and clean energy become points for discussion and inform the design of similar facilities in China, Scotland, and elsewhere. The chapter concludes with investigation of innovation regulation.

Chapter 6 returns the analysis to Indiana and the smaller innovative organizations surrounding the research and development hub of Lafayette, Indiana, and Purdue University. In order to be valued beyond the sites' immediate surroundings, each site's technological and institutional innovations have to be articulated in larger regional, national, and global networks. Local communities have to be recognized as producing distinctive skills and knowledge that can be traded in globally competitive markets. Additionally, recognizing the knowledge and skills clusters in which they participate reveals unique regional assets these networks can draw upon and leverage to add further value to their products and services, following the network and geography work of Marsh (2012) and Moretti (2012), as well as the work in networks and ecologies in rhetoric and TPC research.

Rhetoric: kairos, metis, technê, attunement

Each chapter illustrates rhetorical principles, but three—kairos, metis, and technê—have received renewed scholarly attention from the late 20th century and into the new millennium. The literature articulating each is growing. Thomas Rickert's (2013) use of attunement brings these rhetorical principles together in a cultural-rhetorical binding in the chorus, a return to ancient dramatistic practice (Blakesley, 2002), only, the stage of rhetoric is culture and the chorus sings about techno-cultural decision making: how do stakeholders come to their beliefs and agents act in dynamic arenas requiring action? And how are decision-makers held accountable for their choices? While a renewed interest in each element names frontiers in rhetorical research, these concepts by no means exhaust the rhetorical toolbox.

Each chapter concludes with a summarizing statement given in the voice of the chorus, addressing cultural attunements. Boundaries between the domains of each rhetorical element can become unclear in practice as they describe dynamically churning responses to utterances, text, and contexts organizations produce. In broad strokes, kairos, metis, and technê define opportunity for rhetorical activity in these domestic postindustrial places.

In Chapter 2, at Subaru, kairos is foregrounded because of the way it creates organizational context for communicating across unequal power relationships. Iterative design, in the form of the always improving approach of Kaizen, puts a structure for communicating from the assembly floor to managers' desks, and more importantly, these communications demand the attention of decision-makers. The chapter presents Deming's kairotic presentation of a new management philosophy to Japanese stakeholders in the aftermath of the World War II, a philosophy that has challenged American automobile manufacturing.

It is a form of cunning to articulate effective responses to rhetorical moments when they arrive. Subaru has put in place a conduit for information to flow from those with direct knowledge to those creating applications of that knowledge. It is a literalization of kairos, and transitions to metis—not waiting for the opportune time, but rather creating opportunities for intervention and action by stakeholders. Such cunning is illustrated at length by the plant manager's actions at ADM in Chapter 3: taking advantage of the organization's need for a public relations victory, one individual led a heroic effort to offer a new narrative. Presenting a new face to the public, the plant manager navigated the competing demands of the local organization, the technical requirements of aquaponics, and the challenges of creating new markets for vegetables and fish produced in the Midwest, in winter. Only by recognizing the competing interests and complex variables that make up the cultural context can the postindustrial rhetor succeed.

Chapter 4 illustrates the ecology of expertise in Toledo, Ohio, around the manufacturing of glass, which implicates rhetorical expertise in ecological contexts. It is Chapter 5 that more strongly argues for the power of technê and its application in the context of an emergent technology. Ludington, Michigan's, pumped storage plant is part of an older system of electricity with plutonium nuclear energy production at its heart. Rearticulated for a clean-energy future of intermittent power sources like wind, solar, and hydropower, technologies are improving efficiencies and realizing new applications by utilizing advanced materials, next-generation lubricants, and emergent metering for a smart grid. All these technologies are implicated in an alternative nuclear future, pitting proven plutonium fuel against a new thorium design.

Finally, the conclusion brings the argument back to these key rhetorical principles and connects Rickert's attunements explicitly with the chorus as the voice of postindustrial culture. Technorhetoric finds a rich ground for tracing emergent technologies, and writing a future for postindustrial work.

Notes

1 Later in the study, I reference both Nicholas Negroponte in *Being Digital* (1995) who traces the early internet age using the distinction between atoms and bits, while Lanham, a decade later (2006) distinguishes *stuff* from *fluff*. I do not go so far as to call virtual work fluff—far from it—yet there is no better word I could find to describe my transition from the virtual to the real. Hence my use of *stuff* here, and I hope the specialist reader will indulge the rhetorical flourish designed to orient new readers to the context of the study.
2 See Salvo et al. (2007).
3 The EPI receives a majority of its funding through grants provided by non-governmental foundations. Its next largest funding source is labor unions. www.epi.org/about/.
4 www.epi.org/publication/the-manufacturing-footprint-and-the-importance-of-u-s-manufacturing-jobs/. This is the most recent report available at the time of writing this introduction.
5 Bernan, *Career Guide to Industries*, 2008–2009. Government Printing Office, 2008.
6 *Occupational Outlook Handbook*, Bureau of Labor Statistics: www.bls.gov/ooh/.
7 www.bls.gov/careeroutlook/2015/article/creative-careers.htm.
8 http://idratherbewriting.com/2007/05/24/the-death-of-associations-declining-stc-statistics-prompt-innovation-realigning-of-value/.
9 Wikipedia: https://en.wikipedia.org/wiki/Society_for_Technical_Communication retrieved April 21, 2016. 6,000 members in 2016 is actually a reported increase from the terrible decline to under 4,000 members I had reported to

me in a private conversation, but I will simply state that the Wikipedia entry shows a decline from 20,000 to 6,000 members at the start of the 21st century.

10 For a fuller examination of Braun as worksite, see Chapter 5, as well as Salvo, Michael, Zoetewey, M, and Agena, Kate. "A Case of Exhaustive Documentation: Re-centering System-Oriented Organizations Around User Need" *Technical Communication*, 54:1, 2007.

11 Explained in detail in Chapter 2, Kaizen originated in the United States, was transported to Japan, and then reappears in US manufacturing.

1 Writing working futures

Braun Automotive in Winamac, Indiana, is a representative example of a postindustrial workplace. A globally competitive manufacturer of accessible vehicles, Braun first inspired the idea embedded in the subtitle. What was this company, with sales in Azerbaijan, Dubai, Shanghai, and Zimbabwe, doing along a state highway in a farming town in north-central Indiana? What made this old farmstead, a hundred miles from Chicago, host to a world-class design location and manufacturing hub? This chapter begins by drawing disparate observations into a more coherent vision of the postindustrial future of technical and professional writing. While it is ultimately inaccurate to position the industrial and postindustrial ages as opposites, it is a convenient fiction to begin explaining complex interrelated ideas.

If the industrial age used virgin raw materials, dumped refuse in landfills, utilized a paper-based communication system in top-down hierarchical organizations designed to be stable and long-standing because labor was cheap, automation and mechanization expensive, skies blue, and the environment capable of absorbing a seemingly infinite stream of waste, then the postindustrial reuses, remixes, and rearticulates the outputs of other processes, seeking zero impact on landfills through recycling and reusability, utilizes digital information and statistical analysis to inform agents in flattened network organizations that are pulled together when needed and dispersed when appropriate, and articulates the organization as concerned for the environment and its consumers. What it means to contrast a simple dichotomous industrial-postindustrial binary is by no means clear. Although the transition to deindustrialization has been ongoing for three or four decades, there is no clear line marking the end of the industrial era and the emergence of the postindustrial.

The first caveat in opposing the industrial to the postindustrial is that somehow industrial production no longer takes place. While far less human engagement with industrial production takes place in the privileged first world, factories still produce merchandise, waste, and parts. Richer communities, here exemplified by the postindustrial Midwest, outsource dirtier, more polluting processes to less developed and less well-regulated regions of the world. Automation and mechanization allow higher paid workers to avoid more dangerous and poisonous work. The postindustrial, called deindustrialization in the United Kingdom, is a first-world privilege in which the risks of industrial production are displaced elsewhere.

Braun automotive is located in Winamac, Indiana. The plant sits halfway between Cleveland and Chicago, making it part of the iron and steel network emanating from the Great Lakes northern ore fields to smelters and foundries that had historically been located in Cleveland, Pittsburgh, and Gary. It is no surprise to find advanced materials research and engineering in the postindustrial wake of this most industrial of networks.

For instance, Braun's accessibility designs utilized steel for a long time in the structure of their ramps. Steel is a strong and durable but heavy material. These ramps would fold and articulate, creating a wheelchair-accessible ramp and a safe surface that would allow users in their wheelchairs to enter and leave the motor vehicle in spaces consistent with handicapped parking spaces. The heavy ramps required durable, high-powered electric motors that folded and retracted them back into the passenger compartment of the van. To achieve the levels of durability necessary to make Entervans reliable, accessibility partners added steel retractable ramps and heavy-duty motors. These motors also required heavier, larger-capacity batteries to run. Purdue advanced materials engineering faculty have collaborated with Braun, working to create lightweight alloys and carbon composite materials to reduce the load of access ramps, allowing for smaller motors and lighter batteries, and through efficiencies, to deliver overall reductions in manufacturing costs. But the reliance on advanced materials and effective design distinguishes the postindustrial product delivered by Braun from its earlier models. Ultimately, lower cost, more reliable goods, operated more sustainably, have been delivered to the consumer. Braun, through its collaboration with a research and development center at the university, remains ahead of its competition by delivering better designed, more capable solutions to its niche market.

Advanced materials engineering and next-generation manufacturing represent two local growth areas for Purdue's engineering research and define a point of technology transfer from a research and teaching institution to commerce and the business sector. The reciprocal relationship between the university and local business clusters grows out of a tradition of expertise in industrial manufacturing with campus legacies from the Rube Goldberg Design Challenge to the Grand Prix, and in the Morrill Land Grant University tradition. Purdue has a strong legacy of industrial design and production, embodied in its identity as boilermakers of both locomotive engines and industrial steam machines.

It is no accident that Purdue hosts the National Rube Goldberg Machine Competition.[1] I hadn't quite understood why it was hosted here until I started visiting manufacturing plants across the American Midwest. The idea of creating inefficient machines appealed to me, as it apparently appeals to many in the general population, evidenced by a recent popular OK Go! video.[2] I first saw the practical application of the Rube Goldberg building challenge at Subaru-Indiana Automotive. During an assembly-floor tour, I noticed new tires being fed along a track at the top of one wall. The tires then rolled, moved by gravity, over two working assembly lines. They then plunged down, rolling around and around, and disappeared under a third line, emerging a dozen or so feet beyond and getting conveyed upwards again by a belt-driven elevator. I lost their trail for a while as my attention was fixed on robot-led welding assembly, part stamping, seat mounting, engine installation, and windshield fitting, and then four matching tires mounted on rims emerged ready-to-hand to be installed at the four drive axles, this being a Subaru plant and all cars are all-wheel drive and driven by horizontally opposed boxer-type engines. When asked, the tour guide smiled—happy to put this esoteric bit of trivia to use—and told me the tires roll approximately two miles before they are ever installed on a car. So the Rube Goldberg competition is an industrial-age game requiring the kind of systems design skill in high demand in this manufacturing facility design. It matches need with site-specific constraints: where the tires arrive by train, get transferred to a subassembly area, then enter the manufacturing floor and are needed at specific points in the assembly line, and appear as if by magic at the moment they are needed for installation—carrying near-complete automobiles under their own power for the first time. Since then, I have visited numerous manufacturing facilities across the Midwest—car assemblies, agribusiness, small and large companies, energy—new and old.

In a larger context, research in both advanced materials and manufacturing innovation reveals opportunities for leadership, and information reciprocity is likewise represented by the aerospace research park just outside the borders of the academic campus. Nearby, expanding participation in biomedical research reveals the university's engagement with another concentration of postindustrial technology: the pharmaceutical cluster centered at Indianapolis at Eli Lilly and Company. These are one land grant institution's engagement efforts while gesturing toward emergent trends that present opportunities for technocultural engagement. The university serves as a site for knowledge transfer from laboratories and classrooms into commercial research facilities as well as production lines and logistical systems, making tangible the invisible tendrils radiating from campus, weaving them inextricably into the information age's cluster of institutions being intermingled—or, provocatively, *Intertwingled* (Morville, 2014)—university campus, downtown offices, suburban manufacturing plants, rural farms, and data networks.

Besides being part of the steel-producing industrial Midwest, Winamac is at the southwestern edge of the automobile manufacturing cluster which even today remains in Detroit. Braun's specialty in accessible automobiles reveals its geographical placement at the edge of automotive, medical, and research clusters to be strategically important, allowing information to flow from one network to another.

> Harvard Business School has studied more than 800 clusters in some 50 countries. Nearly all have evolved as a result of two basic mechanisms, which are sometimes intertwined: the development of new ideas, and the use of local materials. Warsaw is an example of the first type of cluster, as is a concentration of scientific instruments businesses in Gittingen, Germany, and a group of aircraft makers in Wichita, Kansas. Examples of the second type of cluster, which are in general by far the oldest, include businesses involved in brick-making in East Godavari in India; pulp and paper production in Sweden; and leather footwear around Oporto, Portugal.
>
> Peter Marsh, *The New Industrial Revolution* (p. 165, 2012)

Marsh is writing about the town of Warsaw in northern Indiana, a town of fewer than 15,000 people situated an hour away from Winamac, which hosts three different specialized orthopedic companies. Warsaw, like Winamac, takes advantage of its geography but also co-creates the micro-cluster of which it is part. It is influenced by Indianapolis' biomedical community as well as the metals and engineering supported by the automotive industry. Coupled with the expertise sustained by participating in automobile supply chains through the industrial Midwest, supplying high-value medical equipment to population centers like Chicago, and sustained by inputs of research from the pharmaceutical industry, Winamac, Warsaw, and Fort Wayne have become its own cluster of highly specialized medical metals. Fort Wayne Metals is another firm that will be discussed at length in Chapter 6 that focuses on homegrown innovation, and also takes advantage of this cluster of expertise and co-location. Marsh calls this not just a network but an *ecology* of expertise.

Marilyn Cooper was an early adopter of the metaphor of ecology for writing situations in "The Ecology of Writing" (1986). The metaphor has been influential and continues to impact how writing researchers see the rhetorical situation. Margaret Syverson's *The Wealth of Reality: An Ecology of Composition* (1999) explicitly develops the metaphor, using it to drive her project. Bazerman and Prior articulate their activity system as ecological (2003) while Jenny Edbauer-Rice self-consciously argues for moving from a situational orientation to an ecological one in "Unframing models of public distribution: From rhetorical situation to rhetorical ecologies" (2005) that informs her book-length study of place, *Distant Publics* (2012). While Edbauer-Rice is concerned with development, particularly in East Austin in Texas, the lessons she draws informs this ecologically imbued study of networks of knowledge and communication techniques. For rhetoricians, an ecology of many competing and complementary discourses has replaced the classical understanding of a simpler rhetorical situation, and has multiplied both the numbers of voices speaking in the ecology as well as the requirements of what counts as a viable rhetorical solution to challenges within cultural contexts. The voices haven't multiplied. Instead it is recognition of the voices as valid and valuable, a redefinition of what sources count as credible input. In this way, postindustrial, next-generation manufacturing forms part of the ecology that technical rhetors address and work within. The postindustrial names a bundle of problems, both tame and wicked, that have presented themselves since the late 20th century.

The postindustrial is an epochal shift that will continue to disrupt accustomed human patterns for some time. The shift has already been underway, whether we ascribe to Bell the foresight and say it was already beginning in the 1970s, or took hold firmly in the 1980s with the advent of the personal computer, or perhaps the internet revolution of the 1990s is more representatively postindustrial and disruptive. This study is less interested in definitions than the larger global flows of patterns of labor and trade, addressing the marginally more manageable challenge of articulating writing in the emergent postindustrial workplace. The study is specifically interested in workplace communication rather than academic writing or activist interaction—Edbauer-Rice's *Public Writing*—to address questions of emergent work and communication practices.

Technology, and in particular digital technology, is used to rationalize all these competing forces of change, but my interest and focus lies with the communication technology that supports increasing opportunities for participation. At its core, the role of the technical and professional communicator in the postindustrial age appears to be linking an expert with the right challenge. Put so prosaically, there seems little to worry about. Yet the challenge remains recognizing the form and shape of challenges—and why Selber and Johnson-Eilola optimistically title their 2012 collection *Solving Problems in Technical Communication*. Long before the field can offer solutions, the challenge is recognizing and articulating problems, and then marshaling expertise capable of articulating solutions, or more likely as problems become increasingly challenging and wicked, of putting together communities of learned experts who dedicate their time and energy to both building solutions and remaining engaged with challenges, as Cushman (2014) articulates: not problem *solving* but problem *setting*. The postindustrial is less a problem to be solved than a context in which we live and work, a lifeworld.

This study concentrates on these lifeworlds, focusing on communication in workplaces and on the ways in which information technology and network theory impact industrial production and open new horizons for realizing efficiencies and putting human beings to work. Jeremy Rifkin's *The Third Industrial Revolution* (2011) argues for the importance of coupling the real and the virtual, of making things, and the management of the processes of making. He explicitly links energy production networks and communication networks. In short, Rifkin describes the first wave of the industrial revolution as linking steam power derived first from wood and then coal with telegraph communication, exemplified by the railroad and the first-generation electronic communication network that literally bound the early United States together with copper wire, as it did Europe and, later, India, following the steel network of railroads. Rifkin describes the second wave of industrialization as characterized by coupling oil and other fossil fuels with telephony: real-time conversation technology and mass access to automotive transportation. This time, the network connecting disparate parts of the globe is the highway. The dawn of the second wave is exemplified by highway systems and the literal paving of pathways across nations—the Eisenhower Interstate System in the United States and the Autobahn in Germany. The internet and digital technologies epitomize the end of the second wave, led by metaphoric representation of the "information superhighway." This second age animated the 20th century and, now waning, allowed this latest third wave to emerge. At its heart, the second wave contrasts personal or individual communication with mass broadcast communication, which is not part of Rifkin's analysis but is important in understanding the emplacement of written communication. Rifkin articulates the third wave revolution as bringing the distributed communication network of the internet to energy production, consumption, and distribution. In effect, Rifkin's forecasts assert an age in which the distinctions between consumers and producers are blurred in the realm of energy as well as information, where new and unforeseeable clean renewable sources of power create a peer-to-peer energy production/consumption network. By representing energy and information as a single thing, Rifkin announces the first of many postindustrial hybrids enunciated and explored here, erasing boundaries between two things the industrial age kept distinct.

However, Rifkin remains silent in two areas of interest. The first is his representation of the industrial revolution. For Rifkin, there are distinct waves and phases of industrialization described by their major technologies. The first wave ended a rural farm-focused way of life and people gathered in large cities with urbanization and mechanization characterizing the first wave. The second wave, now ending, is dominated by fossil fuels, steel, and telephony. The third wave will bring what Rifkin describes as a "post-carbon" future. While new energy technologies are at the heart of many of the sites described in this study, it is important to remember that each successive wave of industrialization includes the continued reliance on deemphasized technologies. Steel and a range of metallurgical products—whether at Fort Wayne Metals or Braun automotive, or other sites—remains necessary if obsolete technologies. Fossil fuels may be diminishing in importance and may eventually run out, but they remain important, imperative, even, for the third wave of clean new energy technologies to emerge. Once invented, technologies are rarely abandoned. We continue to derive most of our conventionally produced electricity, whether fired by coal or natural gas for fuel, by steam power. Even nuclear energy produces electricity using steam-age technologies. Ironically, we've never left the steam age. Now we take the technology for granted, and it is no longer the cutting edge of research and development, which is another way of asserting that it is obsolete. Similarly, telephony has not disappeared; we just use it differently. Indeed, wireless technology has ushered in a new age of connectivity through mobile phones, and communication and information have driven the power of this convergence. Further, each successive age of technological and communications innovation has made it possible to remove human labor from industrial production.

The removal of labor from the production of goods has proven most disruptive to our social and political institutions. It remains a wicked problem, difficult to conceive let alone creatively engage, let alone solve. How would one solve a problem in the midst of its being made? Interestingly, there were corresponding shifts in labor from rural to urban and from farm to factory through earlier stages of the industrial revolution. For good or otherwise, wealth accumulates in the hands of the owners of the technologies of production, which in simple Marxist analysis, leads to inequalities of wealth and power and growing instability. Others have trod this well-worn path before me, and it is not the purpose of this volume to address underlying issues of justice, wealth production, or social stability. However, where these issues become culturally important phenomenon, the argument needs to be informed by labor history, formation of unions, and the rise of labor rights through earlier waves of tension between owners, producers, and consumers, or between capital and workers. Language use reflects and constructs the realities of peoples' experience of the emerging economy and its underlying assignment of wealth and value, no matter how symbolic, symbiotic, functional, dysfunctional, or fair it may be to observers at given viewpoints. Suffice it to say, these are complex and layered issues. Postindustrial hybrid products, like accessible vehicles and industrial-agricultural products, also rely on hybrid *thinking*. Andrew Feenberg (1995, 2002), Mikael Hård, and Andrew Jamison (2013) state that to understand multiple facets—different ecological niches—it is necessary to comprehend ongoing change. I am indebted to the insight provided by these and others' analysis. Latour's (in)famous essay "Why Critique Has Run Out of Steam" (2004) ushered in the postcritical with a lovely pun on steam power, and freed those of us arriving after the Frankfort School to be less concerned with the loss of the high culture they longed for and more concerned with the insights into culture their analysis supports.

Not since the Great Depression and the 19th century before that has the United States faced a similar challenge to its underlying social compact. The violence and conflict of 1867–1890, most clearly illustrated by the events of the Great Railroad Strike of 1877, should not be minimized or forgotten, and the terrible working conditions of railroad workers, nonunionized laborers, children and immigrants, and many new, uneducated workers displaced from agricultural employment should not be forgotten. Nor should the challenges of the Great Depression be lost to history. These two periods are of particular importance to recall as we ponder today's challenges because they represent similar economic and social disruption that Rifkin's analysis glosses over. Unclear is whether the third industrial revolution arrives peacefully.

Narratives and engagements with stakeholders make space into place, a process that supports a complex agglomeration of research, leisure, ecological, and social activities into a community. Communities—cultures— are sustained through even more complex relationships, maintained through written, spoken, and technologically mediated communication. Two groups are most strongly impacted. First, professionals will do their work better, and more effectively, by being attuned to rhetorical and cultural aspects of their exertion. These folks are professionals in fields concentrating on specialties other than writing. These engineers, scientists, programmers—technical specialists—spend a great deal of their time communicating, often mediated by digital technologies. The second group—writing professionals—may already be familiar with many of the arguments on the rhetorical side articulating what it is symbolic-analytical workers do. William Hart-Davidson (2001) articulated core competencies for the professional communicator, assertions that have been widely understood and have driven the preparation of writing specialists in the early 21st century. What has resulted are fairly deep case studies of particular workers in specific situations, yet few studies have attempted to describe common aspects of the variety of places and situations of the work of writing and communicating in this complex age of globalization, deindustrialization, and labor insecurity. By concentrating on digital businesses, we have assumed aspects of high-technology workplaces. As the focus shifts to other sectors of the economy, to advanced manufacturing, energy production, and agriculture, what makes a particular workplace information-age, postindustrial, or symbolic-analytic? By treating one location in each chapter and analyzing the ways communication work is being accomplished, a profile emerges of the postindustrial technocultural communication specialist across a range of industries and communities rather than a description of a single worksite or an individual job. This distinguishes this book's approach from those of others. Clay Spinuzzi (2003), Jeff Grabill (2001), Michelle Simmons (2008), and Carol Siri-Johnson (2009) each pursue exhaustive investigations of their own, which reveal numerous details and documents through deep and extended engagement with a single site. Grabill (2007) studies a pair of sites, which allows for comparatives. Deep attentiveness defines the field's early 21st-century workplace research at individual or paired sites. Stephen Doheny-Farina (1992) and Huatang Sun (2012), however, provide two place-marking boundaries in the field's research. Doheny-Farina's study traces the introduction of new digital technologies across a range of workplaces, where Sun's study pursues interesting emergent examples at numerous organizations in Asia to provide transcultural context. Published twenty years apart, Doheny Farina and Sun's studies share more in common with the approach followed here, with emphasis on emergent regional examples illustrating the challenges of postindustrial writing and communication, challenges of which include dimensions of what are often called science in the public interest, sociology of science, and science and technology studies. Inclusion as part of my approach is meant not to give these methods short shrift but rather to maintain focus on emergent practices at workplaces rather than get lost at a single site (see Lather for the advantages of *Getting Lost*).

Designing culture: sites of labor

Each of these jobs from the steel manufacturing control room in Gary, Indiana, begins with the oceangoing transport moving iron ore to the Indiana foundry from Sao Paolo, Brazil, or from Western Australia. The ore is transported first in railcars from Newman in the interior to Port Hedland, then across the Pacific Ocean, through the Panama Canal (or even around the southern tip of South America if the ship is too large for the canal: post-PANAMAX), then is transferred to smaller ships that make their way through the Sault Ste. Marie Locks in the northern Great Lakes, around the northern tip of the mitten of Michigan and into the port of Gary, Indiana. The global networks are staggering and almost completely invisible, although a recent subgenre of literature has arisen tracing these networks of commodities around the world, like *Cod* (1998) and *Sushi Economy* (2014). Alain de Botton traces tuna from ocean to boat to store shelves in *A Week at the Airport* (2010). Tracing flotsam atop ocean currents, *Moby Duck* (2011) is the king of these network tracings, following bath toys as they land across the Pacific coast of the United States, a genre I first encountered through social histories like Whatley's *Scottish Salt Industry* (1987). Mark Shepard's *Sentient City* (2011) literalizes many of the discursive connections and mappings of these tracings, offering a glimpse of the future of network analysis.

The authors of each of these books, the miners in Australia and Brazil, the ship's captains, mates, and crew members, the producers of iron in Gary, Indiana, as well as the lock operators in Panama and Sault Ste.

Marie, Michigan, are staring at and manipulating symbols on screens that are amazingly similar and built to very exacting standards by similar networks of expertise that construct the Apple iPod. The iPod itself comprises dozens of parts assembled around the world (yet proudly "designed by Apple in California"). These global supply chains take advantage of expertise distributed around the world, distributing high-tech work. Johndan Johnson Eilola, in *DataCloud* (2005), beat the recent buzz surrounding the use of cloud computing, and reminded us that whatever industry we inhabit, we were, following former Labor Secretary Robert Reich, symbolic-analytic workers. Central to defining work in the information age is manipulation of symbols, at the screen of what has been called the "soft machine" or the *Smart Machine* (Zuboff) that, because of its ability to change interfaces, can become (almost) anything the user needs. We take it for granted that the hardened glass interface of our smartphones morphs from calculator to note taker to web browser to telephone, and this expectation is being applied to the multiton metal-forming presses at next-generation automobile manufacturing where shapes and dies can be swapped out like smartphone applications. Somewhere in the turn of the millennium, human beings began treating physical artifacts like digital software, and that switch in mindset and the corresponding shift in communication radically transforms physical work and manufacturing as well as the machines—misnamed *computers*—that handle the manipulation of symbols and information.

The virtual has leaked into the real, and accustomed relationships with digital information display have infected expectations of the real world. As I describe in Chapter 2, automobile manufacturing can turn out body assemblies on demand. Mass production techniques have been remediated by the software industry, and the once-unique practices of Silicon Valley are no longer restricted to software programming or designing hardware. Software development, and the disruptive technology of personal computing, has driven the development of professional and technical communication since the 1980s, and while computer documentation will continue to employ many graduates from academic writing programs, much of the groundbreaking research is in place. Spinuzzi's *Network* (2008) along with Selber's *Multiliteracies* (2004) effectively articulate the endgame of writing for the digital industry. Many technical communicators will continue to be employed in production of software and hardware but it is a context of diminishing returns, while the reinvigorated manufacturing and energy production sectors just begin to understand the implications of incorporating iterative design, process analysis, and user-centered theories to their workplaces. The challenge now is to understand the shift back to the real, or what McGonigal (2011) has described in gaming studies as broken reality. McGonigal's argument demonstrates that knowledge work is not limited to digital products but reengages our physical existence, integrating the virtual and the real. While McGonigal and gamers generally are focused on gameworlds, we share an interest in mapping impacts learned in virtual spaces back onto the real world. She aims to repair a broken world, an ambitious project. Mine is far more limited; I am interested in applying the lessons learned in Silicon Valley and web businesses to the practices of traditional manufacturing in the postindustrial Midwest.

The hallmark of the information age is that all workplaces are high-technology workplaces. Management of so-called creatives—working in design, prizing agility, enjoying flattened hierarchies, and contributing innovations to global supply chains—such descriptions of work are among many shifts that have become a new stability for internet and digital businesses. Information is animating and, in Morville's provocative neologism, *Intertwingling* (2014) all organizations whether they produce goods and services for the international market, supply energy locally, or feed population centers. Those informating innovations thrive in the industrial-age communities of the American rust-belt, the corn and soybean producing heartland, and these communities participate in knowledge clusters every bit as viable as those found elsewhere, nationally and internationally, waiting to be animated by information-age transformation.

This East-Midwest area commands the great inland seas and its northern mines which are rich in metal ores, including iron and copper, along with proven reserves in manganese, nickel, and titanium. Clay, sand, gravel, peat, granite, limestone, and silica sand for glassmaking, salt in Michigan, New York, and Pennsylvania, old- and second-growth timber, and the largest reserve of surface fresh water in the world form the foundation of the Midwestern resources that established the area as a valuable source of industrial raw materials as well as an economical form of transport by ship across the lakes, connecting Thunder Bay, Kingston, Windsor, and Toronto, Ontario, Canada, with Duluth, Milwaukee, Green Bay, Chicago, Gary, Detroit, Toledo, Cleveland, Erie, Buffalo, Rochester, and Niagara Falls. Bound by the Ohio River to the south and the Mississippi to the West, the East-Midwest region is historically, economically, as well as geographically distinct, and has through the 20th century been an important global source for materials.

Ward (1981) maps immigration patterns, and Clark (2010, 1981) presents the postindustrial in geographical perspective. Clark's regional mapping, which he calls East/North Central, includes Wisconsin. While including Wisconsin is appealing, it would expand the scope of the research presented here in this study. For now, and for this text, East-Midwest as defined by Clark exemplifies the territorial focus of *Postindustrial Writing*. Ward's East-Midwest presents an historical rationale for studying sites in Illinois, Indiana, Michigan, and Ohio.

Looking at Ward's map and his East-Midwest label, the label postindustrial and the fate that has befallen Detroit is worth reconsideration.

Chicago is pulsing and vibrant, Indianapolis is holding its own, Cleveland seems to be a bit threadbare, yet attracts new businesses. Pittsburgh has emerged as a vibrant new center of commerce. Detroit and Pittsburgh, then, are opposite ends of a continuum: where Pittsburgh planned for its revitalization, Detroit has allowed the 21st century to elude it. People in both cities, in thriving Pittsburgh and forlorn Detroit and all the cities between, form a continuum of success, those benefiting from planning and those suffering the impacts from poor planning or deferred response. In *Remaking the Rust Belt* Neumann (2016) compares the responses of Hamilton, Ontario, and Pittsburgh, Pennsylvania, to deindustrialization, revealing distinct strategies as well as the limitations of Canadian and American responses. The critique compares strategies—the role of innovation, taxpayer and private funding, as well as labor and management roles in promoting change. Writing of Hamilton, Neumann asserts:

> While downtown redevelopment in the two cities exposed a different range of ideas about for whom cities should be remade, plans for the mill neighborhood laid bare the renegotiations of urban citizenship that were part and parcel of postindustrialism.
>
> (136)

Neumann narrates both cities' recognition of the international context in which their actions were being taken, gesturing toward both cities' awareness of similar global competitors like Glasgow and the Scottish reinvigoration of the River Clyde after shipbuilding and Spain's Bilbao successfully attracting the Frank Gery–designed Guggenheim museum to revitalize its riverfront (Neumann, 187). The outcomes are uncertain, risky, and high stakes, particularly when looking at the fates of once-powerful cities like Detroit.

Urban spaces embody the outcome of cultures of planning and design, representing their founding principles and underlying values (see Sánchez, 2016). Iterative design drives planning for Pittsburgh, where industrial areas are being remade into shopping and living spaces, or Chicago where slaughterhouses have transmogrified into hipster hangouts, full of young craftspeople who believe in their emerging lifestyle (and irony) imbued in the all-under-one-roof, do-it-yourself, urban homesteader aesthetic. These cities are both victim and site of American design aesthetic taken from design-build-teardown-renew modern models rather than the iterative ethic of build, redesign, tinker, renovate, assess. This is not unlike the distinction Alexander and his colleagues express in *Battle for the Life and Beauty of the Earth* (2012). The title may be a bit dramatic, yet Alexander's articulation of patterns and networks of behavior, Alexander's Plan A, resonates. *A Pattern Language* (1977) of hermeneutic looping, of Kaizen, of always better, seems well suited to the challenges of the postindustrial, of its fickle markets and quick turn-arounds. But the cities like Detroit waiting for outside capital to renew its core will be waiting longer still as neither state nor federal budgets seem likely to bring revitalization funds to the fore. Compare that with Boston's Big Dig, and the fates of our cities seem very much connected to political will and farsightedness—and lack of vision.

Traveling to inchoate worksites has provided unique opportunities to learn about new practices and emergent innovations. Global contexts become discernable in contrast with locally situated narratives. Many of these innovations, like smaller work teams, design thinking, and new management practices, have been imported from the digital world, from Silicon Valley, and the information revolution. Digital hardware, software, internet, and web firms have contributed important insights into how many practices considered natural or necessary were neither and were ineffective and wasteful instead. Here, research in the earlier work of technical communication, specifically in software documentation and the networks of knowledge work were exemplified by Clay Spinuzzi's work, particularly *Network* (2008) and *All Edge* (2015). In *Network*, Spinuzzi specifically focuses on telecommunications workers: bits and bytes abound but nary an atom is perturbed. The "adhocracies," or functional problem-centered work teams that are the focus of *All Edge* concentrate on what it is like to work in these postindustrial workplaces that emphasize flexibility and fluidity at the price of stability and sustainability. I am grateful for this work insofar as its existence allows me to focus on the transfer of the innovations represented in these and similar studies to the manufacturing workplace.

Geography again asserts itself as an important consideration. California's Silicon Valley and San Francisco Bay have different constraints than does the Silicon Prairie of Austin, Texas: Google, Apple, Dell, HP. So too the postindustrial East-Midwest, the land of Ford, General Motors, US Steel, and Eli Lilly and Company, have different challenges and certainly a different (and longer) legacy. Other innovations arrive from other industrial clusters as well—digital workplaces do not monopolize innovation. Just-in-time manufacturing, environmental set asides and other protections, and innovative policy-making have been developed and can be adopted and deployed effectively at a variety of sites. Finally, and perhaps most promisingly, there are home-grown innovations created and nurtured in the postindustrial Midwestern United States—like deep recycling and industrial-agricultural hybrids—poised to emerge globally and impact best practices.

Local advantages are leveraged effectively for global impact, and local practices, resources, and community know-how enable success. Challenges remain regarding how to communicate these advantages to both partners and competitors, and opportunities are passing whole communities, not because their skills are not potentially valuable but because their representations of their work are no longer compelling. It is change, and the rules and strategies of play change as well. As a teacher, I have come to terms with preparing students for a job market that, after 4 (or more) years of study will have invented new roles and new titles, which is why I tell students I cannot tell them what jobs they are preparing for. The fact is, we simply do not know. And students will be accepting future jobs with titles and responsibilities we are just learning to name. Even the organizations they will be joining may not yet exist. Rather, the program I direct prepares students to recognize the power of their primary and secondary research skills, coupled with the ability to articulate relationships among scientific and technical knowledge, cultural situation, and institutional context. Students need to be able to analyze and determine which arguments—which available means of persuasion—are more or less likely to be effective at any given moment, and to recognize when opportunities that invite their intervention arise. Recent graduates find themselves empowered, challenged, and engaged by the rhetorical knowledge of how research and planning become reality. These values are at the core of what gives rhetoric both longstanding and renewed impact, particularly in the postindustrial Midwest, and by extension through the postindustrial economy.

Communicating advantages

User-centered design, as articulated by Norman's *The Design of Everyday Things* (1990, 2013) places human beings at the center of the design of artifacts, be they programs, interfaces, or machines. Prior to Norman's text, organizational communicators were unable to articulate key challenges facing them in their work. Called on to represent the needs of their audience, technical communicators became increasingly aware of the problems in their exchange with engineers and programmers—a relationship routinely inscribed as technology producers separated from their consumers by a gulf of understanding. Until there was language that recognized distinctions between system-centered and user-centered design, it was difficult if not impossible for these technology producers to break out of their system-centered mindset; no language described an alternative, so there was no alternative. Since articulating the relationship in this way, Robert R. Johnson (1998) has enabled technorhetors to demonstrate a range of different relationships among the elements of technological production and design: producers, users, artifacts, interfaces, and the mental models of use. While valuable, this language of user-centered-ness has accomplished what it was designed to do (Johnson, 2010). No system can (or should) be completely user-centered. Rather, we have learned to represent different aspects of design as existing on a continuum of more and less user and system centered. Customization, interface, and signposting require high levels of attention to user need.

Elements of the user experience give rise to a new sector of expertise and professionalization known as user-experience designers, interface engineers, and information architects. User-centered design places the user at the center of technical communicators' experience of their work and represents an important development in postindustrial experts' accountability: how will this idea, design, or alteration be received, and how can it be best positioned to do what the user needs to accomplish? Ethical implications of design work emerge through such user-engagement, exemplified by tensions between traditional refuse dumping and limited energy resources, of encountering users in the moment of their frustration or satisfaction with design. Even the U.S. Army values design thinking, claiming it saved lives in Iraq and Afghanistan.[3]

Reuse and recycling have important roles to play in every home as well as throughout businesses and organizations. One surprise has been that costs of recycling have been outweighed by the benefits as well as unforeseen efficiencies. Reuse of materials saves significant energy versus procuring virgin materials through mining, smelting, manufacturing as well as savings in transport. Behind this current reality of widespread consumer and business recycling there are important ideas about sustainability. The cultural acceptance of total costs like assessing the carbon cost, carbon footprint, as well as cradle-to-grave costs, are now becoming more widely accepted. The cradle-to-grave concept traces the cycle of a product's total cost of procurement and use, from its creation to disposal, to which cradle-to-cradle recycling is now added, which traces the difficulty of the next use of the refuse. Metals, like aluminum, are almost infinitely recyclable, and have a positive cradle-to-cradle rating, while paper products have a poor cradle-to-cradle cycle and eventually end up in landfills or burned.

Sustainability vaguely offers broad definition and tries to move the audience to less wastefulness and more attention to sustaining processes over many generations of use. Cradle-to-grave recycling travels alongside an artifact, providing a narrative of its existence where efficiencies can be realized and reuse accomplished. The term describes ongoing efforts to find and eliminate wasteful moments in its trajectory. If a material is energy intensive but gains efficiencies from recycling, like aluminum, its cradle-to-grave sustainability may be low, but adding another category, cradle-to-cradle, allows the material to have its creation spread over multiple lifetimes of products. For instance, a cast aluminum item like a notebook computer case may be resource intensive. Ore is mined, smelted, and then transported to where the item is eventually cast, and then milled to specification. After the years of use for the computer, a cradle-to-grave analysis might reveal a hefty carbon footprint. But, if after a full life cycle, that case is either recycled into another computer or into multiple beverage cans, the cradle-to-cradle assessment makes the original carbon footprint and cost to create more sustainable. I also use the phrase *deep recycling* throughout this text to refer to the way business clusters recycle skills through many cycles of the economy. Abilities and expertise do not become obsolete in the way specific management philosophies or manufacturing technologies age, but rather become part of the local economic skills reservoir—abilities, proficiencies, and procurement strategies are retained by local populations long after specific factories and industries leave. Deep recycling animates the work of redefining and redeploying these skills in new contexts, a hallmark of the postindustrial age where a variety of skills forged in the industrial age are reassigned. The challenges for deep recycling are in reconnecting existing but underutilized expertise to add to perceptions of value of communities to global networks, reinvigorating existing, underutilized clusters.

Coupled with deep recycling of materials and skills, engagement is another important component of postindustrial action. Engagement describes nurturing innovation for local advantage and global value. My reading of Michelle Simmons' and Jeffrey Grabill's (2007) work on community engagement informs the ways in which technocultural work requires the expertise of a rhetorician to trace the feedback, map it, and then comprehend its potential meanings. Only then can the observations be laid back onto the community, making sense of their present circumstance, to prepare not for a mythical stable future of repeating opportunity but rather for instability. Timely opportunities characterize a wired world where markets open and close with destabilizing quickness. Advantages other cultural formations have in terms of regulation, inclusion, opportunity, and cohesion provide global contrasts to American norms, giving rise to the global challenges American manufacturing and management face. Kaizen, the Japanese concept of "constant improvement," resembles iterative design while challenging the slower pace of workplace change in the United States. It was an American managerial consultant who, as described in Chapter 2, had his ideas rejected in his homeland but found an interested audience in postwar Japan. Seen as a Japanese innovation, American car manufacturers were among the first to face the competition of what has been described as *The Toyota Way* (Liker, 2004). Had Detroit recognized the value of iterative design and constant improvement, the United States might still hold managerial and manufacturing hegemony. Design, recycling, and sustainability, coupled with recognizing local innovation, and combined with knowledge and awareness of the value of work and how it structures identity and community can keep civil society sustained and healthy.

Work defines identities, self-worth, and communities. Change is disruptive, and the future of postindustrial society is as turbulent as urbanization was at the dawn of the industrial age. The end of mass employment in agriculture did not end food production, just as industrial output is not declining with deindustrialization. Rather, pollution and danger to workers accompany low-end manufacturing while high-quality production is done with fewer workers in richer nations. For the transition, managing change is the wicked problem, to use Rittel and Weber's language. Bell's prophetic visions, in the process of arriving over three decades and more, did not articulate the transition, nor offer salves for ruptures and disruptions. Making tomorrow better than today, Kaizen as iterative improvement offers one means of utilizing design thinking to engage with the arrival of new configurations of work and productivity. Kaizen does not claim to solve problems. Rather, it addresses them and makes them a little bit more manageable. Not taming them, not at first, but over time making wicked, wild problems into tame, domesticated matters of concern.

Cultural study reveals opportunity

In the introduction to *Critical Power Tools* (2007), Scott, Longo, and Wills argue for a cultural studies approach that puts power relationships at the center of discussion and moves away from a transactional and culturally reproductive approach to technical and professional communication:

> Cultural studies can push our research, pedagogy and practice to critically assess and problematize the hegemonic values and functions of technical communication. Instead of only seeking to explain technical communication, we should evaluate its ethics of its functions and effects, asking such questions as "Whose values does technical communication privilege?" and "Who is included and who is excluded by these practices, and how?" and "How are these practices beneficial and/or harmful?"
>
> (Scott et al., 13)

By applying a cultural studies approach to investigating emergent practices, this study interrogates the postindustrial and assesses the powerful historical and cultural discourses informing the most compelling parts of the new order of work as well as emergent workplace cultures. My essay in *Critical Power Tools* is titled "Rhetoric as Productive Technology" and distinguishes analysis from rhetorical action. The approach revises cultural studies, envisioning critical action in the world—returning to an active cultural engagement. In the first 1997 edition of *Doing Cultural Studies: The Story of the Sony Walkman*, DuGay et al. suggest a circuit of culture that remains analytical and discursive: never engaging the musical culture the artifact of study engages. As I have argued, however, the circuit of culture has to extend beyond academic analysis to engage producers and consumers of technologies to create a conduit of communication moving data from the laboratory to the sales floor and into peoples' homes, and then delivering information through usability feedback to design and production personnel (Johnson et al., 2007).

In its attention specifically on the user-centered design practices of usability work, Bradley Dilger argues for the "important discursivity, cultural context, historical context, implied order or subjugation, and self-reflexivity" (64) in an essay in the same volume of *Critical Power Tools*:

> Cultural studies is especially valuable, since its broad approach prevents the task orientation of usability from myopic exclusion of discursive, historical, and cultural contexts. Cultural studies demonstrates the relevance of considering the history of usability and provides strong justification for broadly construed and implemented concepts of usability. Additionally, paying attention to cultural factors strengthens usability by allowing practitioners to account for and address troublesome environmental factors as part of usability methodology.
>
> (65, ibid)

As designers say about good design, effective writing is only noticed in its absence. The irony is that writers seem only to be noticed—writing only acknowledged—by its lack and in its limits. In a value-added organization, invisibility like this is deadly. Add to that the Midwestern reticence to call attention to one's own competence and, well, invisibility leads to being taken for granted. This is where knowledge of history of writing becomes important. Professors of rhetoric and writing have complained about poor writing among college students for a very long time—James Berlin's favorite reference was to 19th-century Harvard professors complaining about near illiteracy among the young republic's future leaders.[4] Earlier still—about 4,000 years earlier—Plato has Socrates complaining that writing corrupts knowledge and students will be ruined. Indeed, "they will be tiresome company, having the show of wisdom without the reality" (Phaedrus). Connors (1982) chronicles the split between "practical" engineering education and proselytizing humanists trying to fix their technocratic impulses. And it leads to C.P. Snow's (2012, 1959) oft-cited definition of two divided cultures in which scientists and engineers rarely understand the concerns of humanists, let alone take their criticism to heart. This book is not explicitly about this history, but there are elements of the history that have disproportionate impact.

Walter Ong reminds us of important connections to this history (1982 and 1958). First, we know of Socrates through Plato because Plato wrote things down. Socrates defines the emerging age of print by questioning the effectiveness of the technology. We know of Socrates only because his student Plato values writing—thereby preserving his teacher's words. And so Plato participated in this age of written records. Berlin's attention to 19th-century American context signals the dawn of the age of mass literacy. The Enlightenment, which had given rise to the progressive idea of democracy as described in the US Constitution, required mass literacy sufficient for voters to make reasonable choice. The emphasis on reason and choice has been much described, and much criticized, in the postmodern, but it is important to recall that historically, American Civil War epistolary communication provided widespread evidence of growing numbers of literate citizens who would petition their government and, in the post–Civil War financial meltdowns in the 1870s, provided the first stirrings of labor rights activism that became prominent in the 20th century. The Civil War also gave rise to the land grant institutions and the idea of widespread practical higher education, accelerating the agrarian to industrial transformation of American culture.

While Plato, Socrates, and Phaedrus provide one record of the emergence of literacy and writing as a phenomenon and an epistemological shift, 19th-century American context demonstrates one example of mass literacy and its powerful impacts that continue to be felt. Today, we see evidence of another shifting, from a literate book culture to emerging digital and electronic media. Historically, other books do this work better than I can in this short recap. See JoAnn Yates, *Control Through Communication* (1993). Memos—perhaps the 20th century's most ubiquitous form of communication—is, in Yates' telling, co-emergent with railroads and 19th century industrialization and expansion of both mass education and literacy. Today, email, micro-blogging and social media attract much research attention. It remains to be seen how exactly electronic recordkeeping and communication will change our culture in lasting form; entire libraries of books have been written on the literate, business, and scientific transformations attending the digital revolution. Some evidence is already available.

Digitization has brought about disruptive, radical change for scientists and engineers as well, particularly in the increase of data. Some estimates have the rate of increase in the production of data doubling frighteningly quickly—every 11 hours or so. However, this estimate only looks at the rate of increase of data. Information is slower, and knowledge slower still. We've moved from an age of information scarcity to information ubiquity, and where we once fought to figure out how to remember it all, we now see the important role strategic forgetting has to play. Many current battles, like those over intellectual property rights and copyright, have to do with industrial age concerns with scarcity of information, where scholars and prognosticators have pretty well followed Richard Lanham's path in asserting that the information age is one of information glut, and economics will shift to account for ubiquity. Yet we continue to produce scads of data. For Lanham, this is an age of the *Economics of Attention* (2006). With so much vying for our attention, we turn to aggregators and taste brokers to help us each make sense of the deluge, whereas the previous age was one of content scarcity.

Skills we bring with us from the industrial age into the postindustrial include defining what literate action might look like as the traditional activities of "writing" are reformulated by emerging digital media. Furthermore, traditional activities, like primary and secondary research, are pivotal skills to bring forward into the new age of secondary orality. It is particularly important to articulate the ways in which these traditional skills and activities are reformulated (or re-mediated) for the information age and, perhaps most importantly, what these activities look like situated in postindustrial workplaces. By situating practices, emplacement moves us beyond speculation toward emplaced practice, articulating a suite of skills and knowledge.

Recent work on the *chôra*, on the Greek chorus, links these knowledge-making practices to the ancient art of rhetoric. In ancient Greek drama, a personified voice of the people in mass would appear on stage as the chorus. Rickert opens his *Ambient Rhetoric* (2013) building theory for a cultural rhetorical awareness where the chorus is not a voice but a place that *attunes* the rhetor to the expectations of the public. Rickert presents a beautiful articulation of rhetorical ambience and the expression of public mood, but the information age likes its data, and this chorus is best represented in the work of Nate Silver, a statistician who first became famous for predicting baseball statistics with uncanny accuracy. He rose to greater prominence in 2008 with his accurate analysis of a variety of political races, and accurately called nearly all the November 2012 election results. Silver's statistics are analogous to the chorus, the voice of culture, but statistics are descriptive, and Silver reminds his readers again and again that his work is about probability: the likely outcomes of cultural phenomena. Silver's 2012 book returns to the modernist analysis of telephony, *The Signal and the Noise.*

But statistics cannot account for newly invented options, for innovations. Rhetoric can. Rhetoric, like statistics, is probabilistic and concentrates on what is *likely* to happen in given situations. Science does not appreciate the uncertainty of either statistics or rhetoric. This is the realm of statistics, and statistical analysis can certainly be an important and valuable input for decision making. However, design requires that technorhetoricians be interested participants rather than passive analysts. Design needs to be articulated not just as user centered but also as a way to create the best possible of alternative worlds—with active participants rather than passive observers. This is about world-building, about inventing alternative versions of what is and envisioning what else can be. But it is also very seriously about the constraints of such design.

Bent Flyvberg, a Danish expert in estimating economic as well as social costs, offers powerful analysis of a special kind of design in megaprojects. Megaprojects develop on a massive scale, like Boston's Big Dig that required billions in federal funding over a decade of construction. Most clearly expressed in *Megaprojects and Risk: An Anatomy of Ambition,*[5]

Flyvberg opens his analysis with critique of the idea of *frictionlessness* as a key component in globalization. Friction euphemistically eliminates human beings from business, at least from the perspective of entrepreneurs, as it articulates the infrastructure and labor necessary to move raw materials, processed goods, and even people around the world with a minimum of trouble and maximized efficiency. Tracing these global webs is at the heart of network analysis similar to tracing the iron ore to steel manufacturing and shipping networks, as described previously. The idea of frictionless capitalism, which Flyvberg attributes to Bill Gates of Microsoft, depends on smooth-functioning infrastructure and unregulated automation to remove friction:

> Infrastructure is the great space-shrinker, and power, wealth, and status increasingly belong to those who know how to shrink space, or know how or benefit from space being shrunk.
>
> (Flyvberg, 2)

Historical analysis reveals—not in an attempt to halt or undo the necessary work of societies (hence the status as a postcritical investigation)—the places where important stakeholders are ignored, where necessary input is lacking, and where opportunities for more sources of input are apparent and need to be incorporated into the information available for decision making. So Flyvberg's analysis is not meant to halt megaprojects but, based in historical precedent, to articulate previous oversight in cost estimations to understand the potential problems in current mega-project planning, to use history to better prepare for the future. His work does not fetishize history, does not get lost in details or in tale telling, but focuses on articulating important lessons learned from previous experience and using these lessons to better understand future plans.

So, too, experts in communication, professional writing, and the technological-cultural shift, must be able to apply the lessons of history, learned both through cultural sifting and analysis, through linguistic and textual analysis, to participate in the creation of the future, and to learn and digest important lessons of the past. They must keep the focus on participation in future-making and articulation of just, functional, participatory systems of technology and knowledge flow that allow for input from a variety of stakeholders. Indeed, the task remains in many ways to continue showing how failure often arises from omission of key stakeholders and silencing of necessary input. Whether Rifkin's version of the *Third Industrial Revolution* (2011) accurately comes to pass or another's vision proves more accurate, communication of information pertaining to the production of cleaner energy, effective design and realization of megaprojects, and cooperation among hyper-specialized and technologically sophisticated organizations built to communicate and realize these plans will define the future of work both in the United States and around the world.

While these changes deemphasize traditional roles for and genres of technical communication, there are as many, if not more, opportunities for rhetorically trained communication specialists—in addition to professionals in engineering, business, investment, and government who will continue to rely upon their specialized knowledges—to make ideas into plans, coordinate huge amounts of data, and focus on revealing the important relationships among those data points. The shift in responsibilities for these specialists is about articulating a working future in which varieties of expertise are recognized and valued. That is, a bright future exists for technical and professional communication.

Companies that seemed like they would monopolize, or at least control, markets for long periods of time are no longer the powerhouses they once were. Microsoft may come to mind, but Yahoo! and Netscape are equally startling examples of large organizations that lost their way. Google and Amazon dictate current discussions of innovation. The history of Bell Telephone's innovation laboratory, subject of Jon Gertner's book (2012), was the mid-20th-century precursor to the current digital shift and provides warning for those seeking insight into contemporary changes. Leading companies can quickly find themselves behind when they become complacent. Leaders adopting the always-improving model of iterative design may prove themselves formidable players. Throughout this articulation of the third wave of industrialization and other descriptions of the current cultural zeitgeist, technical and professional communicators (TPCs) can drive innovation, and engineers, designers, scientists, and managers can teach and emulate the representative included in this study. Nothing I have learned from these sites offers clear rationale for where innovations occur within organizations. Popular representations of "geniuses" like Amazon's Jeff Bezos make him unrelenting and Apple's deceased visionary Steve Jobs as unwaveringly brutally adherent to a design philosophy. This introductory chapter opens with Ralph Braun and his company, which is also driven from the top, by a visionary. In contrast, Chapter 4 describes agricultural and agriindustrial innovations that emerged from the facilities director, who is amid the middle of their hierarchy. In Chapter 2, at Subaru, the structure of the organization *is* its innovation, and there are rewards available to people anywhere in the organization to communicate suggestions for beneficial change. In Ohio, Michigan, and elsewhere in Indiana, workers themselves are organizing into new collectives—tinkers and makers—working to flatten workplace hierarchies. Many examples of innovation championed in the creative digital economy come from middle and lower levels of the organizations, so long as there are mechanisms for hearing the voices of people contributing those ideas. Other innovative organizations use organization itself as a site for change. With these models in mind, it follows there are potentials for transformation among those with industrial-age skillsets working with hammers, welding, and forges, made more efficient and powerful wedded to 3D prototyping and on-demand digital technologies.

At the heart of all these next-generation postindustrial configurations is the importance of effectively communicating new knowledge. In *Opening Spaces* (1997), Patricia Sullivan and James Porter argue in favor of postmodern mapping, which brings together Bordieu's sense of habitués and concept mapping into visual rhetoric. Here, I draw upon more literal maps of states, cities, communities, and workplaces. The people at these sites represent the source of the "friction," and the "frictionless" utopians ignore people's need for community, for fulfillment, for family, and for institutions beyond employer, government, and formal education. These literal maps reveal the importance of interconnections among a variety of networks and weavings, from singular networks to networks of networks, to mesh. Place is where people, their lives, and communities are located. Place gains new importance, or at least regains the importance in people's minds, but the value has always dwelt there. It just hasn't been valued, and emplacement—location— emerges with renewed importance, particularly as fossil fuels become increasingly expensive and global transport becomes both a financial and environmental liability. Along the way, some attention is given to how these places became important to begin with, and how resources were made into persistent local advantages. These advantages of place reveal problems with the idea of frictionlessness and the important advantages some places have over others for indigenous strengths, knowledge bases, and skills traditions. These places have become not only geographically but also culturally important, revealing why they exist, why they endure, and why they are unique.

In an attempt to describe the importance of place, I discuss the American Midwest in the postindustrial age. The East-Midwest region of Michigan, Illinois, Indiana, Ohio, is now poised for reemergence as the center of high-technology clusters of advanced materials and next-generation manufacturing, supplying advanced products and materials. Digital and physical resources, once the exclusive domain of high-technology organizations to establish their ethos as leaders in research, now support new manufacturing sites, clean energy production, and reutilized urban spaces. Technical and professional communicators (TPCs) understand well the genres and practices of original research, product development, acceptance, and popularization.

Notes

1 www.purdue.edu/newsroom/rubegoldberg/ (Accessed May 6, 2016).
2 www.wired.com/2010/03/ok-go-rube-goldberg/ (Accessed May 6, 2016).
3 The Museum of Modern Art sustains a website in which the Army Field Manual and its attention to design thinking are subject to an inquiry: http://designandviolence.moma.org/army-field-manual-5-0-the-operations-

process-u-s-military/ More interesting, perhaps, is Chapter 2 of the manual that describes iterative design as Army Design Methodology and "operational art." I am not arguing for militarizing design but rather for understanding the widespread reference to and adoption of iterative design. In a field that looks to Roman military manuals as its classics (see Spaulding and Bliese), mention in the latest version of the US Army Field Manual is an important historical marker. The Manual is available online:

http://www.apd.army.mil/epubs/DR_pubs/DR_a/pdf/web/atp5_0x1.pdf (Accessed May 29, 2017).

Spaulding, Oliver. The Ancient Military Writers. *The Classical Journal* Vol. 28, No. 9 (June 1933), 657–669. http://penelope.uchicago.edu/Thayer/E/Journals/CJ/28/9/Ancient_Military_Writers*.html.

4 See Berlin's footnote quoting Kitzhaber in *Writing Instruction in Nineteenth-Century American Colleges.*
5 Bent Flyvbjerg, Nils Bruzelius, and Werner Rothengatter. *Megaprojects and Risk: An Anatomy of Ambition.* Cambridge: Cambridge University Press, 2003.

2 Subaru as postindustrial iterative automobile manufacturing

My students' recollections of the Subaru Indiana Assembly (SIA) plant are strongly connected to spouts of welding sparks. The trajectories went up 10 feet into the air from the robotic arms performing the welds, and 10 feet out from the assembly line, showering the robots with orange-hot plasma. The robots performed a kind of hypnotic dance, taking pieces from the fresh stack of parts and welding the panels together to form doors. The arms had no bodies but were bolted to the floor as they worked in complementary routines: new panels, weld, weld, weld, door panel, transfer to finishing station, new panels gathered and centered, and weld, weld, weld, to station two. One line was assembling right-side doors while the other assembled the left. Weld, weld, weld. A robot carrier arrived just as the previous carrier was filled with door assemblies, as the last robotic arm placed the last door on the stack. The robot cart beeped, and off it went to the assembly line to deliver the doors. Weld, weld, weld. The new empty cart received its first pair of door assemblies. No pauses, the doors accumulated, spark and fire, with one human being sitting behind a Plexiglas shield, watching the robot arms dance and the robot dollies beep and sputter and carry the still-warm doors to assembly.

This line of robotic door choreography is what a number of graduate students report as their clearest memory of the last tour of the SIA plant. The fire meteorically rising and falling to the assembly floor in spellbinding rhythm, the coordinated making of door panel parts for Subaru automobiles. Robotics, while taking repetitive jobs from human workers, also keeps frail human bodies safe. My discussion with SIA moved toward collaborating with human partners, making the muscle work the domain of machines. But right now, robots are fenced off. Recent accidents, rare though they are, are often the result of the robots' inability to comprehend context, and unable to distinguish steel from flesh. So even co-habiting space would be a step in the right direction, which again opens the opportunity for research and development, a theme of cooperative, even collaborative, human-robotic hybridity.[1]

Collaborating with robots has the potential to change manufacturing, and it is also some time off given the current limits of robotics in manufacturing. Requiring dedicated manufacturing floor space labeled a clear danger to humans, robots are currently rather "dumb" terminals, and all the promise and potential are a stark contrast to the current reality.

The largest arcs were actually across the plant at the Toyota line, rising 20 feet in the air and 20, 25, even 30 feet away from the robotic assembly arm, repeatedly fusing metal door panels together. The larger ballistic trajectories were due to the higher welding temperatures of the Toyota line. "Higher temperatures must mean higher quality," one curious student queried. "Not at all," our tour guide responded, "the weld has to be made at the right temperature according to the needs of the metal being joined, the demands put on the welded joint, and a number of other factors." The tour guide continued, pointing out that while the other welds were certainly dramatic to watch, there was no reason to presume them superior.

Our tour guide went on to demonstrate an impressive knowledge of the assembly line and its procedures, standards, and expectations, pointing out that the Toyota welding attachments wore out much quicker at those higher temperatures and consumed more resources to produce. And then our guide reported details about how the SIA associates had made a suggestion that saved the company a significant amount of money and resources.

After sweeping the dust from the factory floor, standard practice had been, to no one's particular surprise, to toss the dust in the aptly named dustbin or garbage pail. But on the suggestion of an employee, the floor sweepings were collected and examined. They contained high concentrations of copper, steel, and other metals in large enough amounts that it was worth SIA's time to gather the dust and send it out for reprocessing. While on the tour, as our eyes were drawn to the dramatic welding bows of fire, we overlooked the mundane details those meteors represented when they cooled on the floor. Subaru mines its own dust. And it values the input of its associates, even those sweeping up the industrial tailings.

When the Subaru plant was designed and first built, Honda was already producing the Accord at its Marysville, Ohio, assembly plant. Honda had started building motorcycles in 1979 and cars in 1982. According to SIA's history, Isuzu and Fuji Heavy Industries reached an agreement to cooperate on a US-based facility in 1987. They searched and found suitable sites that year, and broke ground in 1988. Interestingly, many of the sites scouted by Fuji Heavy Industries, Subaru's parent company, in West Virginia, Kentucky, Ohio, and Southern Indiana, now have other Japanese transplant factories. "[Thirteen] 13 sites were eventually chosen for further consideration in seven states, including the state of Indiana" (SIA website, history). The first cars rolled off the SIA assembly line in fall of 1989: "The annual phase 1 production of 60,000 Subaru Legacys and 60,000 Isuzu pickups and Rodeos began on September 11, 1989. The plant was officially dedicated on October 16,

1989 with a week-long grand opening ceremony."[2] Change was coming; Japanese investment had begun, and the American automotive manufacturing scene would never be the same again.

Before that first Subaru could roll off the assembly floor, the factory had to be designed, created, staffed, and prepared. As I think about the quick turnaround from Isuzu-Subaru's agreement in 1987, site selection and groundbreaking in 1988, to the first cars rolling off the assembly line in 1989, the speed of completion is astounding. And knowing what lean manufacturing means to Subaru, there must have been industrial hydraulic press orders already in negotiation when Subaru-Isuzu officially agreed to collaborate. Factory designs must have already been in progress when teams were searching the Midwest for appropriate sites. And management teams were already in training in Japan long before the final site was even selected for the factory, the factory that was eventually located less than 8 miles from the Purdue campus.

The large Komatsu stamping presses that form lines A and B in the Subaru plant represent Subaru's innovation and leadership as a global manufacturer. These large industrial presses were quite different from what was being used in the United States at the time, and they have become industry standard since then. But at the time, the Komatsu Transfer Press was revolutionary.

When the Komatsu presses were delivered to the Subaru plant, they arrived through a combination of sea, river, and highway travel. Manufactured only in Japan in the 1980s, the presses have since become industry-wide standard. A three-axle transfer press capable of producing 800–3,200 tons of pressure, the presses have the capacity to press, form, cut, and deform metals into a range of shapes and configurations. These huge, powerful presses are at the heart of automobile and other heavy manufacturing, and are a tremendous expense to the manufacturer. The classic industrial age configuration has a large die permanently affixed to the press repeatedly brought into contact with the metal to be shaped. This is also the reason for things like "model years." The stamping plant would run near-identical parts as quickly as its human attendants could manage to load new steel "blanks" into the stamp, and the human worker attended to the machine at work, loading raw materials (usually raw steel) into the jaws of the press, extracting finished parts from the press (or nearly finished as parts needed to be sanded, smoothed, etc.). These parts were stored, or warehoused, until they were needed.

Model years became a way of turning the industrial press runs into a feature. Nearly identical parts would be run off the press line and assembled into finished cars. The summer months would be "retooling"– time when the presses were not running, and the presses were reconfigured with new dies and newly designed body panels that distinguished each new year's design from the previous year's design. The fins that appeared in 1957 cars, from the Cadillac El Dorado to the Ford Fairlane, defined American mid-century style, but they were an unintended consequence of the way the parts were manufactured. By 1959, the Cadillac El Dorado design had already gone too far and created an iconic look that consumers just weren't buying.

And in 1959, it appeared that there would be no challenger to the success of American automotive design, assembly, and consumption. The 1970s oil crisis shook the automotive world, giving rise to a desire for not only economical but also efficient cars, able to squeeze more miles from the gasoline they consumed. And by the 1980s, Japanese imports from a variety of companies like Honda, Toyota, and Subaru-Isuzu had been selling well enough in the United States to warrant overseas factories separated geographically from their parent companies in Japan. It is important to recognize this as an innovation: transplanting the factory to the location of its market, the Japanese car companies created a global supply chain but kept design and engineering jobs in Japan. The scheme retained high-value jobs in the home country and exported problematic dirty assembly and manufacturing at the automobiles' ultimate market, in the United States. Built by US workers, and mostly managed by Americans, these plants produce the cars that American consumers bought by the millions. Today, the drive from Lafayette, Indiana, to Lexington, Kentucky, passes four major Japanese car manufacturers, and a detour through Columbus, Indiana, would pass Honda's major assembly plants. Strikingly, these facilities are also within an hour's drive of major research universities. Purdue is less than ten miles from Subaru, University of Kentucky is close to the Georgetown Toyota plant, University of Southern Indiana borders the Princeton Toyota Plant, and Honda's major facilities are 41 miles from the Ohio State University's main campus in Columbus, Ohio.

Traditional design ideologies tend to replace one flawed system with a new flawed system. Traditional replacement design introduces new unintended problems. Each new design results in problems that require users to accommodate the limitations of the artifacts rather than allowing users to incorporate the designs into their lives, into their routines. A power differential between designer and user results in limited agency on the part of users, what Feenberg (1999, 2002) named the "right of refusal," which is a take it or leave it decision, a choice between accommodating the artifact as-is, or abandoning it unutilized. Furthermore, older designs were replaced by new designs; problems were not addressed but entire systems created and abandoned without addressing user-level concerns. Systems-centered design is prescriptive in that the design worked only as long as the designer's mental model was understood and accepted by the user (again, see Norman, 1990). Through application of an alternative, a user-centered design approach, and utilizing inclusive, descriptive language, design can become not a system-centered replacement of one flawed approach with a new flawed design, but an incremental approach that retains the underlying system and addresses problems as users articulate them. Rebecca Pope-Ruark provides an effective introduction to iterative design principles as a component of Agile development in "Introducing Agile Project Management Strategies in Technical and Professional Communication Courses" (2015).

Too often, however, "design thinking" means reifying the designer's vision. Stakeholder awareness defines part of the next generation of user-centered design as it moves beyond a single variable: the user. It begins to articulate many kinds and types of users who have different interests—stakes—in the design process. Successful designs have to work for many people in different contexts, and they have to accomplish these goals with the same artifact. Digitally, interaction designers have created multiple user-interfaces. With objects, the options are more limited.

As Johnson and others continue to remind us, this is largely a shift from systems-centered to human-centered thinking and design. And even recent calls to return to systems thinking have been impacted by human-centered and user-centered design. Usability as a professional practice and ethical orientation challenges designers to incorporate the needs of the users, calling attention to the very nature of these systems—as if the fish realized they were in water. Once this point is made, cognition never returns fully to the previous way of thinking: the very fact of calling a branch of design *systems-thinking* illustrates this point. Prior to user-centered and participatory design gaining popularity, the systems perspective would simply be design. There is no way to un-ring this bell. Meadows (2008) *Thinking in Systems* illustrates this perspective. And, as many have written but none no eloquently as Kidder in *The Soul of a New Machine* (1981), computers changed culture by making computing machinery available broadly and democratically, yet workplaces remain highly hierarchical in many traditional industries. Computers allowed the emergence of new institutions with their own architectures of power:

> computers altered techniques but not intentions and in many cases served to increase the power of executives on top....A more likely place to look for radical change was inside the industry actually producing computers.
>
> (12)

These changes allowed the field of technical communication to emerge and flourish as attendant to explain how to program and use these liquid machines, support hardware and software, and consult as generations of information technology professionals, web designers, and system architects.

> Generally, that industry grew very big and lively, largely because of a single invention.
>
> (12)

Everything since then serves as footnotes to Kidder's observations, and the book remains in print (even as he has moved on to other interests and no longer writes about technology). Except now the digital revolution, and the lessons learned from hardware, software, and web design, are indeed inspiring transformations if not revolutions—radical change— within institutions.

Gesturing toward universal design while recognizing its impossibility, Graham Pullin's *Design Meets Disability* (2011) reads like a manifesto. Nevertheless, value exists in articulating the destination and naming the goal. Pullin offers brief, cogent definitions. Resonant design offers designers and culture-at-large a phrase for the kind of responsive, use-centered, stakeholder-involving, context-sensitive artifact creation methods he advocates. At its most extreme, design is inflicted upon users, and Donald Norman reminds his reader of this straw man position with the (in)famous teapot for masochists, or one in a series of impossible machines by the artist Ai WeiWei. WeiWei's bicycle for two has two riders in opposition, facing each other in the saddle, connected to the same front wheel that will neither turn nor travel.

Iterative design recognizes that, in a new realm of design like software, the future is wide open and the result of many failures. Fred Kemp writes about this phenomenon as the "User Friendly Fallacy," where the user is reduced to a mechanistic caricature of a technology-using human being. And if it were just thousands of unplayable games, or poorly thought-out user interfaces, or fantastical unusable designs, that would be one thing. But we are doing it both to our cities as well as our social contract, not to mention our workplaces. In recently published work, Fernando Sánchez (2016) traces the question of what we mean by "design" in technical communication, insisting that being aware of our intentions is, perhaps, more important than any particular place on the continuum of design engagement a project may take. Ultimately, he recommends TPC:

> develop an intentionality about moving from one point of engagement to another in order to develop a fuller comprehension of design.
>
> (Sánchez, 26)

Advantages of iterative design are exemplified by the practice of Kaizen. Instead of a rough cycle of replacing one failed design for another, iterative design with a healthy respect for input from users has changed the relationship that stakeholders have with artifacts. In its simplest terms, iterative design requires continued engagement between designers and users over time so that the second design emerges from an ongoing dialogic relationship between designers and users. The attention to design processes and their values encourages development of and awareness of TPC's relationship to design and, as illustrated by the example presented by Sánchez, reveals why practitioners have opportunities as well as responsibilities to engage design as a part of their professional identity and practice.

Moving from version 1 of a design to version 2 requires multiple versions, or iterations, of the design. Of course, the representation of moving from I-it to I-thou brings a new ideological component, which is sufficient only for shorthand. To believe that one moves from broadcast to dialogism by simply listening to users ... well, that is equally utopian. Iterative design itself has a history, which occurs most clearly to me in the progression from Donald Norman's *Design of Everyday Things* (1990), Robert Johnson's (1998) recognition of user-centered design, to Michele Simmons' (2008) naming of various user roles, allowing users to be represented as stakeholders, over three and now four decades of research and engagement with design.

Design itself is being redesigned, rethought, reemployed, and reiterated as a more effective version of itself, striving to recognize the various inputs, to recognize the many ways users can participate in the design and redesign of artifacts they use in work and play that they have employed in their lives as important and valuable.

Iterative design over the lifetime of a product or artifact requires decision making. What changes are included in the next iteration, and which are held for the next design generation? Iterative design is an important update to user-centered design. Central, especially, to manufacturing, iteration cannot start from scratch. Rather, each new design is built upon and dependent upon the last design.

Subaru of Indiana Automotive, Inc. (SIA) utilizes an iterative design strategy called Kaizen—continuous improvement—as an example of an emergent strategy that changes the relationship between workers and management and among workers, their working environment, and their expertise. Also described as a Japanese manufacturing innovation, the underlying management philosophy was proposed by an American automobile executive, Edwards Deming, and rejected in post-war Detroit. Kaizen found a home in the war-ravaged reconstruction of Japanese heavy industry. Iterative design requires flexibility and creative engagement with work and cooperation where antipathy has been the norm and expectation. Iterative design, in the form of Kaizen at SIA, transfers application from resource management and time, labor, and materials saving to a company-wide commitment to recycling, environmental stewardship, energy efficiency, and communication among various workplace stakeholders. Each iteration of SIA as a workplace makes incremental changes. These "virtuous changes" depend upon effective rhetorical interventions, allowing information to flow from the manufacturing line to managers' offices, from the desks of original thinkers to enable change in everyday practices, and to fit new innovations into the mundane practices of the automobile manufacturing floor. The workplace exemplifies the change from a systems-centered design to an iterative user-centered approach. For more on Deming and Kaizen, see Ishikawa (1988). But before describing Subaru's innovation and the way iterative design has established a new status quo, it is important to understand Fordism and American automobile manufacturing at the end of the 20th century.

Ford, Fordism, Detroit

Fordism has come under considerable attack from both the political right and left. On the one hand, Ford was not quite innovative enough and the assembly line did not move far enough along into scientific management or incorporate quite enough of Taylorism. On the other hand, the work was reductive and over time eroded the power and authority of workers—removed the craftsmanship from work by reducing jobs to their most repetitive and least rewarding. However, as Clemens chronicles the devolution of Michigan through Budd as his representative example, we see the fabric of Michigan society unraveling as the lynchpin of Fordism is removed. Ford, first the man and then the corporation, paid significantly higher wages than the average. Racing to the bottom of the pay scale has revealed significant weaknesses and the impermanence of the wealth created as Clemens bemoans the erosion of middle-class prosperity. But Faigley is critical of Fordism in *Fragments of Rationality* (1995), continuing a separation between the workplace studies of professional writing and the more critical discourses of composition while Clemens bemoans the loss of the source of middle-class stability in America, regularized, consistent manufacturing work, unionized, and well remunerated.

Clemens' prose is beautiful and rather than try to recreate his tone and butcher it, I quote it at length. Note the central descriptions of the presses and their dies as heavy, imposing, semi-permanent, and responsible for downtime. Like artists' prints, the dies eventually start to wear, and late-run parts have a tendency to display less precise formations, fit less tightly upon assembly, and produce more blemishes during production. The parts are not as well made or as precise as the dies age after running thousands upon thousands of parts. They will also rack, or even explode, sending shrapnel throughout the stamping plant, harming workers, sometimes killing them. This is no silent or relaxing workplace, and even if the presses themselves do not harm the operator through failure, disaster, or accident, the noise will damage hearing.

> Most of the behemoths in the Budd press shop were, by brand, either Danly or Clearing. Whatever their make, the main components of a stamping press are, beginning from the bottom, its base, its bolster, its die, its ram, its crown, and—running from base to crown—its side columns, on which the crown sits and between which the ram slides.

(Some call the ram the slide for this reason.) The one impermanent piece of the structure is the die, which will be changed out depending on the part. Each stamped part has a specific die that produces it; though necessary, die changes create downtime along a press line. In a state-of-the-art stamping plant, die changes are quick—a matter of minutes—and completely automated. Budd was not state-of-the-art. A spring 1987 plant newsletter, the Budd Communicator, ran an article on the Budd Detroit die transition team, which competed against the Budd plants in Philadelphia and Kitchener, Ontario, to see which plant could complete die changes most quickly. The photograph accompanying the piece pictured thirty or so men on the team—"truck drivers, crane operators, hook-up, die setters, maintenance, sanitation and supervisors." A caption beneath a photograph of a group of men guiding the die noted that "teamwork and muscle are required." Philadelphia won the inter-plant contest. Detroit, where "the elapsed time was 89 minutes," came second.

(27–28)

The ecology of businesses begins to reveal itself. Imagine the many firms producing the presses throughout the modern age of American industrial dominance. Danly[3] is now subsidiary to the MISUMI group headquartered in Japan,[4] and Danly continues to manufacture tools and products for die creation. Like high-end programming, Danly continues to make the tools that produce new tools: the forms in high-technology metals and precise engineering that requires advanced education in metallurgy and cutting-edge new-generation materials. These deep skill sets and advanced abilities do not dissipate because the final assembly plant has moved to follow cheaper labor. It is, however, interesting to see how the die manufacturing firm has been purchased by a Japanese multinational and kept in business producing high-end dies for transplanted and American-homegrown industries concerned with retaining skill sets needed to create the machines-that-build-other-machines in the postindustrial Midwest. Clearing is represented online only by a series of late World War II posters and advertisements and entries regarding patents and filings like Ansley's (1957) *Manufacturing Methods and Processes*. It also produced a series of equipment pamphlets, the most intriguing of which is titled *The Hall of Giants* published in 1947. Once rich with historical linkages and suppliers and networks of animating expertise, Clearing seems to have disappeared from industrial history.

Like the fabled John Henry, the best team in the best of circumstances at a competitive event could keep up with a routine die change in an automated Kamatsu press. Of course, it doesn't take "thirty or so men" to change the Komatsu die. It takes two trained associates. And the Komatsu line can change the whole line of dies—up to five—simultaneously, with two workers per die. Ten workers in 45 minutes to change the whole press line in a sustainable, rationalized process versus a team of 30 at their best to change one die under ideal conditions … in 89 minutes.

Clearing and Danly manufactured the machines that punched the parts, Budd created the line that manufactured the parts themselves, then the parts were gathered together with the engine and transmission works and assembled at yet another plant, the final assembly line. And while the military mass production of jeeps and tanks that valued interoperability and volume production, and relied on the ability to swap operators (soldiers and their training were just replaceable parts, after all), the age of information requires more nimble production coupled with an ability to customize for special orders, take special requests, and morph the basic automobile platform for numerous different orders and different contexts of use on the fly.

Detroit failed not because of failed workers or labor demands run amok. To the contrary, management and labor share their failure to understand that their system of static design, redesign, and innovation had broken. Both workers and managers came to believe that their first-generation industrial production would forever rule the international scene. As we have painfully come to understand, that is not the case. Sadly, management and its political allies have attempted to obscure the shortcomings of their ideological approach and rather than redesign their failed ideas seek to (unconscionably) change reality, or at least the perception of evidence, and assert that labor was responsible for industrial decline. It simply isn't the case, and SIA, Subaru, and the car industry in the United States reveal that managerial failure.

The industrial press rollers immediately distinguish the Japanese designed facility from the description of the Budd plant. The city of Detroit seems to be the symbol, on one hand, for all the ways American management and workers failed to adjust to the new challenges of manufacturing. It is also a symbol of resistance and of overcoming long odds. Current politics require that Detroit will have to be self-reliant rather than depend upon a central government to provide resources. It is important to remember, though, that Detroit, the United Auto Workers (UAW), and General Motors did not fall overnight. Rather, a slow decline was punctuated by moments of insight with events and warnings that might have resulted in mid-course corrections by all the stakeholders involved: missed opportunities for small improvements made along the way that, in aggregate, change manufacturing and change the relationship between managers and workers.

I knew that the presses in the Subaru plant were very different from those I had seen in previous plants. Over time, I had come to understand how different the Subaru plant was from previous industrial concerns and how this thoroughly automated manufactory site differed from its contemporaries. There was something in its national origin, yes, because this is a Japanese transplant company manufacturing in the American Midwest using Japanese techniques and practices. Most impressive was the distinction in its management style.

Designed in Japan, put to work in Indiana, based on principles of Kaizen, lean manufacturing, and iterative design that were driving efficient manufacturing and effective marketing, Subaru is at once a Japanese success story, an American tale of de-industrialization, and a postindustrial irony. Once in place, the Komatsu presses revolutionized the automobile industry and left the Budd plant and American manufacturing, as well as management, behind. Of course, it didn't have to be that way.

Iterative design as new normal

By the mid-1980s, the Japanese had created what has become industry standard: the ability to replace dies and press molds on the fly as if they were programs. The Komatsu stamping press is revolutionary because it allowed the dies inside its 800 ton press to be removed and reset through an automated process, allowing new shapes—new car body parts—to be formed with only an hour of down time between stamping runs. In effect, this allows the highly accurate, highly automated stamping press to be programmed on the fly, using physical dies as object-oriented programs that can swap a current model year fender for one from a design used in 2005. Or run 500 more hoods and 500 additional door panels only when orders and forecasts indicate the need for 500 additional cars to deliver to markets. The combination of just-in-time production with statistical modeling and data-driven decision making is quite astounding, particularly when we think back to what was happening in American automotive manufacturing.

Even after the oil shocks of 1973 and again following the Iranian revolution in 1979, American automotive manufacturing did not have the flexibility to respond to changes in the automobile market. Honda's timing seems almost magical, as gas-sipping Civics and Accords rolled off assembly lines at American-based manufacturing facilities as GM and Ford continued to produce high consumption, large engine models as well as poorly designed, poorly manufactured smaller cars that earned comparison not to their Japanese competition but to the French Citroën, so close to the French for lemon, *citron*, that the Vega, the Pinto, and the Gremlin earned the title as some of the ugliest cars ever produced. They were also among the most unreliable. See Kimball (2006) and Pflugfelder (2016) for more on rhetorical automobility.

The revolutionary Komatsu presses, designed in Japan for a new style of auto manufacturing, sat idle in Japan waiting to be transported to the American Midwest. The Komatsu presses would likely be delivered to the United States through the Panama Canal today after its recent expansion, and the East Coast ports of Baltimore and Norfolk are expanding to accommodate the new standard "Post-Panamax" transport, which accounts for only 16% of ships but 45% of shipping capacity worldwide.[5] Had the newly reopened, expanded Panama Canal existed then, the story may have been different, but in 1988, the Komatsu presses surpassed the capacity of the canal, requiring a trip around the southern tip of South America, around Tierra del Fuego, up the eastern coast of Brazil, and into the Gulf of Mexico. They were loaded onto barges and shipped up the Mississippi and onto the Ohio River, where they were transferred to specially designed cargo-carrying trucks up interstate 65 under the darkness of night, closing parts of the interstate, redirecting traffic, and going around overpasses too low to accommodate the massive presses.

Mike Mattingly, the tour guide who told this version of the story, added a few unconfirmable details that are just simply delicious and provide some insight into the nature of global logistics. Apparently, the planning team had some tense moments as the ships were held in the central Pacific Ocean waiting for storms to clear from the South American coast. It is a powerful reminder how the combination of predictive technology and global communications really have changed shipping practices, as a management and design team waited sleeplessly for weather to pass while the tremendous cargo ships idled, halfway to their ultimate destination, in the middle of the Pacific. Imagine half a century earlier, without effective Doppler radar weather tools, how the huge Japanese industrial press might have been damaged, delayed, or even sunk without the ability to see an oncoming storm and wait out high seas and damaging winds. Literal connection to metis, the ancient arts of sailing, are unavoidable as technology informates the process. Would Subaru have been able to ensure the press without access to real-time weather forecasting? Since widening the canal, the distance traveled would be halved. These various elements—ships, ports, radar, traditional shipping routes, and predictive computing power—coming together into logistical networks to allow for safer, smoother passage across huge distances and wild oceans culminate in advanced industrial technology that is delivered, installed, and operating just down the road. This stamping press has become a naturalized part of the larger story of postindustrial manufacturing in the United States in the 21st century.

In contrast, recent work observing the dismantling of Detroit has earned the name disaster or ruin porn, with photos of once grand homes and hotels, neighborhoods, and infrastructure abandoned, like the infamous pictures of the Detroit railroad terminal, Michigan Central Station. The Design Observer Group catalogues the outpouring of literature and film about the demise of Detroit[6] while the group See Detroit supports a website of images of the city's deteriorating infrastructure[7] from a local activist perspective. Local artists like photographer Dave Jordano[8] and the Heidelberg Project[9] represent hope for a better future while French photographers Yves Marchand

and Romain Meffre[10] take a documentary approach. Rhetoric offers a hopeful voice in Jeff Rice's *Digital Detroit* (2012), which traces the signs of life from the hacker and maker communities in the city that take advantage of the idle talents of local artisans and inheritors of Detroit's industrial heritage. But perhaps the most striking narrative of the deconstruction of the city is Clemens' *Punching Out* (2011) that tells of the slow work of disassembling, packing up, and shipping the Budd stamping plant to Mexico, Brazil, and parts of southeast Asia.

Clemens' narrative reveals key components of the contrast between the late industrial manufacturing practices of the United States and the Kaizen-driven lean manufacturing of Japan. There is far less enlightenment to be found in labor-management relations than there is to revealing the chimera of labor relations. Clemens' narrative insinuates that executives and representatives of management heightened tensions with labor in order to mask overall poor decision making and lack of imagination and leadership, replacing vision and long-term planning with hackneyed attempts to crush resistance and demands for fairness. Tracing these technocultural networks reveals deep dysfunction in decision making and vision, and even in research and development.

The disassembly of the Budd presses in Detroit in 2010 can be articulated as the end of the process begun with the arrival of the Komatsu presses in Lafayette in 1988. Budd characterizes the end of a static form of industrial assembly characterized by industrial-age modernism: the creation of the model year, of static presses lining huge press and assembly lines. Clemens narrates the fate of smaller single-die presses, attended by unionized autoworkers, demanding higher pay for fewer hours. According to Clemens:

> At the time of its closing, Budd Detroit was solely a stamping plant. There are all kinds of auto plants, and there are auto plants of all kinds in Detroit, but the three predominant types, by size and conspicuousness, are stamping plants, engine plants, and assembly plants. Assembly plants are the final stage, where the auto body parts from stamping plants and the engines from engine plants and the countless other components, big and small, come together to make a car. Poletown, for instance, is an assembly plant. Fisher Body was a GM stamping plant. New Center Stamping—stamping. Ford Wixom was an assembly plant. The Ford Rouge, as originally conceived, was all-inclusive. Some of these plants, such as Budd and New Center Stamping, are, or were, suppliers. Others belong to the Big Three. But all belong to the same industrial ecosystem.
>
> Assembly plants are distinguished by their assembly lines—Henry Ford's great innovation—that produced middle-class prosperity as surely as movable type made possible widespread literacy. Similarly, stamping plants like Budd are identifiable by their press lines—the

linked presses, arranged in rows, that stamp out auto body parts, with each press performing a separate but sequential operation: blank, form, trim, pierce.

(Clemens, 25—emphasis mine)

Ford's Rouge is the closest equivalent to Subaru's all-inclusive design. Subaru builds four-cylinder engines, fabricates parts, and assembles cars under one gigantic roof in Lafayette, with some smaller subassembly of wire harnesses, seats, tires, and glass being manufactured and shipped for final assembly. Specialty subassembly parts are part of the larger car-assembly ecosystem that Detroit still centers, and which Toledo contributed auto glass, with tires produced in Akron, nicknamed Rubber City. Detroit continues to design cars and centers a more diffuse automobile manufacturing cluster with fewer assembly plants in Michigan, yet American automotive assembly continues at Toyota, Honda, Mitsubishi, and Subaru plants further south.

Kaizen at SIA

Kaizen[11] is Japanese for continuous improvement, or change for good. It is based on the idea that institutions and processes are never complete but that there is always room for improvement. This contrasts with the idea of genius or one-off design in which old processes are replaced by new with each instantiation of the process. This designing from a clean slate, or the myth of the *tabulae rasa*, is where many unintended consequences are introduced.

Participatory design and user-centered and focused design methods draw strongly from this tradition of continuous improvement. Widely used social media tools like Facebook now rely on the cascade of user feedback that comes with every incremental change. It is both a process aimed at approaching an ideal state while realizing that goal is a chimera, an unattainable ideal, while also demonstrating that users are enculturated into a system, whether it is a virtual or physical system. Interestingly, it has become something of a joke to watch the screens of Facebook light up with user complaints no matter how small the change is. Over time, these complaints die back, and users continue to use the system. It is an interesting phenomenon, and reveals the sense of ownership users have over a system they use regularly, that the immediate response to change is resistance, and finally, that most changes quickly become renaturalized as a new status quo, and users forget their initial resistance.

Kaizen received much attention in Graham's 1995 book about Subaru-Isuzu, *On the Line,* but in hindsight the resistance seems misplaced. So much of what she and the UAW had feared either has not come to fruition or has been renaturalized into a "new normal" that it hardly seems important to rehash those arguments, particularly in light of the ethical concerns that emerge when considering her method as she did not reveal herself to be an academic researcher either to the company or to her coworkers. There are, however, certainly gaps between the description and ideology of Kaizen and its practice on the Subaru and other Japanese auto manufacturers' assembly and manufacturing facilities.

Graham's research practice has been informative. For each site I wished to visit, I introduced myself as a researcher writing a book about postindustrial communication and emergent practices. I avoided any situation in which I would be asked to sign a nondisclosure form as I only wanted to speak with people in their official capacities and about materials and processes the firms were comfortable with making public. I was direct and honest about my interest and desire in disclosing, in sharing, and in analyzing the materials, people, and processes with which I interacted. This study has also been in development for years before publication, further distancing the feeling of breakthrough technologies being guarded secrets, but close enough in time that they have not yet become mundane practice and everyday technologies. I am not studying humans but instead the places they work and their relationship to the organization structures and institutions they are part of and participate in creating. The institutional review of research practice, human subjects research review, is an important element of self-policing and protection of human subjects. See *The Belmont Report Revisited* by Childres et al. (2005) for more about this important institutional innovation designed to protect citizens engaged in research processes, and the process of integrating human subject research review into research organizations is an example of the kind of design-for-change this study emphasizes. In short, everyone I spoke to knew I was writing a book about workplace practices, and they invited me to talk with them about their workplaces knowing I was writing about their work. Talking to people about their work in workplace settings consistent with their job descriptions is simply not human research as defined by Belmont or IRB, the Institutional Review Boards responsible for protecting the interests of human subjects of research. I was speaking with people about their work as described in publicly related information, generally from websites and other published materials, and was only interested in their work as evident through work title and organization affiliation. That many workers are connected to their workplaces through publicly available information is a significant change between the postindustrial and the industrial. On the one hand, contemporary regulations are designed to protect human bodies from physical harm while the workplace itself maintains astounding amounts of information about each individual worker as well as the work being done. I emailed 8–10 potential participants and for each one who responded to me, and I winnowed this list of potential interview subjects down to approximately three potential subjects for each example that became a representative site study. What was most interesting to me was the gap between what I expected to find in conversations, tours, and site visits and what was in evidence. I expected noisy factories that matched my older expectations and instead I found worksites that were quiet and clean, resembling healthcare facilities and college campuses more than the factory floors I had imagined. Subaru and Braun were particularly quiet manufacturing floors, testifying to the change marking new manufacturing.

Evidence of change is striking. Each bolt and screw is accounted for today, examined for potential savings and rethinking. Even the packing materials in which bolts arrive at the plant have database entries as well as narratives representing their inclusion in the assembly process. Standard procedure today, history shows that the early 20th-century workplace was much less precise. In the history of foundry floor and back office work that Carol Siri-Johnson chronicles in *The Language of Work* (2009), there was not even a master list of workers. Foremen managed work teams, paid them in cash, and often did not necessarily know the men's names—and the vast majority of workers were men at the time (see Oldenziel, 2004; Ware, 1990). This longer historical view paints a different picture than that told by either management or labor, and it isn't until we begin to reflect on the deindustrialization of the upper Midwest, in comparison with the emergent narrative of knowledge and media jobs, that we begin to gain some perspective. In his concluding chapter *From Counterculture to Cyberculture*, Turner asserts that

> The New Communalist celebration of information, technology, and experimentation has two implications, one for our understanding of postindustrial society, and another for our understanding of the counterculture's role in the spread of both computing and the networked mode of production. Since the early 1970s, a series of sociologists and geographers have chronicled the growth of a new, knowledge-based form of economic production.
>
> (240–241)

The collaborationist spirit and emerging social network make labor-management relations obsolete, and empower citizens to use their free time in interesting and productive ways, to create whole new realms of what used to be called hobbies, but what Clay Shirky (2011) celebrates as *Cognitive Surplus*: as a powerful source of social power, or social and cultural *capital*. Turner is more explicit about what makes both management and labor concerns fall away:

> Yet, despite their differences, these scholars have tended to agree that, starting sometime in the late 1960s or early 1970s, a postindustrial mode of development emerged as a dominant force in society.
>
> (241)

The postindustrial mode was first characterized by the application of decentralized, collaborative management structures to the computing industry, to software development, then to hardware development, and then to the internet and online social networking environments. This postindustrial mode of knowledge work is poised to continue to radically change manufacturing and take advantage of the powerful tools created for managing information work innovated and used in the United States, as well as developments like Kaizen and lean manufacturing, that make the next generation of manufacturing revolutionary, innovative, and effective.

The perceived obsolescence of unionization and labor is persistent and lies at the heart of long-running conflicts beyond the scope of this study except to point out that labor relationships are fraught and come into heightened contrast when comparing books like Graham's and Turner's which seem more like battles between modernism and postmodernism, or industrialism and postindustrialism. More productive modes of engagement, like that narrated in *Inside the Ford-UAW Transformation* (2015), offer a vision of cooperation and an understanding of the challenge facing American manufacturing and labor, to the point that the co-authors are a United Auto Workers Union Leader, a Ford corporate executive, and an automotive industry consultant. *Inside the Ford-UAW Transformation* represents the power of iterative design and the slow change of institutions necessary to address the challenges of wicked problems as described in the introduction rather than either the unfortunate rhetoric of assigning blame of Graham or the utopian foolishness of Turner. The organizational change necessary to transform the confrontational relationship between management and labor into a cooperative negotiation takes persuasion and patience but ultimately pays off in tangible results. Remember here that Ford is the only major American automobile manufacturer not to declare bankruptcy in the great recession of 2007/2008.

> Ford believes a commitment to developing your business internally is one of the most reliable methods by which you can weather an economic storm. If you're developing new products and services and finding other ways to enhance your business from within, you'll become much more strategically diverse and self-sufficient as a company.

Building from within, building resilience and flexibility, and building alliances among stakeholders: each of these assets are perhaps less tangible than the unit cost per bolt, or the value of 100% recycling, but the benefits are no less real as Ford has won over consumers skeptical of large corporations either unable to weather economic challenges or swift to take government assistance. While Kaizen has aided the emergence of

Ford as a flexible postindustrial manufacturing concern, the underlying myths of modernist replacement design—the use of the word transformation in the book's title—reveal that acceptance of iterative design is far from universal or transparent. Nor is the collaborative relationship between the United Auto Workers Union and Ford's executive management taken for granted.

At the heart of Kaizen and its arrival in the United States first with Honda and then shortly thereafter with Toyota and Subaru is that continuous improvement, and total quality management, and even lean manufacturing, were the ideas of an American business consultant and professor. My Kaizen books and materials, ones with publication dates in the late 1980s and early 1990s, are withdrawn from Wabash National, Caterpillar, and the Krannert Business School at Purdue. Kaizen, total quality management, lean manufacturing, and its offspring Six Sigma have been operative in the Wabash Valley for a quarter century, impacting not just advanced manufacturing, but healthcare and education.

Jeffrey Liker in *The Toyota Way* and Masaaki Imai both name W. Edwards Deming as bringing the ideas of total quality management to Japan. Deming was a frequent consultant to Japanese businesses rebuilding during the post–World War II allied occupation, and it seems ironic that Deming engineered Ford's turnaround in the 1980s after American automobile manufacturing had fallen to the very concepts he championed. The Deming Institute carries on his legacy, and he is considered a hero in Japan, although he was largely forgotten in the United States through the 1960s and 1970s, the years when he might have had the most to offer American manufacturing. During the occupation, the programs Deming headed were referred to collectively as Training Within Industries, or TWI. According to Masaaki Imai in *Gemba Kaizen*:

> The TWI programs were developed in the United States fifty years ago. They were designed to play a major role in boosting industrial production to the levels required to win the Second World War. Even though TWI did this very successfully, after the war the program's usage dropped off until, in 1992, they are hardly used or even known in the United States.
>
> (106)

Imai continues, asserting that postwar domestic American production turned to efficiency through scale rather than quality, and it showed in the reliability, dependability, and customer satisfaction with automobiles as well as a whole generation of American-manufactured goods:

> In 1992, even though the programs have changed little since their arrival in Japan, they are well respected in Japanese management circles and are viewed as important enough to the national interest

to be overseen by the Ministry of Labor, which licenses instructors and upholds training standards throughout the country.

(ibid)

It is one of the postindustrial ironies articulated in this study: an orphaned American innovation finds a home in postwar, rebuilding Japan and then arrives back in the American Midwest in the late 20th century and continues in the creative destruction of US homegrown automotive manufacturing techniques. Deming develops and successfully implements a system of statistical quality control in the United States that aids the war effort, and then in an act of goodwill, joins the American occupation in postwar Japan. He contributes significantly to Japanese redevelopment and postwar industrial growth, while his ideas and values are lost to American manufacturing, and only after losing ground to Japanese automobiles imported and then built in the United States with US labor are his ideas once again valued. As Liker asserts:

> Part of the problem was that mass production after World War II [in the US] focused on cost, cost, cost. "Make bigger machines and through economies of scale drive down cost." "Automate to replace people if it can be cost justified." This kind of thinking ruled the manufacturing world until the 1980s.
>
> (Masaaki Imai, 109)

Liker's *The Toyota Way* concentrates on the lean production system that Subaru and other Japanese car manufacturers brought more broadly to manufacturing. Indeed, it seems that "advanced manufacturing" requires some adherence to lean, *gemba kaizen*, and supply chain management. Deming's innovative model of manufacturing was rejected by American manufacturers in part because it was such a sweeping transformation of current industrial practice, so different in fact that I represent it here as a key theme distinguishing postindustrial from industrial manufacturing. It is no small distinction to call attention to the important tradition of management represented by Taiichi Ohno and his 2012 book *Workplace Management* (reissued for its 100th anniversary), a contemporary of Ford and Taylor. Ohno represents a significant local innovator who distinguished East Asian management style from Euro-American management.

Kaizen is not limited to Deming's statistical quality control, nor is it limited to manufacturing. Recent developments have brought lean cyclical development to healthcare, programming, and technical communication (see Simmons & Zoetewey, 2012). Central to all these is the analysis of process as well as outcomes, how goals are set, how communication is accomplished, how decisions are made, and how the next iteration of production cycles can be improved. It concentrates not only on efficiencies but also on quality.

Kaizen gets slammed as a management fad (one that has been operative since the 1960s in Japan and successfully working in a variety of manufacturing workplaces in the Midwest since the late 1980s). It has resulted in millions in savings and untold thousands of gallons of saved fuel—diesel, gas, and coal—that did not need to be consumed. While Six Sigma and Kaizen and total quality management can be mocked, it is nonetheless operative. Kaizen and Six Sigma are ripe for ridicule, but both operate and support innovative action. It functions. Perhaps, as Latour writes in *Aramis*, it is a show of filial love, all this mockery. Our beloved technologies are our most lampooned. They are taunted but they function; they are derided, but they shape the experience and extend the capacities of individual human beings within the system. Kaizen is an input stream that impacts the functioning of the institution. It is perhaps an early step, a temporary fix, that does as much to call attention to the power differential between those who work on the assembly line and those who manage the factory, the organization's strategic planning, design, marketing, and engineering of the automobiles. The ethic of always improving through small iterative adjustment is an institutional innovation, a soft social technology that embeds positive, cyclical, recurring change throughout the institution—an organization built to change. See "Institutional Critique" by Porter et al. (2000) for more on the role analysis plays.

When I first visited Subaru, they had already embarked on their project to realize 100% recycling. They reached the goal more quickly than many had anticipated. By 2007, they could claim to be recycling 100% of their waste stream, putting nothing in the local county landfill. What had begun with bottles and cans in the cafeteria had grown to include lunch scrap composting as well as a sophisticated system of barrels, process analysis, and worker-management cooperation.

Central to Subaru's marketing identity, to this organization's corporate branding, is its environmental policy and perceived sustainability. My careful language in the preceding sentence should not be taken so much as criticism or skepticism but careful description of the company's commitment to its environmental policy. Nothing is spent on recycling, cleaning up its manufacturing operations is seen as opportunity to articulate new recyclables, and the team is always seeking additional efficiencies. Each of these recycling sites is examined for potential marketing opportunities. The way their actions are interpreted, described, and presented to shareholders and customers, to managers and regulators, feeds back into the stories the organization tells itself and its customers. SIA is a subsidiary substantially owned by Fuji Heavy Industries, and FHI is traded in Japan on the NIKKEI index rather than in New York, London, or Chicago. As such, it is required to publish its carbon dioxide output and to quantify its carbon footprint. Other car companies and leaders in other industries have followed suit, but Subaru was early in this level of transparency and shared data on numerous aspects of its environmental impact, both as a part of FHI, but also as an early adopter of ISO 14001. Central to ISO 14001 is an articulated continual improvement process (CIP) that is both consistent with and responsive to Kaizen philosophy, and which has three dimensions for proving compliance with the International Organization for Standardization: expansion, enrichment, and upgrading.

Subaru expanded a modest strategy for recycling at two sites: first, an employee-sponsored recycling program for containers and food in the canteen and a cardboard and packaging recycling program begun on the assembly floor. The program expanded in the canteen to include all packaging, switching to more easily recyclable and compostable materials, and composting food scraps. Enrichment took the form of encouraging employees to use compost generated through recycling as well as finding markets for recycled materials generated at the plant. Upgrading took the form of moving from recycling what was easily accessible to stretching and articulating a goal of 100% recycling—zero landfill impact. Now, this is an historical narration of this program because Subaru has been certified as a 100% recycling facility since 2007, certified zero waste. Its new goal, discussed below, is even loftier. But, first, it is necessary to describe the process of achieving zero waste.

Line workers first suggested their nut and bolt suppliers reuse the cardboard cartons that parts arrived in, and after 10 or 12 uses, these boxes were themselves recycled. Later, reusable plastic totes replaced the boxes. Suppliers who were required for various reasons to use cardboard had custom-designed boxes that used materials more efficiently, and in some cases, they redesigned their boxes to use less material by shortening top tabs. That is, the boxes never really closed the way cardboard boxes do. There was a small opening on top of each box that retained the structural integrity of individual boxes and of stacks of boxes, but less material was used in constructing the shipping and storage containers. The extruded foam packaging in which engine transmissions and other imported parts were shipped was sent back to Japan for reuse, marked each time through the process, and reused up to 20 times, carrying 20 transmission assemblies across the Pacific before being recycled themselves into new polystyrene products. Then the industrial boxes and pallets into which polystyrene-encased transmissions were themselves redesigned so they could be stacked, empty, 12 deep instead of 3, and transported back to Japan to be refilled. Each of these processes represents many dozens, then hundreds, and eventually thousands of small, incremental changes that were made to the delivery, packing, and shipping processes.

During my visits, I heard about negotiations with parts suppliers over packaging materials, of switching to more expensive plastic caps that were more easily recyclable—replacing red and blue plastic with high-quality undyed plastic that could be more readily turned into other products after their lifetime of use. This process demonstrates that paying, for example, an extra 2 cents at the point of procurement more than made up the savings realized by reusing the marginally more expensive part many times. Apparently, in the long run there is more money to be made in investing in quality design and processes than in a race to the bottom of cost for each individual part, and economies of scale go so far but then information and informed design, research, and contextual awareness make strategic investments pay off in the long term.

Communication and persuasion are an important part of iterative Kaizen process. Particularly when a short-term savings is offset by long-term investment, it can be a battle to convince reluctant managers to consider the more expensive alternative. The institutional advantage of iterative design may not offer an immediate payback but through the accumulation of additional adjustments, makes disruptive changes less necessary while returning long- and medium-term return on investment. Whether a technical or management specialist looking to influence the practices of their workplace or a writing professional with communication as a primary organizational responsibility, the role of the communicator is both challenging and potentially powerful. In an organization designed to learn, change, and grow, rhetors are capable of impacting the development of their organizations. Communication specialists who manage to articulate advantages will accrue growing influence and trust from above as well as below, and participation and articulation of functional alternatives will reward the successful practitioner in the form of a reputation for making effective suggestions and having foresight.

Steel and other metals arrive in large industrial rolls from foundries across the upper Midwest. These metals are being produced in the old industrial centers: US Steel in Gary, Indiana; Dotson in Mankato, Minnesota; Timken's in Canton, Ohio; Rouge Steel, Rouge, Michigan; among 25 others still operating in the United States. Often, the steel is higher quality than commonly used in automobile manufacturing, and steel is imported from China, India, Brazil, and Russia in part because it is lower cost *and lower quality.* Imported steel is not high enough quality for Subaru's needs. After first negotiating higher and higher quality, with fewer and fewer contaminants, blemishes, and imperfections, negotiations turned to other issues. Working with their suppliers, Subaru negotiated different custom widths of the rolls of steel to minimize waste. They have even gone so far as requiring that the steel and other manufacturing materials be covered with reusable, weatherproof tarps during transit. These tarps enable Subaru to use more of each roll of steel without discarding surfaces exposed to air and weather during transit; the cost of covering materials during transit added negligibly to the overall costs of the materials. And they now have the drivers of their suppliers involved in Kaizen redesign efforts, informing foundry forewomen and shipping and receiving managers that they need to pay attention to the demands of their customers in order to ensure continued collaboration and business with this internationally respected automobile manufacturer.

But to reach zero waste is a goal both powerful and marketable, laudable beyond the accusations of green washing that dog less enthusiastically idealistic concerns. It is fact that around 5% of total waste is burned to generate electricity, and this is the lowest level of recycling because of the amount of carbon dioxide created as waste and the paltry amount of energy produced. However, there are numerous realized and planned recycling processes that are both more impressive and more technologically innovative. It is, perhaps, a cost of marketability. It represents the power of saying zero waste rather than 99.9% or 95% waste free. See Anderson (2009) and Arielly (2010) on the importance of the difference between zero and any other value. But that is a cultural concern beyond the scope of marketing Subaru cars in the marketplace, the agora. Indeed, what they have achieved is impressive.

There are plans to convert the solvent-based paint process to a waterborne process. This will save significant amounts of both energy and materials. The most wasteful process right now at the SIA plant is paint and finishes, and this is true of most painting and finish work because of the nature of waterproofing and the chemistry of rust. Protecting the metals and other materials that make up the outer shell of the car body that is exposed to weather, atmospheric, and road conditions are hugely important, and are one face the company shows the world. The gleam of its finishes, defying years of road grime and salt, represents Subaru's durability. As it is, solvents are treated and recycled, reused as many times as possible, before being disposed of. These solvents—or what is left of them after what cannot be further concentrated and distilled for reuse and redeployment—account for a significant part of the waste burned for electricity. Advanced paint is a polymer. Polymers are plastics. The waste paint-polymer now is filtered out of solvents, kept as industrial sludge, and incorporated into plastic parking barriers by a company in Ohio. The polymers were of a much higher grade than what was required for plastic fill in this application, but the polymer was given new life, not taking up space in the landfill but redeployed as a parking bumper. If, in Latour's world, significance lies in a speed bump being called a sleeping policeman (Latour, 1992) then what added layers of morality arise when the sleeping policeman is made of recycled plastic?

If it sounds like this analysis promotes Subaru, I must disagree. Instead, I am drawing attention to the way the organization is devised to welcome and accumulate modification. Over time those adjustments accrue and result in what appears to be transformation. But conversion is not disruptive. It is a realization, perhaps, that there is more to gain through cooperation and mutual respect between management and labor, and that the age of raw muscle-driven labor really has past. Again, the Japanese have a useful concept, *muri*, which is one of three forms of waste. *Muri* means impossible work, or unnecessarily hard work. John Henry, beating the mechanized hammer with brawn and muscle, can be understood as postindustrial warning rather than as industrial hero. If the mythical John Henry ever had a chance against industrial hammers, he has absolutely no chance in an age of 3,200 ton, three-axis programmable presses, where experts are paid not for their ability to stack machined parts as quickly as the press can spit them out, but in understanding that the steel scrap produced in that press is itself worth something. Let that unpleasant, dangerous, dehumanized, deskilled work get automated, and allow the human brain to examine the process so it can create innovations and revisions. Perhaps I am guilty of cheerleading, but I am neither acquiescing to those who hold that management is powerful and therefore right, nor willing to accept that there are not legitimate concerns about the shortsightedness of some labor unions and their representatives. I am leading a cheer for iterative change.

The innovations at Subaru move far beyond mundane items transformed. Working at SIA means construing waste differently. It means reconsidering the cast-off products of assembly and finish not as unfortunate but unavoidable costs produced at the point of manufacture, as garbage to be dumped. Rather, the same economy of scale derived from the economic advantages of mass production can be brought to bear through rationalization and statistical analysis in conjunction with a concomitant drive to improving product quality and environmental sustainability. What else can these products be used for? What if the definition of efficiency were turned to include not just the short-term reduction of cost but also the cost to culture of wasteful use of raw and natural resources, of the medical cost of dangerous workplace injury, as well as accounting for many as-yet unaccounted for elements in bookkeeping. Ecological economics, here represented by bookending essays by Clive Spash (1999, 2015) expand the notion of economics to include not just what the direct costs to the company are but what the costs are to culture for utilizing scarce virgin resources. For instance, what is the cost of replacing the marsh's ability to filter wastewater, protect against storms and tidal surge, and support a complex ecosystem versus the economic benefit of however many waterfront condominium units? How much does it cost in the long term to dump plastic polymers rather than find a factory building plastic parking bumpers? Usually, the economics of conservation and careful stewardship of resources outstrip the promise of opportunistic development, and put environmental degradation in a different context. Far from mechanizing or devaluing nature, this economic trend articulates the richness (and riches!) of supporting cradle-to-cradle recycling. Once feared by environmentalists (and still a source of concern for environmental ideologues), use has to be balanced by cost, and the timeline and deep value of resources assessed.

Iterative design is restless. Kaizen, defined as virtuous change, or change for the better, is a mechanism for institutionalizing change. Critics like Graham certainly have their points. First, Japanese transplants to the United States have proven themselves to be able competitors. Also, the UAW, union shops in general, and the rise of "right to work" legislation has unleashed a torrent of innovation ripe for criticism, and soft tissue injury and morning calisthenics and the like seem minor compared to the suppression of worker rights and widespread management abuses of disenfranchised workers, who are displaced by growing automation and robotizing. Kaizen itself is striking and certainly not beyond reproach or criticism. Yet my analysis reveals not that Kaizen is a dehumanizing practice. Instead, Kaizen reveals existing inequalities and striking power differentials between assembly line workers and top management, with well-paid but still comparatively low paid engineers, office workers, and salaried employees. These middle-earning associates were rightly proud of their work and provided access to their working worlds. The jobs, the work, being done at Subaru are good jobs that pay well and provide good benefits. They are worthy of the information age, of postindustrial context, and manage risks as well as rewards of emerging opportunities.

Balance is the goal and there are trade-offs. Some emissions need to come from burning fossil fuels. There is a loss to mechanical inefficiency, and there always must be waste products produced in heavy industry. Iterative design recognizes that there are ways of improving, of getting from what works now to where we want to be, of articulating attainable short-term goals, challenging mid-range goals, and articulating wild blue-sky potential. The challenge is to create regulations and articulate risks appropriate to these challenges, and reward the organizations, like SIA/Subaru, that value environmental stewardship, community collaboration, and humane treatment of workers. Advocate for higher pay and greater benefits, but recognize the benefits an employer and global player like Subaru provides both the employment landscape of Indiana and Lafayette, as well as its entanglement in the high-technology research and development network. Such are the challenges of writing the postindustrial age: they are representational, technological, political, social, and cultural all while demanding factual accuracy and an engaging style. Add the challenges of technological relevance, findability, and search-ability, and the professional challenges of being a writer in the postindustrial age begin to come into greater focus.

ISO 15001, 50001: SIA's blue sky future

Subaru's blue-sky goal is to reach carbon neutrality by 2025. If carbon neutrality sounds like an unattainable goal, consider the organization's history and what it has already attained. While all recommendations are considered, those that contribute to realizing its long-term goal of carbon neutrality are given precedence. I interviewed Denise Coogan, who at the time was Safety and Environmental Compliance Manager for Subaru of Indiana Automotive. Since conducting that interview in 2014, Subaru of America has appointed Denise Environmental Partnerships Manager[12] and has moved from the Lafayette assembly to the New Jersey corporate offices.

Subaru is aiming for carbon-neutral car production. This is a lofty goal, but Denise thought 100% recycling was impossible, and it only took 5 years to realize. Subaru has begun pursuit of the goal with an energy consumption spreadsheet. Workers record where their energy expenditures are already occurring. Step one is a descriptive analysis. They have begun reducing lighting and turning off lights not in use. These were among examples of soft options that they had already been doing as part of their regular Kaizen routines. Compressed air represented a source of energy consumption that could significantly impact overall energy use. Compressing air for a number of industrial processes accounts for a good deal of the plant's electricity consumption, and power tools pneumatically powered are a mainstay of the assembly line. It is the predominant sound of the manufacturing line as air is expressed, tools engaged, and metal engages metal. Pneumatic compression is an example of a chokepoint where overnight charging can time-shift electricity use and offer some relief to the municipal power grid during peak consumption. Beyond electricity, Subaru uses significant amounts of natural gas which hydraulic fracturing has made significantly cheaper over the last decade. The biggest consumer of natural gas in the plant is the paint shop. That paint shop draws the interest of numerous inventive thinkers on staff. The painting and finishing department still uses chemical solvents and produces the most concerning waste products in the plant... but for now, well, the attention of this chapter remains on how they use compressed gas. That remains a significant challenge for reducing consumption, but this paragraph, quickly tumbling from compressed air to natural gas and electricity, demonstrates the infectious drive to improve existing processes.

Some solutions considered included time-shifting compressed gas usage. Unfortunately, this suggestion led to production rescheduling. Managers considered reorganizing their shift schedules, going so far as completing a close study of electricity consumption in half-hour increments. Ultimately, the shift schedules have remained in place, but the study did articulate a number of potential solutions for previously unarticulated problems. Some of these produced procedures for emergency situations like flooding and fire. Others addressed less dire conditions. For instance, if the ambient daytime temperature outside reaches 95°, managers created a decision-making protocol to decide if production should shift to late night in order to take advantage of lower temperatures and lower electricity demands and costs. The solution is considered contingent because third shift—overnight, usually 11 p.m. to 6 a.m.—may achieve a greener reputation for time-shifting energy demand, yet overnight shifts are notoriously dangerous and may result in loss in the form of industrial accidents, injury, or (of less importance to workers but high importance to accounting) poor performance and error. And the impact may be as subtle as increasing waste of raw materials with a decrease in managerial presence in off-hours production. Such plans and alternatives are seriously considered, but then decisions about implementation are based on complex communication undertaken among production management and associates working on the line, along with energy production and supply partners and community partners. Changing shift schedules can have impacts on various stakeholders in the community, like area schools that have scheduled start times around shifts and bussing schedules around traffic patterns created by workers getting to and from the factory. Even traffic patterns across town and the timing of traffic lights would be impacted by changes to shift times. "Sometimes traffic engineers adjust lights for just a 15- or 30-minute interval to reflect a factory shift change or even school dismissal time."[13] The research leading to signal optimization translated wait times and stoplight idling into costs and emissions: "optimizing signal timing resulted in an estimated annual cost savings of $472,817, with a reduction in carbon dioxide emissions of 197 tons per year showing the financial and environmental benefits of using systems and processes such as these."[14]

ISO 50001 requires quantifiable environmental measurement rather than vague promises of "improvement" and so the first task is setting benchmarks. ISO benchmark uses the year 1990 following the United Nation's Kyoto Protocol environmental agreement. Because the SIA plant opened in 1989 and was ramping up production in 1990, the traditional benchmark date of 1990 is a challenge because emissions then would be benchmarked on 20% of current production. The agreement made between the local government of Lafayette, Indiana, and Subaru allows for SIA to increase production so long as measured emissions stay level. While ISO would like emissions to decrease, SIA's preferred measurable standard is waste produced per vehicle produced. While waste per vehicle has steadily declined since the plant opened, it makes reconciling SIA's carbon production difficult to measure in the terms understood by the ISO, and by extension, the United Nation and the Kyoto Protocol.

Subaru also markets its environmental stewardship. Working closely with the state fish and game authorities, they have set up a recognized wildlife refuge and mushroom hunting fields (but they are keeping those secret—available only to associates of SIA), and they fight battles with invasive species like honeysuckle and thistle. An infamous beaver family had been expanding, but has been sequestered to a far-off field. Deer, turkey, and foxes have all been sighted on the campus. Prairie grass grows on 30+ acres on the side of the factory facing the interstate highway. SIA approved the proposal for the restored prairie on a report that included an accounting of the resources needed to maintain bluegrass that had been on the site. Accounting for the gasoline and diesel, the human labor hours, purchase, and maintenance of landscaping equipment with the grounds maintenance department made a compelling case for sustainability and economics. Goats keep the edges of the prairie under control. And in the realm of research, a Purdue faculty member has been tracing the prairie restoration as an example to be emulated at other marginal landscapes, as basic research is conducted into carbon as well as ecosystem restoration in prairie grassland habitat. The SIA campus is being analyzed for its ecological diversity and robustness. Even in the drought year 2012, significant savings in diesel and gasoline and maintenance costs have been realized. Furthermore, prairie grass sequesters more CO_2 than trees providing SIA's neutrality efforts with a substantial carbon offset. SIA is already inching closer to carbon neutrality and its 50001 ISO certification. Numbers of plant species seems to multiply carbon sequestration; grassland reestablishment certainly allows more species per square foot of prairie.

Steel is currently an object of scrutiny, and associates are rethinking the need for high-quality steel that is carbon-intensive to produce. Some associates concentrate on creating less scrap steel either through reduction of waste (cracking, splitting, poor use of steel blank rolls), or replacement with other materials, like next-generation alloys, or even nonmetal carbon fiber composites and high-end plastics—soy- and plant-based materials have been considered in place of petroleum-based products. Handling is also improved so there is far less loss through waste and rejection of substandard materials. Subaru pushes its suppliers to deliver its metals in pristine condition, covered for transport with anti-corrosion coatings, which also increases the overall efficiency of the production line as there are fewer pauses for inspection of materials before they are put into production.

Denise Coogan reported that the paint shop is an area for long-term research and development of solutions for both waste production and energy efficiency. A long-term replacement research project is searching for a waterborne painting process. The bumpers are already being manufactured and painted using far less volatile compounds. Subaru car bodies themselves still use a chemical primer and clear-coat process. Consumer's expectations for shine and durability keep the chemical-intensive process in place, and Subaru finishes consistently win awards. The waterborne process that wins Subaru's contract will have to be spectacular to become a replacement process for the current finishing, but scaling up production numbers while maintaining or decreasing emissions will require creation of a water process. Waterborne primer would take a significant investment first to test the process and then to determine if long-term quality is maintained. The car manufacturer does not want to lose their industry-leading regard for their durable paints and finishes, but there is pressure to realize a waterborne painting and finishing process. Already, the solvents are recycled, cleaned, and reused which reduces their impact, but it also is an energy-intensive process that presents a challenge to the goal of carbon neutrality.

IDEM, the Indiana Department of Environmental Management, is another stakeholder, protecting the interests of the state in environmental stewardship. Indiana has a troubled history with major polluters, although SIA reports a good collaborative relationship. In my interviews with SIA, IDEM was reported to display ties "to older technologies," and had difficulty understanding how SIA was innovating and decreasing its emissions so consistently. The Federal Environmental Protection Agency, the EPA, "is maturing," "is increasing their understanding" of new manufacturing processes (Interview). But it was striking to hear how Subaru, the corporate parent of SIA, wanted their competitors held to the same environmental standards they held themselves to, to challenge other local companies to adopt an iterative design model when it came to emissions and wastes, and rather than penalizing certain emissions benchmarks to instead ask for continuing improvement. In effect, SIA is creating pressure to make iterative design the norm, and rather than penalize competitors for current levels of emissions and waste, Subaru is encouraging accurate benchmarking and commitment to long-term emissions reductions. SIA's perspective was articulated to me as moving beyond the "shop cop" model, and instead working with stakeholders to measure current practices and the waste they produced, and articulating reasonable short- and middle-term goals. SIA's goal is to iteratively redesign automotive manufacturing globally by collaborating and creating new relationships, like the Japanese car manufacturing transplants generally strive to do. Having establishing functional relationships between labor and management—sustainable relationships developed over time—competitors like Ford are up to the challenge.

Denise brought this episode of our long-running far-ranging conversation to a close with a powerful statement: "You have to pay for better technology." In a manufacturing operation at the scale of SIA, there is significantly less cost overall as waste is reduced. Even if technology increases costs, fewer loads handled at higher cost result in lower overall cost, and less waste over time per load results in greater overall efficiency. Above, I mention SIA's waste per vehicle. Over a decade of iterative design, of small Kaizen-based iterative improvement, SIA has gone from producing 49 pounds of hazardous wastes per car produced to 0.7 pounds. That is less than 12 ounces of hazardous waste produced per vehicle—seven-tenths of 1 pound of hazardous waste material produced per automobile; 11.2 ounces per car of hazardous wastes, which include paint wastes, metals, anything considered harmful or toxic reduced to ounces of material per car unit assembled. It is an amazing statistic, and has probably been reduced further in the time that has elapsed since this interview was conducted. The organization has committed itself to reducing these and other wastes. Likewise, over 5 years, they have realized a $10 million benefit—$10 million saved over 5 years!—by reducing regular waste products that are normally dumped in municipal landfills. The figure started at 459 pounds of waste generated per vehicle in 2004. In 2013, the year's target was 229.5. And their last environmental audit showed they are producing 227 pounds of solid waste per unit. While carbon neutrality remains an elusive goal, it is more in the realm of possibility than anyone might have thought possible. SIA and Subaru are, indeed, global players. More importantly, they are also responsible neighbors providing access to excellent working conditions and rewarding work for which the local community feels justifiably proud to host.

SIA, Subaru of Indiana Automotive, is but one point in an advanced interconnected manufacturing network—and an advance guard of emerging practice. It is somewhat ironic to label an automobile manufacturing firm *postindustrial*, yet no better post-Fordist title yet exists to describe the quiet manufacturing floor, the forms of deep recycling, and interrelated expertise and supply-chain networks—knowledge and logistics together that form new, functional, powerful configurations of car building. Advanced manufacturing does not capture the cultural and community aspects that distinguish SIA's practices from Detroit's, and to traditional Fordist assembly-line production. Inseparable from its advanced manufacturing practices are its entanglements in both management history as well as the convoluted history of management theory after World War II and through the late 20th century that makes Japanese and now European transplants to the American Midwest such a delicious and inspiring site for studying budding new constructions of work and communication. Understood as an American innovation based in research and development, Kaizen is an important concept. American management rejected iterative design, committed as it was to the centralized military-industrial hierarchy of postwar assembly plant management. Perhaps it is both less foreign-feeling to an American audience as well as more globally powerful when its widespread adoption is considered in the context of growing collaboration between managers and workers. Far from ideal, the movement toward cooperation and collaboration illustrates a key argument of this study. Innovation does not replace older practices but subsumes what works. The industrial is necessarily part of the emergent postindustrial order.

The chorus calls out from culture: manufacture cars in cleaner, more sustainable ways. Those with the means will purchase vehicles that cost marginally more to support an organization known for effective environmental stewardship coupled with the best safety record in the United States. The ability to recognize the opportunities—and the timing—for a transplant Japanese automobile manufacturer in the Midwestern United States reveals a depth of understanding of kairos. Metis is literalized in sailing the Komatsu presses across the Pacific. Technê, in the form of both technique and technologies, animate the assembly floor in the dance of robotics to assemble and transport what are emerging as automobiles from raw materials of plastic, steel, and electronic components.

At the core of these nascent economic practices are new theories and practices of design. No longer classical or even modern, postindustrial manufacturing relies on better and more constructive relationships between workers and management, between new and forthcoming modes of design. User-centered and iterative design methods require a different, more collaborative style of management that acknowledges, values, and even celebrates contributions from a variety of sources, from stakeholders recognized as partners in the company's progress and (partial) source of competitive advantage, encouraged to both speak up and to contribute. The challenge remains to reward these contributions fairly and articulate the role of contributors. And that role of articulation maintains the focus of this study on writing, communication, and persuasion.

Notes

1 See Morato et al. (2014) for more about safety issues when humans and robots inhabit spaces together.
2 http://subaru-sia.wix.com/indiana#!about/cq65 (Accessed April 28, 2016).
3 www.danly.com/CompanyInformation.html.
4 www.misumi.co.jp/english/.
5 www.bbc.com/future/story/20120326-slippery-ships-and-cramped-canals.
6 https://placesjournal.org/article/motor-city-breakdown/ (Accessed May 26, 2016).
7 www.seedetroit.com (Accessed May 26, 2016).
8 www.wired.com/rawfile/2013/01/detroit-dave-jordano/ (Accessed May 26, 2016).
9 www.heidelberg.org (Accessed May 26, 2016).
10 www.guardian.co.uk/artanddesign/gallery/2011/jan/02/photography-detroit#/ (Accessed May 26, 2016).
11 Why use Kaizen instead of *kaizen*? It seems a subtle difference: capital letter with standard font versus lowercase and italicized. The argument in this chapter is parallel to the one provided on the blog linked below. The author of the blog is a language and cultural learner's diary, with interesting entries on the challenges of learning Japanese and culture in Japan. The author claims that Kaizen is a new English word with a complicated history rather than a transplanted Japanese word, and is consistent with the argument regarding iterative design I present. In short, Kaizen began as an American innovation but could not find a home in Detroit, making its way back to the United States through Honda, Toyota, and Subaru. So Kaizen will appear with a capital letter rather than lowercase with italics, indicating

a new English word rather than indicating a foreign word used in the text. www.homejapan.com/2009/03/debunked-kaizen.
12 http://media.subaru.com/newsrelease.do;jsessionid=B68DC2B8AB3C0C8 CD5A976013B648D84?&id=920&mid=1 (Accessed April 28, 2016).
   http://media.subaru.com/newsrelease.do;jsessionid=E03FC2D1F23FB333 823D67D649DE9A88?&id=920&mid=1 (Accessed April 28, 2016).
13 http://wlfi.com/2016/05/18/news-18-investigates-traffic-light-timing-part-2/ (Accessed May 27, 2016).
14 www.purdue.edu/newsroom/outreach/2012/120702BullockLafayette.html
   http://wlfi.com/2016/05/17/news-18-investigates-traffic-light-timing/ (Accessed May 16, 2016).

3 Illinois and hybrid industrial agriculture

When I visited the Decatur, Illinois, Archer Daniels Midland (ADM) Plant, the company was in dire need of a public relations success. Still reeling from the lysine and citric acid price fixing scandals of the 1990s,[1,2] *The Informant* had been published in 2000 and the movie of the same title was released in 2009. Students at nearby Milliken University refer to the ADM plant as "Gotham" due to its resemblance to a postapocalyptic urban cityscape complete with larger-than-life dumping equipment, mysteriously unrecognizable industrial and agricultural machinery, belching smokestacks, and huge plumes of steam rising from its cooling towers. It is most recognizably a workplace, and it announces itself as dangerous through the many signs warning of hazards to human respiration as well as to human bodies. Signs even warned of threats to the structure of passenger vehicles not designed for the rigors of mechanized labor. In short, it's a hazardous place.

ADM once marketed itself as the supermarket to the world. The huge plant began capturing its excess heat emissions to warm a hydroponic vegetable and aquaculture farm in 2008, from which they shipped organic cucumbers, lettuce, herbs, fish, and shrimp all over the Midwestern United States. To understand the size and financial power of ADM, it is important to state that, although the hydroponics and aquaculture farm is a million-dollar investment, ADM calls it an experiment. At most it is a sideline business; it is most accurately described as research and development. Meanwhile, the main business of ADM's plant in Decatur turns corn and soybeans into a variety of products. It produces fish and animal feed. Cooking and industrial oils, ethanol, and industrial gasses like carbon dioxide and liquefied nitrogen are also produced at the site. The Decatur plant also grinds up tons of used tires, mixes them with ethanol and spent grain on-site, and produces electricity that powers the ADM production campus and supplies electricity to the city of Decatur. The power plant mixes limestone into the furnaces, which drastically reduces the amount of sulfur dioxide released into the atmosphere.[3] The primary fuel used for combustion is coal, but these additives are used to both increase efficiency and reduce emissions into the atmosphere.

One major by-product of this process is massive amounts of heat. Fuel boils water, and the power of that steam turns gigantic turbines. Steam-produced electricity is a late 19th-century technology, based on 18th-century development of coal-fired steam power that first turned heat into mechanical energy. This was the dawn of the locomotive age, offspring of what we might assume is the long-gone steam age, but the process has been redeveloped, redesigned, and refined through many iterative generations of development. At the heart of electricity production in the 21st century is the 18th-century steam engine, turning heat into electricity. Over time, steam power has been made more efficient and effective through the application of mechanical and digital technology, and space-age materials.

ADM produces dozens of products, foodstuffs, energy, industrial and building materials, chemicals, compounds, gasses and vitamins, fish, shrimp, and organic vegetables because it sees itself not only as an agricultural business but as a site of a range of agricultural, industrial, pharmacological, and human and animal nutritional processes that begin with corn and soybeans as raw products.

The cooling tower that was never built is perhaps the most striking example of ADM's inventiveness. In the mid-1990s, the small city of production facilities in Decatur was ready for expansion. One element of that planned expansion was the addition of a second cooling tower. The current plant and operations manager first suggested that ADM use the heat produced through the steam-powered generation of electricity rather than waste it through dissipation in the cooling tower. He used an economic argument with ADM's management: if the experiment failed, all ADM had done was defer construction of the cooling tower. Accountants like to defer construction, managers like to slow decisions, and while the greenhouse offered potential for long-term public relations and environmental gains, the short-term promise of deferred construction pleased key stakeholders within ADM's decision-making structure. So the plan was approved.

The greenhouse design redirected the flow of the heated water away from the cooling tower and pumped it through a large greenhouse, heating it. The greenhouse produces herbs, cucumbers, lettuce, and other vegetables and heats a large aquaponics facility. Faculty and graduates of numerous Midwestern universities participated in designing and continue to consult with ADM on this aquaculture enterprise, which ADM still regards as an experiment. Tilapia, an African freshwater fish, is raised organically, without chemicals or hormones or genetic modification. ADM is expanding their aquaculture facility, and are beginning to ship what are marketed as organic freshwater tiger shrimp.

Aquaponics brings together hydroponic plant horticulture and dry land fish-farming, a new world that strings hydroponics and aquaculture together. The plants and fish create a loop of production and feed wastes from one process as input of another. The fish excrement becomes rich manure for the plants, and the fish use the carbon dioxide produced by the plants. The plants produce enough oxygen that ADM employees were monitoring concentrations to be sure the atmosphere in the greenhouse would not become explosive. Even at this relatively small scale, the fish-to-plant relationship was providing excess oxygen as well as vegetable and herb harvests and regular fish yields.

Two things at the greenhouse surprised me. First, the entire farm is soil-less and takes place on an industrial-age conveyor belt three and a half feet off the ground. But the combination of industrial technology and a decidedly nonindustrial product—organic vegetables—indicates that this is not industrial but postindustrial. The modern separation of industrial products from agricultural products is gone, and ADM has created a farm-factory, a postmodern hybrid consistent with the forecasts of Haraway (1997) and Latour (1993) and the kind of technoscientific hybrid discussed in Hård and Jamison's *Hubris and Hybrids: A Cultural History of Technology and Science* (2005). Plants grow hydroponically in a nutrient-rich flow of water, and when the plants are mature, harvest takes place ergonomically. Workers stand at tables, harvesting, washing, and packaging produce. Even though this is a farm, there is no backbreaking bending, squatting, and reaching by workers. ADM is less dependent on the weather, as water is available from wells rather than in the form of capricious rain showers. Sunshine is still necessary to ensure photosynthesis—although nutrients can be adjusted to lessen the effects of cloudy days on the growth of the crops. And there are full-time workers on this farm, hired to work a conveyor-driven landscape that operates year-round, even in the dead of winter, providing employment and fresh produce during the darkest and coldest months of the Midwestern winter.

ADM's wastewater heated greenhouse is the central artifact of this study of postindustrial Illinois. Layers of complex technologies make the ADM campus particularly interesting, from next-generation electricity production using a mixture of coal, limestone, spent grain, and recycled tires, to boundary crossings where the distinction between agricultural and industrial production is blurred, to the production of oxygen that needs to be measured and dissipated from the aquaponics facility to minimize risks of fire and explosion. Yet it is the facilities manager who made the proposal to redirect funding and super-heated water to warm the experimental aquaponics production facility that makes this site of particular interest to technical communication scholars. The facilities manager brought together the contextual, organizational, and cultural issues with the institutional and legal challenges and economic constraints and articulated these elements into a meaningful proposal for a future economic and public relations success.

The ADM cooling tower illustrates a technocultural agent, in this case the manager of Decatur's physical plant, and offers a solution at the crossroads of various discourses that are institutionally, technologically, socially, and historically valuable. Many different agents could act effectively at this node in the network: manager, programmer, line worker, writer. I am not arguing that only the technical communicator is a viable agent here, but the preparation and training provided in humanities-based technical communication programs uniquely situate the techno-rhetor to be effective, balancing competing narratives of tradition, history of innovation, institutional identity, and business context. Kairos, technê, and metis are implicated here in unique and powerful ways; effective action will determine the ability of the rhetor to establish ethos.

Kairos, or Greek καιρός, is the opposite of chronos. Kairos is opportunity and recognition that conditions are favorable for one action over another while chronos is more like clock time. Since Kinneavy (1986) argued that Kairos has been a neglected concept, it has been made the subject of numerous scholarly studies and brought back to the fore as an important element in effective speaking and institutional intervention. Here, the manager of the physical plant—an engineer—was able to articulate a technical solution that addressed numerous needs within the organization, and along the way created an innovative new postindustrial model for agricultural and industrial production that shattered the distinction. Corn and soybeans are raw materials used for production of plastics, medicines, alcohol, livestock feed, and electricity without any concern for separation. Industrial gasses and building materials—cinder blocks—are captured from effluent streams and recycled as components of new products rather than dumped as waste from industrial production cycles. Every part of the process of turning corn and soybeans into useful products is analyzed to turn what was once considered waste— including heat generated in the production of electricity—into an ingredient in another process, harnessed and recycled in order to gain every efficiency that can be wrung from the rather dirty job of turning raw materials into finished products. ADM's contribution to the innovation network centered at the Decatur plant involves taking agricultural production from around the Midwest and turning the yield into a variety of products, from the hybrid production of finished goods, foodstuffs, energy, industrial materials, to knowledge and expertise.

Time, kairos, opens up the moment of action. Related is metis, a rhetorical concept that Pope-Ruark (2014) points to as neglected (not unlike Kinneavy's call to pay attention to Kairos and context decades earlier). For Pope-Ruark, metis is counterpoint to phronesis, favoring flexibility and opportunity over set goals and detailed planning. Invoking the work of Hawk (2004) who proposes a "post-technê" approach, Pope-Ruark remains concerned with software development, specifically so-called agile development that creates quick prototypes and engages users to redesign and rerelease iterations of the design. Metis, however, is originally a sailor's expertise where basic understandings of the sea and wind lead to smooth sailing and opportunities for taking advantage of favorable winds and fortunate tides. Metis is as valuable at ADM and Subaru as it is in Silicon Valley. In *The Social Life of Information* (2000), Brown and Duguid call it "improvisation," and it grounds their approach to maintaining expertise and discipline in the face of novel, confusing, and opportune circumstances.

Hawk (2004) develops a pedagogy for what he labels "post-technê." Hawk labels as technê the tradition of instrumental engagement with technology, and his use of the "post-" prefix here is not unlike the approach described in this study. In Chapter 5, the Ludington battery is described as a quasi-object, and while Hawk is less inclined to use that terminology, it is preferable to post-technê if only to limit confusion with all the post-prefixes in circulation: post-technê, postmodern, post-human, postcritical. The term *postindustrial* seems to encapsulate them all. Technê, as Pender argues (2011), is both useful and teachable, and while that use-value makes it more likely to be categorized as instrumental, kairos, metis, and technê together sketch a much more elastic practice, perhaps less opportunistic than a strongly third sophistic rhetoric might encourage (see Vitanza, 1997), but such is always the borderland between theory and praxis.

Metis is further implicated in use of the French mètis used to describe hybrid tribal identity, whether referencing people of mixed racial heritage or the necessary mixing of indigenous tribes into mixed collectives. Métis, or mixing, is at once boundary crossing and the making of new identities, practices, and communities; navigating and establishing boundaries are emergent forms of work in new context.

ADM's postindustrial hybrids

So ADM grows organic fish and vegetables. The multinational concern that has legions of agricultural scientists working on the next breakthrough in genetically modified organisms, creating trademarked and copyrighted hybrid beings for our consumption, also produces and markets organic vegetables. There's a great postindustrial irony here, and I do not want to come across as Pollyanna-ish, or as an ADM cheerleader. There are real problems, both ethical and cultural, represented by these agribusiness technologies and the business models that support them. Yet it is important to state that ADM's research and development investment is beginning to pay off both economically and environmentally. Rather than choose between efficiency and environmental responsibility, ADM is creating efficient, environmentally friendly processes. One major way they realize efficiencies is by linking once-separate processes, using the by-products and waste of one process as the raw materials of another. The process might be called wholesale recycling, but it is specifically postindustrial in its boundary-crossing, mixing production of agricultural and industrial products, pharmaceuticals and neutraceuticals, of recycling cast-off waste products such as car and truck tires and using them as fuel, and mixing limestone into coal-burning furnaces to remove harmful sulfur dioxide from the air.

Since visiting the ADM plant, numerous sites similarly composed have popped up across the Midwest. A student in a recent graduate seminar reported an old Chicago Slaughterhouse was converted into a similar organic greenhouse-aquaculture arrangement—aquaponics—and effectively repurposed the abattoir as a hipster hangout, adding a micro distillery and brewery to the site. This long-abandoned building was being reused as a locally produced goods showcase, with farm-to-table produce picked from the roof gardens and greenhouse served alongside fish raised under the same roof. These fish were fed the spent grains from the brewery and distiller. And again, the greenhouse was producing so much oxygen, the levels had to be monitored to be sure the greenhouse was not becoming explosive. In turn, the fish wastes were used to fertilize the greenhouse, and greywater from the brewery and kitchen watered the plants. All this recycling and reusing required great patience on the part of city officials because regulations were written in an age of command and control in which innovation was happening elsewhere in the business cycle.

These regulations were designed to ensure uniformity and safety in a different technological ecology. Both require worker safety as much as possible while maintaining consumer safety. However, many odd contemporary challenges emerged from this rather paternalistic and outmoded form of regulation because food is bland and uniform but safe; produce is available in winter months at northern latitudes, but summer tomatoes lose their most pronounced flavors and juiciness. Raw milk, for instance, is handled the same way explosives are handled at customs. Cheeses like Mimolette are not only treated as potentially dangerous substances, but regulatory practices require the sequestration of suspect stocks.[4,5] Foodies are concerned about losing their access to the cheese they want, the taste they want, claiming that raw milk cheeses and dairy products have different taste and texture profiles than those pasteurized. The challenge is balancing safety overall with the desires of producers and consumers to have access to the wide variety of food products and experiences that postindustrial as well as traditional and artisanal methods make possible. Just as steam technologies underlie existing digital culture, people crave tastes coaxed from artisanal methods of production, but require a balance between guarantees of safety through stringent regulation and recognition of the differences between production processes. Aquaponics probably will not yield tomatoes with the sweetness of those picked ripe from an August field, but dill grows tasty under the greenhouse glass, and in March, the advantages of fresh herbs grown locally and transported miles from the greenhouse to local kitchens may outweigh the disadvantages of transporting produce across the country. Moving produce from farm to table over kilometers outweighs the cost in fuel and environment in a cross-country transportation network.

The shift comes in the form of the quality of the subjective experience. Here, locally produced products are given pride of place and celebrated for being fresh, taking advantages of being produced nearby. In an earlier age, Chicago was concerned with keeping any contaminants out of the food supply. Chicago was transporting meat produced throughout the mid-American heartland and out to the world. Chicago's meat supply had to be kept not only healthful and free of disease, but also maintained as safe in the *imagination* of the global public. Chicago's export, its identity as Hogbutcher of the world, depends upon being held to the very highest standards. Historically over-regulated in an age of growing but incomplete sanitation and food safety, the 21st century has seen its share of foodborne illness, but these outbreaks of salmonella[6] in poultry, produce, peanut butter, mangoes, and even hedgehogs imported as pets, *Escherichia coli*[7] in spinach, lettuce, sprouts, and hazelnuts have been tracked to individual farms or distribution centers. It is the lasting impacts on perceptions of safety often more than the safety concerns themselves, like the 2008 Korean riots in response to fears of importing US beef. The concern was mad cow disease.[8]

All these concerns are raised by ADM's greenhouse: food safety, traditional regulation and control, innovative regulation that accounts for the challenges of aquaponics (just how much oxygen is considered safe?). Local production versus national and international transportation, as well as the rights of consumers to accept some risk in consuming artisan-produced foodstuffs are raised in this site of agricultural/industrial hybridity and the decision to defer construction of the cooling tower. The tower-that-never-was remains a potent symbol for writing this analysis.

At ADM, the company was looking for a public relations boost after the embarrassing events surrounding the lysine and citric acid price-fixing convictions. The need for expansion and building a new cooling tower was a practical as well as a local concern. Decatur needed more electricity and was producing more superheated water than the current towers could process. But that tower was expensive. The solution articulated by the physical plant manager responded to many needs simultaneously and minimized costs (and deferred investment—expenditure—in a new tower structure), as well as delivered a marketable innovation.

Instantly, the discussion changed from ADM's past behavior to the new ways in which it was innovating and creating sustainable jobs. A suspect multinational corporation greedily cornering the market and hiking up prices in echoes of a bygone age of Robber-Baron monopolists gave way to representations of a space-age new economy in which summer foodstuffs would be available in winter and health-conscious consumers would have expanded access to inexpensive, locally produced fish.

It is the ability to recognize, articulate, and respond to the various flows of change that empower the physical plant manager at ADM to claim expertise and accomplishment. He is satisfied—ecstatic, really—to establish the aquaponics facility and realize his dream of innovation and next-generation agriculture at an industrial scale. Marketing gets its sought-after success: the ability to put the price-fixing scandal behind it and join other corporate rebranding efforts at greening the company's identity. Accounting is satisfied because the expense of the cooling tower is deferred to a later start-up date, shifting costs from the multiple millions to hundreds of thousands, and budgeted over time. These institutional-cultural discursive strands define my interest in the site. This is the role of mêtis, in the ancient sense of the sailor's expertise, able to read the conditions of the fluid sea and sail safely to harbor and deliver the goods, services, and messages aboard ship.

The cooling tower is but one part of an innovative suite of technologies, our technê, which is at the heart of technique. The heated water is an outcome of electricity production. The greenhouse and the decision to build it at Decatur reveal a rhetorical nexus in numerous competing discourses. The fact that the decision to build satisfied so many different stakeholders with differing interests in hindsight makes the greenhouse seem an inevitable addition to the campus. Yet its existence was no more assured beforehand than the as-yet-unbuilt next-generation personal rapid transit Latour describes in *Aramis*. What new structure, what new investment, will look inevitable in hindsight next?

The coal-fired electricity plant on ADM's campus is already innovative. When I visited the campus, coal was being burned alongside shredded tires. To reduce the production of SO_2, sulfur dioxide—the main component of acid rain—crushed limestone was added to the mix to produce a cleaner flue gas. Coke was also produced. The heated water was seen as a waste product and transferred to the greenhouse, where it was not treated as waste but as an important input in the aquaponics operation, providing warmth that would otherwise need to be produced through other energy-intensive means. ADM utilized its waste streams and captured efficiencies that would otherwise be lost.

Here, let us leave Decatur as it stands now, and ponder what new opportunities may arise in the future. ADM has already identified wastes—used tires, spent grain, ethanol, lower-quality higher-sulfur coal, heated water—and articulated them as new inputs. These decisions and shifts already mark the organization as highly innovative and resourceful in demonstrating economic benefits of green engineering. Research and development, reported in numerous scientific journals and sources, present additional efficiencies that can be squeezed out of existing coal-fired plants. The US Environmental Protection Agency (EPA), in order to bring together many of these scientific advances into transferrable technological artifacts, have issued significant reports on the viability of clean coal technologies.

Below, I concentrate on the promise of one particular report that gathers many emergent technologies together into a coherent strategy for wringing every efficiency out of coal and producing as much electricity as possible while protecting the environment from both SO_2 and CO_2. While many of these efficiencies are marginal, producing less than 1% gain in overall effectiveness, their impact must be taken collectively. For instance, if a marginal gain of three quarters of a percentage point in efficiency is added to and contextualized alongside a carbon capture and sequestration strategy, the long-term impacts are sizable. Here the public perception of these technologies, their impacts upon quality of life and the quality of the environment, as well as the costs to consumers that are passed on by energy production companies remain rhetorical and cultural problems of acceptance of new economies and new technologies. They are not challenges of science, engineering, or technology in large part because the technologies exist. The need is for the confluence of forces, as with the aquaponics example, where stakeholders recognize how their interests and needs are being met.

Limestone reduces SO_2 emissions

In attempting to address these stakeholder interests, the EPA has created a series of grants that are now producing reports under the heading of Emerging Technologies. The 2010 report titled *Available and Emerging Technologies for Reducing Greenhouse Gas Emissions from Coal-Fired Electric Generating Units*[9] addresses the challenges of increasing the efficiency of coal-fired plants. Significantly reducing the sulfur dioxide produced by burning higher-sulfur coal increases both the economic efficiency as well as the life span of the fuel supply. Higher sulfur coal, usually bituminous, has an average sulfur content of 1.68%, compared to subbituminous 0.34% and lignite at 0.86%. But bituminous also produces more energy at over 10, 500 btu per pound:

> The combustion temperature of a FBC boiler (1,500 to 1,650°F) is significantly lower than a PC-fired boiler (2,450 to 2,750°F), which results in lower NOX formation and the ability to capture sulfur dioxide (SO_2) with limestone injection in the furnace. Even though the combustion temperature of a FBC boiler is low, the circulation of hot particles provides efficient heat transfer to the furnace walls and allows longer residence time for carbon combustion and limestone reaction. This results in good combustion efficiencies, comparable to PC-fired EGUs.
>
> (Fellner and Hutson, EPA, 2010, 13)

The sulfur affixes to the ash and that ash is also used as a product to produce new materials, like cement and cementitious bricks—cinder blocks. An entire postfurnace, postboiler industry has arisen: Boral, Titan America, and Cemex all proudly announce that they use fly ash from coal-burning electric plants in their products, and Aggregate Research hosts a website (aggregateresearch.com) aimed at articulating the industry's news, regulation, and opportunities.

There are real and dangerous by-products that result from burning coal. Just the immense volume and weight of slag, ash, and tar are themselves problem wastes, but mercury and other heavy metals are also concentrated when coal is burned. Mercury is useful, as are many of the by-products, but they need to be accounted for and handled responsibly. Coal also contains trace amounts of uranium and thorium, harmful radioactive elements if allowed to go up the flue after burning.[10] While these processes are collectively referenced as "clean coal," I want to acknowledge that significant challenges and wastes remain in effective utilization of coal resources. Recalling the amount of work represented in each BTU, we remain in the grip of the industrial mathematics Roger Osborne (2013) articulates when describing the amount of work done per person in industrial versus completely organic societies. We cannot return to pre-industrial relationships with work yet seem unable to escape the limits of the industrial.

Most important is the ability to monitor and measure what the power plant is burning, how the by-products are accounted for, measured, and re-processed for use and safe disposal, as well as making honest and measurable attempts to always minimize and mitigate the damages inevitably caused by fossil fuels. Sequestering sulfur is low-hanging fruit. Reusing hot water is, as described above, inventing new and innovative uses for waste products. And the separation and collection of metals—themselves needed for a variety of industry, research, medical, and as-yet unarticulated uses—make the smoke and ash viable new materials for further exploitation. Once the coal has been mined, the challenge is to use all its riches for as many processes as possible, to squeeze out all its potential value, akin to SIA's recycling efforts that include mining their own dust to separate out the gold, copper, and iron that can be recycled and reused. So, too, uranium and thorium are useful inputs in the nuclear industry, just as mercury has numerous applications. The challenge is to recognize both the value of capturing it as part of the fossil fuel electricity production process, as well as regularizing and institutionalizing—creating infrastructure for—the processes of mining the effluence, as carbon sequestration is discussed in coal gasification below.

Sustaining large-scale power plants

While the world waits for the ability to escape fossil fuels while supporting our energy-intensive lifestyles, advanced coal-fired generators produce efficient electricity around the world. These do not yet sequester their carbon, nor are they attached to the kind of laboratory experiments for sequestering carbon; nevertheless, they are hugely efficient and represent a leap beyond traditional electric turbines. This technology not only exists in laboratories but produces electricity, most notably in Poland where it supplies major cities and energy-craving Germany with power. While Germany produces the most renewable electricity, the EU leader continues to import electricity, mostly from nuclear generators managed by the French nuclear regulatory agency, which is discussed in Chapter 5. The salient point here is that, unlike the future potential of numerous electricity production and carbon sequestration technologies, these technologies exist and are at the heart of systems operating reliably and consistently around the world, as examples of large-scale technological artifact design, installation, and sustainability:

> Atmospheric CFB boilers have successfully been scaled-up and are operating at a number of facilities throughout the world. Exhibit 2–4 presents a simplified schematic of the major components of a CFB boiler EGU. Calcium in the sorbent combines with SO_2 gas to form calcium sulfite and sulfate solids, and solids exit the combustion chamber and flow into a hot cyclone. The cyclone separates the solids from the gases, and the solids are recycled for combustor temperature control. Heat in the flue gas exiting the hot cyclone is recovered in sections of the boiler to produce steam. The superheated steam leaving the boiler then enters the steam turbine, which powers a generator to produce electricity. Like PC-fired EGUs, CFB boilers can be used with either subcritical or supercritical steam cycles.
>
> (Fellner and Hutson, EPA, 2010)[11]

These systems are sequestering sulfur, thereby increasing carbon sequestered passively in forests without damage from acid rain. Part of the efficiency of high-pressure systems stems from their ability to remove solids from the smokestack—the "cylonic" action described in the technical description quoted at length above. Central to the decision for selecting this quote is its assertion that these boilers can be used with both sub- and supercritical steam cycles. Supercritical steam is the technical reference to steam under pressure, over 3,200 PSI of pressure, assuring more efficiency as the water never reaches boiling action because of the pressure. Suffice it to say that there are efficiencies to be gained in this highly technical process of pressurized water heat transfer. Advanced as the process is, the underlying technologies remain at least theoretically connected to the lineage of the first steam engine—they would, more or less, be recognizable to Newcomen, Watt, and Trevithick. Solar cells? Solar cells would baffle these engineers, fulfilling Clarke's assertion that "Any sufficiently advanced technology is indistinguishable from magic." I do hope, however, that while we are venturing to the edge of the possible, I have not lost readers who are shaking their heads and asserting we've ventured into the impossible. The impossible is a horizon always being overcome by current events.

PFBC is a next-generation technology that requires whole new machinery and design: really, it is a series of new turbines built with new technologies and advanced materials designed to extract as much electricity form the coal as possible. These are expensive machines, actually large assemblages of many machines working together. Like oil processing and refining plants—another whole family of new technologies I do not treat here in this analysis—a next-generation coal/steam turbine plant will not be a single fuel hopper feeding coal into a single furnace chamber (or, as is quite common now, numerous similar hoppers feeding many furnaces) but rather a series of interconnected subassemblies and after-processors that scrub the coal, dry it out to remove water, extract useful metals and materials, and sequester contaminants. A primary ignition chamber will create electricity under pressure, while the pressurized steam will then drive secondary and tertiary turbines in order to extract additional cycles of useful energy. Ultimately, the hope is that linking existing traditional turbines as secondary systems will recycle obsolete systems while generating more electricity from waste heat and pressure.

Pressurized fluidized bed combustion, as described by the EPA:

> More advanced second-generation PFBC system designs use a pressurized carbonizer to first process the feed coal into fuel gas and char (solid material that remains after light gases and tar have been driven-out during the initial stage of combustion). The PFBC burns the char to produce steam and to heat combustion air for the combustion turbine. The fuel gas from the carbonizer burns in a topping combustor linked to a combustion turbine, heating the gases to the rated firing temperature of the combustion turbine. Heat is recovered from the combustion turbine exhaust in a HRSG to produce steam, which is used to drive a conventional steam turbine. These systems are also called advanced circulating pressurized fluidized-bed combustion (APFBC) combined cycle systems.
>
> (Fellner and Hutson, EPA, 2010)

Once pressurized to supercritical levels, the steam drives with incredible force. Supercritical steam also produces turbine-driving pressures without actually showing signs of physical boiling, bubbling, transitioning to gas, and other signs of observable sea level changes to water's states. Through research and experimentation, it was determined that pressure creates efficiencies and ekes out additional kilowatts from each pound of coal. However, achieving supercritical pressurized water demands even more advanced engineering and building, as well as large-scale investments in education and research—to provide staff with the technical capacities necessary to accomplish the daily requirements of running the plant in addition to the highly advanced research driving the building, design, architecture, engineering, and invention of next-generation materials to withstand the increased wear, and regular as well as irregular maintenance demands.

For instance, Caterpillar has designed a generator engine rated to run for a million continuous hours. These engines have redundant piston assemblies than can be shut off independently, allowing a 16-piston engine to run temporarily on 14 or even 12 pistons. The oil, lubrication, and fluid systems are independent and can be changed on pairs of pistons while the remainder of the engine continues to run. Routine maintenance, like replacement of spark plugs and even spark plug assemblies and similar subassemblies, can also be undertaken while the rest of the engine continues to run. It requires an advanced design where the pistons can be isolated from the power stroke of the other pistons—a "soft" camshaft design where pistons can be taken off the line in pairs. Similarly, advanced steam technologies have layers and layers of electricity-producing technologies that can be individually maintained and taken offline for maintenance and put back into service as appropriate.

In the EPA description above, next-generation PFBC turbines are only marginally more efficient than their atmospheric, or noncritical, cousins. However, the efficiencies introduced later in the cycle as water, returning to noncritical pressures, can be used to drive current standard atmospheric turbines. A waste product in the form of hot water transitioning from supercritical to atmospheric pressure is reused as a new input, driving traditional generators. These generators have themselves been redesigned and refitted with the latest advanced materials so they are more efficient electricity producers, with reengineered fan blades and rare earth magnets to maximize the electrons generated, and so the real efficiencies utilize recycling to drive secondary generators after the electricity produced by the first-stage supercritical pressurized fluid-bed combustion power plant.

The technology addresses two important questions simultaneously:

- First, why invest in the new generation of PFBC boilers for a modest return in efficiency?
- Second, what is to be done with the first-generation atmospheric turbines and the huge investment in both expertise and materials they represent?

The answer to the first is that supercritical steam is itself a useful and usable product that, once created, can be used to generate work at the supercritical phase as well as after the water returns to atmospheric pressures. And the second is addressed as the second part of the PFBS hybrid process: as the supercritical water returns to atmospheric pressures, it retains enough power to generate massive amounts of electricity in the first-generation atmospheric generators. And that process utilizes both existing equipment (that has been retrofitted, reengineered, and refurbished) as well as existing expertise in keeping these massive machines in good working order. The PFBC process, as described by the EPA, further improves the coal burning process by removing contaminants harmful to the environment, as well as mercury, other metals, and radioactive elements. And, as the EPA describes, water, carbon, limestone, and dolomite can be added or removed as necessary to allow the furnace to cleanly burn a wide variety of fuels as market forces create fluctuations in the costs of materials and fuels, further enhancing economic efficiencies added to the energy efficiencies described above. The second generation provides answers to many competing questions from a variety of stakeholders, much as the opening vignette from ADM described the single emplaced example responding to that campus' needs, that organization's situation, at the time of their consideration of a new cooling tower.

Hybrid networks

Were agriculture and industry ever separate things? This chapter specifically articulates a hybrid postindustrial agriculture and describes the Decatur site as a postindustrial hybrid. Traditional agriculture includes practices of animal husbandry and plant science, controlled breeding, bringing two different strains together. Through the middle 20th century, the process resulted in what was widely hailed as "hybrid vigor" (see Crow, 1948, for an interesting theory and timeline), yet technologies of genetic manipulation result in what Haraway et al. (1992) titled the "Promises of Monsters." Hybridities, as Hård and Jamison (2005) remind us, leave people uneasy, at least at first. Change is challenging, and, particularly when livelihoods and lifestyles are disrupted and communities uprooted, can be seen as threatening—as monstrous.

Agriculture, and particularly the application of industrial practices to farm production, formed the heart of the land grant university (Johnson, 1981). The momentous if disruptive creation of these institutions after the American Civil War defines the agricultural network, the farm-to-market roads, the production technologies, and even the accounting technologies that keep track of which farm/farmer receives credit for which truckload of grain, and which process—nutraceutical extraction, human foodstuffs, livestock feed, etc.—it is best suited to contribute the most to, depending on its quality and the current market price, moisture content, source seed stock, and a host of other measurable qualities. In order to tame this hybridity, it has been given the name multifunctional agriculture, referred to as MFA in the literature (Jordan, 2010). Both production of agricultural products and research of agricultural processes remain a postindustrial Midwest global export, with information technology and bioagriculture impacting the practice of farming to the point of it being nearly unrecognizable to traditional farming techniques. The networks of university-hosted agricultural extension stations are a case in point. Once central to the land grant education mission, standardization of industrial agricultural practices, professionalization of crop production, and development of agricultural economics alongside bioscience driving crop innovations (note the influx of technocratic language), industrial-agricultural practice required these extension services to rethink their activities (Colasanti et al., 2009, Cash, 2001). But as Haraway argued in 1992, the challenge of monsters is their unfamiliarity, their newness, and that newness conflicts with expectations. So part of this description of the agricultural plant is not to point out its monstrosity but rather to historicize it and draw attention to current change not as troublesome or unique but rather as the latest phase of continuing transition. With fewer than 2% of the population directly engaged in farming activities (according to the Bureau of Labor Statistics 2014[12]), extraction of human labor from agriculture has largely been accomplished (Hamilton, 1994).

Technical communication has engaged environmental and agricultural issues through the Environmental Impact Statement and alternative agriculture. Environmental impact has played a significant interest in the late 20th century with Herndl and Brown (1996) tracing the rhetoric of activist environmentalist culture through Simmons' interest in the disposal of chemical weapons (2007), while contemporary studies shift to "topic-driven" environmental rhetoric (Ross, 2017). Alternative agricultural approaches have also been environmentally focused since the National Academies report of 1969 articulated concern for information centers largely committed to agribusiness concerns rather than more sustainable agricultural processes (pp. 194–196).

Networks of information remain a challenge. How does innovative, sustainable practice get shared across communities and complex networks of people and agricultural practice? How does innovation break through? At ADM, one individual addressed concerns present at multiple locations of the organization. The success of the innovation depended on the technorhetorical ability to assess and address anticipated concerns from a variety of stakeholders. The logic, the factual and scientific basis for decision making, while necessary is not sufficient to carry the argument, and preparation in rhetoric prepares a range of professionals to be aware of the extra-logical dimensions of persuasion, the cultural and social flows that sometimes can only be accounted for in the moment. While these emotive, ethical, identity- and expertise-driven elements may be anticipated, they cannot be surveyed but rather are part of what Rickert articulates as the ambient elements of rhetorical being. Attunements are not quantitative, but the more potential questions the rhetor is prepared to speak or write to, the higher the probability that the innovative solution will be accepted. Any change has the potential to be represented (misconstrued?) as a monster in Haraway's language of technocultural engagement, but change can become less monstrous through familiarity.

Familiarizing the unfamiliar through rhetorical attunement is a key expression of next-generation design moving alongside iterative design, as new technologies like the PFBC supercritical pressure turbines take their place as important components of large-scale electricity generation. They allow for recycling and reuse of older atmospheric technologies, and create a new market for older maintenance and engineering skills coupled to refurbishment while simultaneously supporting a new generation of development, advanced materials research, and engineering design to maximize PFBC, as well as preparing institutions to plan for and design for generations of technologies after today's innovations. The blue-sky technologies now in development, aimed at carbon sequestration and related clean-coal processes, will impact electricity generation and, perhaps even more importantly, will attract capable young minds to the laboratories and organizations performing the research. China's ENN (see Li et al. 2011), with its algae grown in water made carbon-rich with coal flue gas. Coupled to ongoing experiments in algae-based biofuels, foodstuffs, animal feed, and building materials, the opportunities for reuse and recycling multiply. Spent grains—the fibrous solids of corn and soybeans left after nutrients, oils, and proteins have been removed—are used to feed fish and plants in aquaponics systems, used as fertilizers, and burnt as fuel in advanced furnaces. And at each place, at many stages, the need is for clearly communicated well-maintained technical data, the communication of risk, the articulation of innovation and best practices, as well as preparing organizations to recognize and prepare for next-generation change.

At each stage of technological design, deployment, and advancement, there is a need for clear communication of technical data and information. Further, attention to the context of the deployment of these technologies is an important extension and growth opportunity for technical rhetors. This includes working with engineers to articulate technological opportunities and research needs and coupling processes together to squeeze out efficiencies, and working with management to articulate cultural and economic challenges. The citizens of Dacatur may need some convincing about the efficacy of a high-pressure supercritical boiler. Is this a technology they will assimilate into their mundane expectations for electricity generation? How will their awareness of further flue-gas scrubbing impact their impression? Will it make a difference if the relative cleanliness of the advanced design is clearly explained, as well as the economic benefits of having a furnace that can accept a variety of qualities of coal, as well as petroleum, natural gas, and continued use of used tires, spent grain, ethanol, and other recycled fuels—perhaps even dried algae fuel? These are opportunities for highly trained, literate cultural agents: the next generation of technical communication expertise in an age of advanced manufacturing, clean energy production, and cultural emplacement in an age of social media and interconnected networks.

The chorus sings that ADM has public relations problems and that the public is mistrustful after price-fixing on the lysine market comes to light: how can the organization redeem itself? The facilities manager marshalls technê in support of metis: that is, the hero in the story knows he can recycle the heat from electricity production to warm the greenhouse—a workable technology that effectively supports the aquaponics system. The challenge to metis is in figuring out how to meaningfully engage decision makers: defer capital expenditure! The further variable addressed by this solution is environmental responsibility in the form of organic produce. The chorus sings their satisfaction, accepting the innovation as an effective solution that elegantly addresses multiple challenges and multiple variables, shipping organic herbs, vegetables, and fruits, to markets from the Appalachians to the Rockies.

The ADM plant in Decatur, Illinois, is as unlikely a place as any to witness postindustrial innovation, yet the site is home both to a hybrid blurring of the boundary between industrial and agricultural production as well as innovations in electricity production from coal as fuel. While the moniker "clean coal" is problematic because of its marketing as well as grand promises, efficient energy production at scale remains an important goal as well as a remunerative pursuit. ADM and other large organizations stand to make large profits by creating cleaner and sustainable practices. Coal is comparatively inexpensive and abundant, as well as easy to ship in solid form—unlike natural gas. However, coal has numerous problems from its heavy metals content to the dangerous and environmentally unfriendly work of extracting and mining it (indeed, it is cheap in part because demand is down because of its drawbacks). However, like the processes of communication developed at Subaru, innovation is encouraged and celebrated at ADM. Its most innovative employees have to articulate solutions amid competing stakeholders and respond to competing demands. While clean energy is a widely understood and accepted goal for the organization, the value of recycling wastewater was less evident until one engineer, the plant manager, articulated the value of aquaponics. The resulting protein-rich agricultural products are used symbolically to create cultural capital as well as monetary value on the marketplace. ADM could claim itself to be not only innovative but interested in pursuing sustainable farming techniques and organic production while maintaining attention to their core crops. As the chapter shows, these crops continue to be used for agricultural applications. But these crops are used for much more than syrup, feeds, and oils. They are annually renewable sources for fuels that extend the value of agricultural production into industrial use and blur the boundaries, becoming postindustrial hybrids.

Notes

1 www.justice.gov/archive/atr/public/press_releases/1996/1030.pdf.
2 www.justice.gov/archive/atr/public/press_releases/1996/0988.pdf.
3 www.epa.gov/sites/production/files/2015-12/documents/electricgeneration.pdf.
4 www.cato.org/blog/watch-rinds-fdas-mimolette-ban.
5 www.dairyreporter.com/Regulation-Safety/FDA-dismisses-reports-of-US-import-ban-on-French-mimolette-cheese.
6 www.cdc.gov/salmonella/outbreaks.html.
7 www.cdc.gov/ecoli/outbreaks.html.
8 www.nytimes.com/2008/06/29/world/asia/29korea.html.
9 www.epa.gov/sites/production/files/2015-12/documents/electricgeneration.pdf.
10 www.scientificamerican.com/article/coal-ash-is-more-radioactive-than-nuclear-waste/.
11 In describing these technologies for producing electricity from burning coal, I am interested in the innovation and networks of change, technology, and culture they represent. Since writing these paragraphs, natural gas produced through hydraulic fracturing has displaced innovations in coal as a source of cheap electricity and power. So-called fracked gas is as controversial as claims of "clean coal," and indicate the kind of boundary object and cultural touchpoint that this analysis pursues not because of its benefits but because its *perceived* benefits are being debated, not because the value of the technologies are self-evident but because there are significant and long-ranging (often heated) discussions over the meaning and value of these technologies. That the current federal administration has closely restricted coal emissions and halted issuing permits for building new coal power plants makes the discussions about coal-based energy more interesting as a cultural space for engagement. See the EPA's report from which technical descriptions of fluidized coal versus the administration's infographics depicting climate change as just two examples among thousands of potential documents: www.epa.gov/sites/production/files/2015-12/documents/electricgeneration.pdf; www.whitehouse.gov/climate-change. Though extremely interesting, this debate is ultimately beyond the scope of the analysis presented here.
12 www.bls.gov/ooh/.

4 Recycling expertise in Ohio's automotive triangle

Ohio's northern border is largely made up of Erie coastline. On the eastern edge is Cleveland. To the west is Toledo. Along the lake, there are miles upon miles of Niagara grape vineyards, farms, and entertainment like Sandusky's amusement parks. Toledo has the distinction of being the cause and focus of a war between states that resulted in Toledo and the Maumee River becoming a recognized part of Ohio while Michigan gained the Upper Peninsula. At the time, Michiganders thought this unfair, but with the discovery of a reliable copper vein and seemingly endless old-growth forests, it came to be seen as a better deal for Michigan than first thought. Faber's (2007) retelling of the history in *The Toledo War* includes reference to key historical texts in an accessible narrative. Ohio's industrialization has been closely tied to Michigan, and Toledo's fate long associated with Detroit, particularly with automotive assembly and parts manufacturing.

In Ohio's east, Youngstown has hosted automotive assembly plants, and currently assembles the Chevrolet Cruz: Youngstown is connected to key moments in American manufacturing and labor history and Youngstown State University hosts the Center for Working Class Studies. The geographical triangle defining the eastern industrial Ohio cities of Cleveland, Akron, and Youngstown have been a hub of rubber and related industrial research, supplying Pittsburgh's steel and metallurgical as well as Detroit's automotive needs. And with Devo and Pere Ubu, the region also produced key bands in the post-punk postindustrial music scene (see specially Dellinger, 2008).

Like other citizens of the deindustrializing Midwest, musicians attempted to rebuild their future in contrast with their past. While accepting that the golden days of unionized work with guaranteed pensions was gone, they knew that the inventiveness and creativity of the people remained. They built something new and breathtaking amid the ruins of the prosperous if staid industrial past. Travelling around Ohio, I had the impression that there was hope and optimism for a brighter, prosperous future. Solar energy promises clean energy that is sustainable and avoids the environmental consequences of 19th- and 20th-century industrialization. Centered on the Solar Hub in Toledo on the University of Toledo campus, my observations took me from university research laboratories, to advanced manufacturing facilities, and even to automotive subassembly facilities located in the middle of Ohio cornfields.

In Ohio's west, with Owens-Corning locating its research and development facilities downtown along the Maumee riverfront, Toledo is proud to call itself glass city. Nearby, the University of Toledo, with other university and commercial partners, hosts the state's solar energy hub, a technology transfer lab specializing in supporting next-generation manufacturing and advanced materials research.[1] Ohio has two other recognized hubs. Cleveland is home to the Health and Technology Corridor while Dayton supports the Aerospace Hub. All three are built on city identities and traditions, taking advantage of existing strengths and historical focuses and industrial support networks, and each seeks to articulate existing industrial networks, skill sets, and knowledge traditions from the waning industrial age to the new postindustrial age. Each is centered in a city with significant human resources as well as development challenges, and each is seeking to emerge as a leader in the 21st century.

This chapter moves quickly from site to site in order to contextualize an emerging network of university-based research and development, start-up assembly plants in areas accustomed to light-industry, and further-flung sites amid agricultural lands. The people I have been fortunate enough to encounter as I have learned about Ohio's photovoltaic industry have been exceptionally generous. They represent nodes in this emerging network, and as I describe their daily responsibilities, emplacement within their employing institutions, and relationship to the industry as a whole, I articulate their relationship to the web of connections that animate the production and the marketing of solar power in Ohio. It is a daunting task. Throughout, I rely on Jackson's *Social and Economic Networks* (2010) as well as Barabasi's *Linked* (2003) and *Bursts* (2011) to envision these connections as well as Benkler's *Wealth of Networks* (2006). Spinuzzi's *All Edge* (2015b) provides a precursor to the approach followed here, only Spinuzzi's study concentrates on digital economy workers. Here, the players are similarly dispersed but work within Toledo's extensive next-generation glass industry, specifically the areas of research, technology transfer, manufacturing, and education surrounding solar glass and clean energy production. As individuals, each player is interesting in their own right, but it is the sum of these individual people—the invisible linkages of common interests—that bind them into a network that makes them remarkable as a group, defining the upper Ohio photovoltaic mesh. They represent an assemblage of people and technologies. Solar energy represents the first real postindustrial technology, as it does not rely on an engine, steam, or internal combustion, to produce electricity. Skill sets are recycled for new industries, articulating generations of expertise as valuable in new technologies.

Photovoltaic technology was once thought unviable as far north as Toledo. Research and development could be pursued there, but applications were more likely to be installed farther south. Growing installation of solar panels in Spain and southern France, Italy, and North Africa seemed to confirm these early expectations. But with Germany, Scotland, and Scandinavian countries installing significant solar arrays as part of overall clean-energy initiatives, the growing viability of Ohio-based commercial and residential installation businesses came to be realized.

Photovoltaic glass research supports a larger cultural transition from dependence on fossil fuels to next-generation clean energy. As this description attests, Toledo rearticulates existing knowledge and skills for emergent opportunities. None is more striking than the portrait of the daily operations manager of the research hub who has transitioned from a career as an operating room nurse to the logistics administrator of a high-technology research facility. His first job at the University of Toledo was in technology transfer, and a decade creating sterile conditions inside an operating theater provided abilities relevant to administering manufacturing facilities requiring similar standards of precision and cleanliness. His experience at the micro-scale of germs and infection transferred as glass engineering went from micro- to nano-scale manufacturing, requiring sterilization and clean-room technologies orders of magnitude beyond medical requirements. Single molecules and atoms are manipulated in silica matrices to produce advanced characteristics and durability. While these materials continue to be called "glass," they are designed and engineered materials just as advanced as the electronics they encase and protect.

This theme of skills rearticulation is an aspect of what I name *deep recycling*. At ADM, deep recycling includes the ability to recognize the outputs of agricultural and industrial processes, once dumped as waste, as potential inputs for new processes such as an aquaponics production facility. At Subaru, it means recognizing the welding dust on the floor is actually valuable as an ore to be mined and metals extracted for (re)use—mining the factory's dust. Similarly, industrial clusters like Toledo maintain valuable skillsets among its workers, managers, and educators. These skills and experiences sometimes have to be redefined, but they provide significant advantages across the cluster. Here in Toledo, a century of turning silicon into glass has resulted in a population with an understanding of and respect for the needs of advanced manufacturing and research. Rodgers (1998) narrates a parallel example by describing the ways in which Northern Ireland, the city of Belfast, and Queens University reimagined native skillsets to support hard drive research and assembly with Seagate, while Clancy et al. (2001) describe similar phenomenon in the Irish software, dairy, and music businesses. Clancy and collaborators provide the transition from information and high-technology industries to the production of foodstuffs and include ways that dairy represents more than milk and cheese. Music addresses issues of community as well as crossover from so-called "creatives" to manufacturing and general industry.

Elsewhere in Ohio, innovators find new uses for brownfield sites, industrial plots believed to be lightly contaminated with industrial pollutants. Many similar sites exist across the postindustrial Midwest: former factories, storage areas, and assembly plants that ideally would be reused for another generation of industrial activity. In megacities like New York, Los Angeles, and Chicago, the brownfields define older sections of the city and often support mixed-use development and different forms of urban innovation. These sites are often not suitable for housing and certainly not for farming, but contamination falls short of levels considered for major cleanup; that is, brownfields are not Superfund Sites. Instead, these highly regulated and closely watched sites cannot be used for parks, schools, or other municipal or private uses—the very uses vacant lots in urban areas would be put to in order to improve property values and quality of life.

When on a visit to Xunlight in Toledo, Ohio, I heard about an upcoming experiment in downtown Cleveland designed to put a brownfield to renewed use. The idea was interesting, and my contact lingered on discussion of details of environmental stewardship and regulation. One strategy for dealing with brownfield sites is to idle them. Most industrial contaminants in a site, from underground storage tanks to metal shavings to lubricants to fuels, will dissipate over 25 years. While this is not ideal—certainly not for the municipality that would like to put the land back to productive use as park, housing stock, or municipal facility—it is inexpensive and relatively safe. By coupling the need for the land with a relatively safe reuse plan, Cleveland has found a way of reusing urban brownfield sites for solar power generation.[2] While the story offers the benefits of utilizing the land and the marketing potential as well as the practical application of solar voltaic power generation, the story does not articulate the challenges my contact shared with me.

One of the concerns the EPA has with brownfield sites is disturbing the soil. If undisturbed, ancient systems of groundwater filtration seem to do an excellent job of removing metals and other materials from water and soil—the basis of environmental accounting in both ecological economics and full cost accounting. And while the life span of solar voltaics has recently come under some scrutiny, and quality control of Chinese-manufactured solar arrays has been questioned,[3] the 25-year brownfield sequestering nicely matches the projected 20–30 year life span of most solar arrays.

But the EPA warned against disturbing topsoil, requiring that nothing penetrate the soil to a depth of more than 4 inches. Furthermore, the solar array needed to be attached to steel and aluminum supports anchored at least 8 inches deep. Through negotiation and discussion, the EPA granted a variance to allow the anchors to penetrate to the required depth in part because the rated life span of the solar array would cover the entire sequestration period of the brownfield site. Once the array reached the end of its life span, the ground should be clean enough to return to productive and, hopefully, safe, unregulated use after extended testing and analysis. Granting the variance for a one-time soil penetration would allow the urban brownfield site to be productive for its fallow quarter-century postindustrial season while not becoming either blight or hazardous for the community. It is a hopeful reclamation of urban postindustrial land, built on an agricultural metaphor of the fallow field.

Human nodes in Toledo's photovoltaic network

People living in Northwestern Ohio populate, energize, and give meaning to the network of expertise in solar energy, transferring information from research sites to manufactories, to marketing and installers, and back to educational institutions. Here, I begin at the Solar Energy Hub at the University of Toledo and its recent spinoff, Xunlight, a leader in photovoltaics, and follow connections into the surrounding landscape. The hub is well named because of its location at the nexus of this network, but its tendrils splay over the region. Sophia Fisher was working for the University of Toledo at the time, and she introduced me to a number of important players in the solar industry in Toledo as well as in surrounding towns. I retain Sophia's real name here because she was incredibly generous to me in time and effort, and also because she asked that I not anonymize her identity. As a free agent in the postindustrial economy, she thought being represented in this text might be an asset to her, and she would use the reference to demonstrate her expertise in northwestern Ohio broadly in high technology and solar energy more specifically. She was generous and kind, thoughtful and creative, and also open to my project when I arrived. She helped make my visit incredibly dynamic and—looking over my notes regarding four contacts at five sites—I give Sophia credit for making my visit productive. As a researcher, I have been fortunate, and it is people like Sophia Fisher who make me believe in better futures and help me remain optimistic.

Sophia believed in the hub and its solar work, and was a good and diligent employee. But as the day unfolded, I got to see that she was working angles of her own. This rhetoric of motives affords a certain clarity and contributes to articulating the networks of motivation that inspire individuals to act. I know in my day-to-day work, there are emails, phone calls, and requests that are prioritized, either because of immediacy of consequences, perceived importance, or because I could advance cause(s) of my own interest. For Sophia, my research visit represented an opportunity to rekindle connections that had been established but then gone dormant as her grant-supported position matured and the focus moved to newer connections as well as bigger organizations and from regional to national to international networks. With the grant ending, she was looking for her next position. And knowing this, I was able to get out of her way, recognizing that she was going to be working her own angles during these meetings, and that I had to let her take her project forward if we were to remain effective partners. I had to recognize when I could take the lead and meet my own project goals but recognize when I had to let her project—her own self-advancement—take the lead. Upon reconnecting with Sophia, I was happy to learn that she had moved on to her next big opportunity.

It wasn't rocket science,[4] figuring out my contact's ulterior motives. But it did take a moment of reflection, of listening,[5] and of articulating how another is motivated, what interests she is playing out in this pantomime, and thinking about how she might benefit through helping me, and how helping me becomes helping her. So that in effect, she can identify my project as her future. Thanks, Kenneth Burke. Listening led me there. Just-in-time networks. I was using her and she was using me, and as long as we were helping each other's projects, we can be a team, and our alliance was built on recognition of kindred goals. While we were using each other's connections and insights, both were free to end the relationship at any moment, and our relationship was not exploitative. Or at least I am asserting this, and in subsequent communication, Sophia seems to agree even years after the fact.

Sophia introduced me to four people at four sites in the Toledo area connected to solar energy. I have done my best to protect their identities, but have named many of the organizations for which they work in order to maintain the rigor of the research.

- The director of daily operations at the Toledo Solar Hub who has 20 years plus experience in advanced materials engineering, microelectronics, semiconductor manufacturing, and institutional and laboratory management. I call this person George Jansen in the narrative below.
- An education administrator, Samantha Ellsworth for the purposes of this document, runs a program in wind and photovoltaic maintenance at Owens Community College, where she administers the Clean Technologies Associates Degree program.
- An entrepreneur, Mitchell Van Ter Beek, Marketing and Sales Director of AP Alternatives. In a farming town 30 miles from Toledo, Mitch runs a successful solar start-up alongside the family auto parts manufacturing business his father started. Corn rows run right up to the parking lot and assembly buildings, and (along with Subaru Automotive in Lafayette, Indiana) inspired the title of this study.

- Research scientist Pieter Kampinali, a retired University of Toledo faculty member and chief technology officer of Xunlight. Pieter has been part of glass research in Toledo for more than three decades. He took an early retirement buyout package, gave up tenure, and started a solar voltaic company.
- Innovation manager of the Urban Affairs Center of the Solar Hub, Sophia Fisher, has already been introduced above. Hers is the only name that has been left unchanged.

Daily operation manager

George Jansen took an hour out of a very busy day to give me a tour of the facility at 2600 Dorr Street. It is on the edge of the University of Toledo campus, and George's first nugget of information is that it is not a new building but a rebuilt and refurbished space that was underutilized. I do not know details of the building previous to the hub's occupation. During our hour-long tour, George accumulated 14 phone messages, two-dozen emails, and three meeting invites. He also accepted one phone call in which he advised a research scientist how to begin an experiment. George Jansen was the key connector node in the Solar Hub network, and it seemed very little happened without his knowledge or approval. Indeed, I was well aware that he was both sizing me up before granting me access to the research facility as well as providing deep background on the facility and its location at the University of Toledo and northwestern Ohio. He acted as both gatekeeper and tour guide.

At the time, the Solar Hub configuration involved collaboration with Bowling Green State University, University of Toledo, and the Ohio State University along with many regional players including a state-sponsored Regional Growth Partnership.[6] Key industries linked partners with research and design capacities. George Jansen talked about a variety of technologies developed at, available through, and commercialized through the Solar Hub—manufacturing research taking science breakthroughs and working on scalability and mass economic production capacity. Examples include analyzing substrate application to glass and steel, crystal and coating, or the process of moving to stainless steel substrate as opposed to glass or silicon, which Xunlight has both patented and commercialized. At the time, there was renewed interest in common earth materials—copper, gold, cobalt, all mentioned as replacement for rare earth materials. The goal is sustainability as well as profitability.

George articulated a national network of related research facilities and the local network of political, institutional, and social stakeholders. Although located in Colorado, NREL, the National Renewable Energy Laboratory[7] located between Golden and Boulder, is considered an important partner, and Xunlight and the Solar Hub participated in NREL-sponsored events, including industry and R&D conferences and meetings, illustrating an important government role in research. Locally, the University of Toledo sponsors the McMaster entrepreneurs named for Harold McMaster, an important glass innovator as well as a rotary engine designer. Pieter Kampinali, described below, cites McMaster as a driving force in articulating Toledo as a center of glass and photovoltaic research. A philanthropic organization named for McMaster supports numerous education, research, and entrepreneurial programs, as well as education and medical care in northwest Ohio and southeastern Michigan.

Northwest Ohio Regional Economic Development[8] is similar to RGP but with a general business improvement mission and regional responsibilities. Spanish company Isofoton built a photovoltaic factory in Napoleon, Ohio.[9] And finally, individual students, nontraditional returning adult students in particular, are supported by retraining and education grants for displaced workers through Ohio's labor department.[10] Ohio state resources, federal solar subsidies and research funding, labor retraining resources, and local manufacturing, marketing, installation, and educational institutions are all interwoven in their interest and commitment to net-generation electricity-generating technologies. Solar is one face of this multifaceted effort of defining next-generation energy production: the articulation of the underlying science, its application in technologies, development, and design, into usable artifacts, effective deployment, and installation, all relying on consumer acceptance of the technologies as reliable and dependable as sources of electric power at an acceptable price.

Overall, George is representative of so many interesting people who find themselves inextricably linked to postindustrial assemblages. He has designed technology for commercial and academic use in a variety of contexts, and has had a dozen different jobs over decades. He was interrupted 10 times in the first 15 minutes I was with him, balancing the needs of many different elements of the lab's spaces and communities. He designed and built the clean rooms and different research configurations that he was very proud to show to me, as an outside researcher and observer, once I had passed his few probing queries before he decided I was not an investigative reporter or troublemaker. I hope George recognizes himself in this representation, and is as flattered by it as I was truly impressed with his accomplishments and central emplacement in this cathedral of technological research and development. More impressive was that George Jansen had nothing but praise for graduate students and undergraduates capable of completing the research in the lab and spoke about the important relationship the hub facility represented for students interested in working with advanced technologies. The hub, its administrators, researchers, and employees illustrate another face of forward-looking industries in the region, and have parallel equivalents in other regions, as well as nationally and globally.

George also wishes he had less regulatory writing to complete in running the facility. He also reported spending more time with graduate students than their faculty directors and thought that relationship shortchanged the students and faculty both. George Jansen was excited talking about the work the lab was doing, and explained a host of interesting developments, like a fixed laser–focused manufacturing process that displaced the need for the time and expense of a mechanical plotting focusing process. While that detail eludes me as to its importance or even its meaning or application, I include it because it was important enough to George that he know I had accurately described the detail in my notes; for that fleeting second talking with George, his enthusiasm and optimism were so completely infectious, and I felt convinced it was imperative to capture this impression of my visit and of my interaction. George knows his stuff and was a delight to meet. In many ways, his skill set complemented Sophia's, and together they represent two places in the postindustrial organization where students educated in professional and technical communication curriculum will do well in communicating high-tech information and in navigating complex postindustrial institutions. While neither described themselves as a communications expert, both spent their days making technological information accessible, moving complex data between collaborating laboratories and groups of people, and coordinating and troubleshooting technologies that supported the research being done at the research facility. George was doing little research of his own, but he served as catalyst for the research that animated the site. He was the communicative and logistical center of Solar Hub.

Education administrator

Samantha runs programs at Owens Community College where she built a clean technology associates degree. Another autodidact with a lengthy career trajectory, including operating room technician, medical researcher, and university administrator, Samantha knows the Northwest Ohio region and its history of manufacturing and research, and she had an acute sense of what proposals seemed likely to work and what schemes were unlikely to work. While we spoke at length about the different programs at Owens, the most interesting subtext surrounded discussion of the 2-year battle over whether to focus the 2-year degree specifically on solar, wind, biomass, ethanol, or general clean energy. Discussion eventually settled on general clean energy engineering with a two-course concentration on solar, wind, ethanol, or management of clean energy. "It would be easier to shift focus as required," I remember her saying, and immediately connected to the need for both institutional flexibility and the kind of iterative design that would allow students to pursue their interests while maintaining flexibility for the programs.

It is a smart degree plan,[11] flexible to adjust to changes in technologies and institutional funding priorities; it requires classes in science and applied technology as well as humanities classes in technology in society, information technology, and communication. Conversation centered on creating functioning networks to support hiring of program graduates, and talk about putting different aspects of expertise in clean and next-generation energy production together in an effective applied technology and applied science workplace. Overall, Sam agreed with many observations regarding students in 2-year degree programs: lack of preparation for advanced scientific work, unfamiliarity with academic expectations and the role of faculty in the classroom, lack of drive and initiative, problems with work ethic and understanding the demands of the workplace. Sam also described concerns with mechanical capacity but also reported a strong tinker/maker tradition in the region, a gendered tradition with men in their workshops showing sons to build soapbox derby racers, model cars, gas-powered minibikes, and the like in suburban garages. As a result, diversity among applicants lagged behind diversity of the local population. Sam articulated institutional problems in funding and in making graduates from local community colleges of interest to large organizations. Questions and insecurities about the technology/communication mix in the curriculum either were a core concern, or performed more for my benefit with Sam asking me if the described curriculum had the right mix of what she labelled hard and soft subjects. Owens Community College and its administrators were asking difficult questions, with few clear obvious answers. Their focus was on producing effective, well-trained, knowledgeable workers for the clean energy sector in northwestern Ohio, and their decision making was guided by real-world concerns about the employability and sustainability of the local student population and the ability to raise these students' sights and aspirations to meet the challenges of the emergent economy.

The challenges for students and their preparation involve high school administrators and curriculum designers, and require creatively developing education beyond a vague reference to college preparation, or similar euphemistic descriptions. Existing traditions, local economic resources, and durable institutions and organizations—historical business organizations, organized labor, and the foundations they support—are especially valuable within this network of stakeholders working to reimagine education and business to prosper in this age of emerging technologies. How education needs to adapt to a flexible networked future is the worthy subject of a book of its own, and I dedicate the final chapter to envisioning technical communication curricula. Sophia Fisher, as my guide to Ohio's solar voltaic network, demonstrated unimpeachable instincts by including innovative educators. The network needs the input of its educators who demonstrate knowledge of and commitment to the success of the people of northwest Ohio.

Entrepreneur

Mitch Van Ter Beek is a visionary and talented entrepreneur. AP Alternatives, a spinoff from Alex Products, or APInc, that Mitch's father started in the late 1980s after realizing that he was a better manufacturer than farmer, is also an astonishing site that touches on so many powerful themes. APInc is a diversified metal subassembler and manufacturer, a company that specializes in fabricating parts that larger manufacturers put in their assembly chains. For instance, the company supplies metal frames to Toyota that become seat assemblies, and right now it is their largest contract. APInc also manufactures restaurant seating for a company that supplies franchise sandwich shops with standard seating. The Ohio company also takes on other small jobs and one-off opportunities that Mitch describes as "appropriate for a small metal shop." While APInc produces some finished or nearly finished products, others—like the Toyota seat chassis—are clearly supply-chain materials that become part of other finished products manufactured elsewhere. More information is available at APInc's website(s) complete with timeline and historical data.[12]

APInc links today's innovations in solar and clean energy back to its automotive roots. Robotics and lean manufacturing principles are applied from the Toyota supply chain to solar energy production. Looking at AP Alternative's Projects, especially watching the installation videos and hearing about their advanced machinery development, they adhere to lean production, as well as iterative design. They asked me not to take pictures of their installation machines, and I understand why they protect their intellectual property in such a competitive arena. What I saw were robots repurposed from automotive assembly to a solar array frame mounting, as well as three generations of installation machines. First, solar cells are assembled into larger collections of panels, and robots are good tools to assemble these repetitively compiled systems. They worked well in APInc's assembly area putting reliably precision-mounted arrays ready to be installed. Second, and more impressively, these arrays were stacked and ready to be installed by robots of APInc's own design.

These installation robots are persistent examples of iteration and the kind of engineering and adaptation of lean and Kaizen principles that animate discussion of industrial assemblages and slippage between categories and erasure of boundaries. These robot-machines represent innovation that moves proven solutions from one realm to another, from auto manufacturing to solar array installation. Mitchell's business successes relied on proven successes of a precursor, auto parts manufacturing, recycled in the context of the new solar voltaic cell manufacturing and assembly. Central to AP Alternatives' business model is reduction of labor costs. Mitch adapted automotive robots to assemble solar cells into free-standing solar-production units on steel and plastic frames. He also designed a series of robotic assembly line processes that minimize both time and effort in installation. Tracing changes between generations of robots at AP Alternatives reveals iterative design at work on a smaller scale than at Subaru, demonstrating the scalability of Kaizen.

First generation

A custom-built prototype was put into early service on the first contracts because it worked. It takes about 2 minutes to set two stakes and it looks like student projects that populate engineering universities in the spring when senior design projects are due. It works, but it is impractical at scale as it breaks down frequently. Between repairs and time lost restarting the machine were AP Alternative's biggest labor costs when this primitive design was its primary automated installation option, yet it remains a significant asset (alongside the three robots in the assembly area and two other installation assemblies). The prototype looks like it works through sheer determination and luck—and Mitch admitted that it does not inspire particular confidence among clients. In a pinch, the machine is used in large installation projects where any additional help is welcome or on small jobs where an afternoon fiddling with settings is necessary anyway, and the visibility of the prototype is not a problem. While this demonstrates proof-of-concept, the uninspiring and unprofessional appearance is a known and understood problem. Mitch uses the prototype as a teaching tool. He brings it to local schools and public events, and uses it to train new technicians.

Second generation

Another custom-built solution, it would have been model 1 if premature success had not forced the prototype into production duties. It takes an operator just over a minute to set two posts. This second generation exhibits dramatic improvement in build quality. Design expertise is evident in doors that hide clockwork workings from view in a next-generation design that looks both robotic and professional. However, the look is of something cottage-built—clearly custom built and rather rough in some areas. This model established the start-up as a regional and national player, and the company continues to use it at smaller jobs as well as to demonstrate the organization's mechanical competency. This design asserts APInc's independence as it can build the machines that make the process possible, testifying to what the organization is capable of creating on its own. It is an example of infrastructural engineering in that it proves AP Alternative's engineering assets, the capital and investment at its disposal, as well as the can-do spirit of bringing ideas into working prototypes.

Third generation

The third generation is a simultaneously overwhelming and completely mundane example of modular engineering. Closely mirroring Braun and others, AP Alternatives abandoned the idea of building the installation machine from the ground up. Instead, the solar peg installation machine is a standard add-on to a modified John Deere Tractor. Here, AP Alternatives remixed an existing technology and put it to work in the field. This allows for commercialization and scalability, and as Mitch said, enables the innovator to remain focused on their core business, using the finished product of one industrial process as the input of another. John Deere makes tractors with creature comforts and tests them for stability, safety, comfort, and durability. With standard hitching technology, AP Alternatives can tether its installation machinery to John Deere's standard hitch, which allows the operator to work not in an unprofessional good-enough awkward machine, but in a John Deere tractor. It has the added advantages of air conditioning and radio/ CD, as well as a standard operating interface, with the added power of military-grade guidance GPS to automate the process provided by another partner corporation. Maintenance consists of a John Deere– trained mechanic who also knows how the pinsetter works, rather than trying to rebuild the custom truck each time it breaks down. And in moving a tractor designed from agriculture use to clean energy, it is another boundary-crossing hybrid.

Modular design and remixing also allow AP Alternatives to meet expectations for corporate partners and their demands for equipment reliability and replacement/duplication in the field. Mitch mentioned he had lost some contracts because potential partners worried about the reliability of the one-off design of their second prototype and the challenges that unique purpose-engineered parts and lack of off-the-shelf availability presented to efficient and redundant large-scale projects. Partners were afraid to be held captive by an equipment malfunction or parts failure. Modular, iterative design allows the drive system to be as reliable as John Deere tractors, the gold standard in the American Midwest, while a complete second unit of pin setter can be more easily transported to far-flung worksites and replaced while the malfunctioning unit is repaired offline.

AP Alternatives also becomes part of the John Deere Tractor network, allowing itself to be seen as part of a successful and historic tradition of Midwestern reliability. It immediately grounds the new solar installation industry as rather routine and steadfast, removing worry about the tenuous design of the stand-alone system. Simultaneously, it positions AP Alternatives as a desirable partner for John Deere, eager to add innovation and solar and clean energy to its marketing portfolio, a global brand that already asserts reliability, flexibility, and the universality of standard hitching technology. The partnership removes many perceived risks from both companies, as well as representing AP Alternatives as a solid company for the new millennia, while updating and makes the potentially stolid brand of John Deere new and exciting in an age of clean energy production. The standard hitching technology also makes AP Alteratives' design more stable, putting redundancies into the system of solar panel installation. No one step can bring down the whole system: redundancy and system scalability and standardization allow flexibility and resilience.

AP Alternatives spun off from Alex Products in early 2001 during the last economic downturn when the automotive supply chain looked like it might collapse. When the auto industry took a hit, Mitch and his father looked to diversify. Mitch spoke about finishing college and coming back to the family farm, rather than heading out to Silicon Valley, Chicago, Toledo, or Detroit. His title is marketing and sales manager, not chief executive officer (CEO) or chief technology officer (CTO) or owner of AP Alternatives, so the relationship between AP Alternatives and Alex Products is unclear. AP Alternatives may be a completely owned subsidiary of Alex Products. Mitch maintains the websites for both, and the relationship between models is implied but never explicitly mentioned or described. I suspect that, as a single twentysomething, Mitch is working 60–80 hours a week and has not considered what his life might look like a few or even 10 years out and how his worklife is unsustainable.

Mitch learned his trade running all the "alternative" manufacturing from Alex Products' portfolio before starting AP Alternatives as an alternative energy company under his father's established business. Mitch learned to manage payroll and labor, hire and fire, and oversee inventory and logistics by turning out the barstools, medical devices, and "other" manufacturing that accounts for 3–5% of the total Alex Products, Inc. portfolio of products. And he was successful, returning profit to Alex Products and proving to his father, Alex, his business acumen and the potential profitability of clean energy. AP Alternatives, as a subsidiary, began flirting with profitability in 2010, and someone else was put in charge of the "other" category of manufacturing. While the relationship between Alex Products, Inc. and AP Alternatives is murky here, generational connections in entrepreneurial activity and inherited daring-do are more clear. Revealed is the powerful attraction of place as well as tradition. Why Toledo? There's a long history of Van Ter Beeks running metal shops here, and steel and aluminum photovoltaic frames promise to be profitable long into the postindustrial future.

AP Alternatives started with a vertical axis windmill design for suburban and ex-urban use. It was imagined as a farm-based energy production unit to generate small amounts of site-specific clean power to supplement electricity from the grid when windpower was available. It turned out not to be a scalable design, or at least a profitable version eluded Mitch's design and manufacturing skills at the time. He was not able to bring to market commercial numbers at the level of efficiency necessary. Mitch maintains his dreams of a suite of clean energy products, and he just may become the Vanderbilt of the clean energy age, or perhaps the next-generation Henry Ford under the name AP Alternatives. He imagines still a portfolio of clean energy offerings from solar panels, to wind turbines, to small hydroelectric generators, and yet undreamed-of technologies of his design, manufactured with people and robots at his family shop in Northwestern Ohio. His optimism, while certainly contagious, is also built on a solid foundation of innovation and accomplishment, as well as on his design success. Mitch dreams big and works an unsustainable number of hours. But while his dreams for the future are driving his current commitment and accomplishments, they are grounded by his father's experience handling the economic challenges of decades leading APInc. AP Alternatives has recycled those decades of business success as an important ingredient into a component of its own future.

Mitch spoke at length about the connections between Solar Hub and AP Alternatives, mentioning many times he consults with the research organization and the connections it fosters between himself to other suppliers, competitors, and markets. In the future, Mitch will likely look to his regional partners at Owens Community College to find well-prepared students who understand the basic demands of the business he runs. And Mitchel Van Ter Beek will likely be programming his robots to assemble parts based on the technologies and developed at and transferred from the Solar Hub, perhaps licensed or subcontracted from Xunlight.

High-tech research and development

Pieter Kampinali is retired faculty from University of Toledo and has worked on glass for photovoltaic use, leading Xunlight[13] as CTO since taking an early retirement package from the University of Toledo in 1998. Our conversation was wide-ranging. Professor Kampinali spoke in detail about two important themes:

- History of photovoltaic research & development and commercialization in the Toledo area
- Breakthroughs and up-and-coming technologies in the realm of clean energy production.

Harold McMaster started GlassTech for researching and manufacturing automotive glass in the Toledo area. I leave his name unchanged because he is deceased and historically significant. Pieter Kampinali mentioned McMaster as an early mentor and breakthrough engineer in the mid-20th century. McMaster recruited Kampinali, who joined the University of Toledo at McMaster's recommendation. McMaster started GlassTech for tempering glass and shaping/bending glass for the automobile industry. Toledo's tradition of automotive glass in Toledo is guided by McMaster and the companies he established: Permaglass and Glasstech for automotive applications, Glasstech Solar (Arizona), which became First Solar, a precursor to Xunlight. Glass research continues to be centered in Toledo, and many innovations in automotive and photovoltaic glass are discovered in Toledo.

Pieter Kampinali believes in the technology as well as the market for photovoltaic cells. When pressed, he begins talking about interactions with major retailers and a rival Canadian solar company. True North[14] was an example that stuck with him because it was "real money" joining alternative power, rather than the corporate or government grant money that the American public often sees as problematic: government waste or meddling in the marketplace. Sam Walton of Wal-Mart was a substantial investor in True North technology,[15] and when Pieter heard that Wal-Mart was simultaneously redesigning its stores to utilize more natural light and use HVAC more efficiently, replacing conventional lighting with LED lighting,[16] and installing photovoltaics and wind turbines at retail store locations,[17] the potential shifted for the retiring professor to move from solar power theory to very practical promising markets. He had talks with Walton early in Xunlight's existence, and Wal-Mart continues to lead because, first, they demonstrate understanding of the financial implications of cutting their electric and HVAC energy bills both at retail and distribution facilities, and second, because of their tremendous buying power. Wal-Mart has at least 100 stores in California using photovoltaic cells to directly power their stores.[18] Wal-Mart became leaders in driving research into dimmable ballast fluorescents to maintain steady lighting regardless of weather or time of day for their retail spaces, and such change represents huge markets for clean energy technologies that spur innovation. Pieter Kampinali was no idealist, or perhaps better put, he was not a foolish idealist risking his pension fund on Earth-Day feel-good environmentalism but a hard-nosed businessman with a clear understanding of the market and what it was going to take to move from potential to promise of real income and employment for his community. And he happens to think sustainability is also necessary to maintain quality of life in the new millennium.

Over and again smart entrepreneurs articulate the need for smart regulation necessary to ensure a fair market rather than crony capitalism. Good regulation maintains competitive fairness and an open market rather than favoring one or another technology or organization. Understanding what innovation and entrepreneurship means is more important than simple elimination of regulation. Instead, these entrepreneurs want effective regulation, which all players are forced to work within, including fair treatment of workers, protection of the environment, and marketplace transparency that protects intellectual property while allowing innovation to find its market and create competition. Zingales in *Capitalism for the People* (2012) articulates this argument, which remains true to the ideas expressed over and again by these innovative and thoughtful inventors and investors.

Some notable innovations at Xunlight include the capacity to manufacture a photovoltaic structure 36" wide and 2 kilometers long—that is, with an infinite length. With only theoretical limits on manufacturing solar cells, the process of imaginatively integrating photovoltaics into new products will only be limited by the imagination. A particularly exciting example is semi-transparent glass impregnated with invisible photovoltaics allowing for ambient electricity solar generation—that is, creating electricity-producing structural glass. Imagine office buildings that generate electricity at only a 15% difference in the original building price tag.[19] Once the LEED Platinum certification standard seemed impossible to attain. Now, with passive solar electricity produced by the building itself, the very highest LEED certifications seem attainable when buildings create their own power. Energy-producing structural glass adds a 15%–20% premium on building costs at the moment, but these costs will be offset in the short term by the reduction in grid-provided (metered) electricity. As structural glass becomes commonplace, manufacturing costs will approach the cost of other nonsolar structural glass. Imagine the next generation of Apple stores producing more electricity than consumed by the very products they are demonstrating, inside their very own electricity-generating glass boxes. Xunlight has also patented a range of colored structural safety glass, and the first application of this tempered product is for car sunroofs that will both produce electricity and match the design of the automobile. Auto manufacturers have been slow to adopt these technologies for fear that electricity-generating sunroofs would be perceived as ugly, that they would mar the aesthetics of nonhybrid cars.

Pieter Kampinali is deeply involved with a range of emerging clean-energy technologies. Many of the ones he mentioned involve utilizing excess capacity. One application uses excess capacity of electricity to compress air in unused mines. During the heat of the day and at peak demand, the compressed air is directed through the generating turbines, and Professor Kampinali claims large increases in efficiency as the pressurized air aids in spinning the natural gas turbines, providing a boost in production. Called CAES for short, the system is like pumped storage using air rather than water, and compression of gas rather than gravity on water (see Luo and Wang, 2013; Luo et al., 2014). In the United States, a compression system is installed in disused coal mines in Alabama,[20] while in Europe, Germany is installing compression systems in abandoned iron and other mines (BINE, 2016). Both represent reusing what could be considered waste lands as important resources to increase electricity generation, turning derelict mines into significant components of systems redesigned and rearticulated to improve efficiency using the resources at hand, which are now cast-off unintended consequences of the industrial age. Similarly, Google and other high-tech users of massive amounts of electricity are moving closer to the source of their power, such as the Suma Mill site in Finland (Google, 2016), just as Las Vegas has been able to sustain a massive population from the cheap electricity and water resources enabled by the Hoover Dam at the zenith of the industrial age (Manaugh, 2016). Google's network infrastructure is benefited by its inventive place-based electricity generation.

Pieter claims half of the automotive glass in the world is manufactured in the Toledo, Ohio, area. Wherever the automobiles may be assembled, the windshields and other glass components are likely manufactured in Toledo, and certainly the technologies, manufacturing systems, and underlying scientific concepts were if not wholly then partially researched and developed in Toledo, and likely at the University of Toledo. Glasstech continues to be a worldwide leader in the creation and manufacture of glass manufacturing equipment; leadership in the tools that make the tools is a valuable asset both globally and for long-term economic sustainability. These are long-lasting geographically situated forms of expertise and place-based knowledge that cannot easily be transported, outsourced, or replicated elsewhere, and retains for Toledo the tradition of glass begun before automotive manufacturing and fiberglass insulation and that continues beyond automobile manufacturing. These are deep traditions and skills built with the resources that first made Toledo the center of glass manufacturing, and they represent a bright future in solar and green energy research and development.

Safety glass, thin film coatings, and so on, are all part of the Toledo legacy in glass. Solar Cell Inc., SCI, the primary organization in the 1980s, represents older technologies producing far less electricity than is possible using contemporary advanced materials: wafers on glass substrate, and the new technology Cadmium Telluride, now on a substrate of stainless steel in addition to silicon (remember that silicon is a pure glass). The promising change is a shift from rare earth minerals available mostly through China and Australia to more widely available common materials, even if some (like silver, gold, and platinum) are rather precious. They are common in comparison. However, the silica—sand—on which Toledo's glass is built is a naturally occurring locally available mineral. That natural deposit has been turned, through human muscle and brainpower, into the foundation of the city of Toledo, and those assets—human, mineral, and now the expertise as well as the institutions that house that expertise—are rather durable and have resisted attempts at outsourcing and liquidation. These hubs of innovations reapply and reimagine these assets: Toledo in glass and solar, Cleveland in health and high technology, and Dayton in flight.

Ohio has named its three world-class centers of innovation. In meeting both leaders and workers at these sites, it becomes clear that centers of innovation and development and skill sets are persistent regional assets. One important job that continues in importance is the ability to recognize, name, and market the local assets that make work and community not just possible but sustaining of functioning communities. Exemplified by Sophia Fisher and George Jansen, the research, communication, and technical articulation skills that are key components in professional and technical communication programs remain necessary skills in the postindustrial age. As the geographic advantages of transportation over the Great Lakes gain new significance in an age that values clean and green energy production as well as sustainable practices, clean and efficient energy production, in a smartly regulated marketplace, as each of these components of the postindustrial economy favor Ohio's Innovation Hubs, as well as the citizens with advanced degrees and experience to contribute to the emergent research and development missions of these next-generation cities. I return to the promise of a win-win solution represented by Cleveland's sequestration of industrial brownfield sites—20–30 years of clean solar electricity generation atop fields set aside for 25 years to clear industrial contamination. Toledo's Glass City identity is shifting from canning jars to automobiles to structural photovoltaic glass, from agricultural to industrial, to clean, sustainable postindustrial production.

Ohio refocuses its substantial research and development infrastructure toward a post–fossil fuel future, and along the way is retrofitting its industrial infrastructure. Moreover, the skills that made Ohioans employable in the industrial economy are finding renewed importance in the postindustrial. Locally, household photovoltaic installations employ contractors who are as likely to install solar panels and wind turbines as to renovate kitchens and bathrooms. Automotive parts robots are being redeployed and made part of industrial-proportioned photovoltaic array assembly processes. Educational institutions benefit from their ability to revise curricula for new work contexts—transforming ancient lessons to be learned afresh in new conditions rather than deviating too far from effective long-term education and pedagogical principles. And skilled managers are finding their talents and experiences valued in motivating teams, effectively and efficiently using resources, and addressing vexing problems in creative and interesting ways. In each case, an accessible skill set tied into existing networks is rearticulated in newly emerging contexts, effectively recycling the skills from the industrial economy into the emerging postindustrial economy. And while the challenges of numbers stemming from automation and removal of labor present new problems, they are merely that. They are the new challenges of this emerging economy, sharing much in common with the disruptive changes mechanized agriculture ushered in to these same cornfields in the 19th century.

Writing that sentence does not make the transition any more humane, or the suffering faced by displaced workers any easier, but it may just provide another argument—another available means of persuasion—for redefining retraining and educational funding not as government waste but as recognition that the economy demands investment, and that sometimes that investment takes the form of educational reform and training that requires increases in funding from private and public sources—not decreases.

Translating innovation: rearticulating Toledo

Translation has been critiqued, particularly in network typologies. The ideological assertion has been that translating from subject matter experts to the general population, or between two groups of experts, offers insufficient value added to justify the cost of human labor. This assumption requires accepting Gates' assertion of frictionless globalization, that an idea is an idea is an idea, whether thought in Silicon Valley or Chicago or Botswana. Instead, this study with its attention to the unique situation of each place, identifying each expertise, and the uniqueness of the East-Midwest as a whole, has asserted that an idea must necessarily be localized for each place. Localization has been effectively utilized as a concept by international technical communicators (see Agboka, 2013; Maylath et al., 2013; Andersen, 2013). The work of transferring expertise across language and cultural barriers is recognized and rewarded as work. Yet information transferred thousands of miles, from one workplace to another, from one industry to another, even if that business is conducted completely in English, must still be translated from the design to the production, from the context of marketing to the context of sales, over and over again. Yet this is what work is. Moving ideas from one realm to another, from digital to analogue, from idea to execution, from automotive to energy production, and from social application to manufacturing floor.

In this study, the photovoltaic research at Xunlight is a case in point. Toledo is a case in point. To say that the ideas that emerge from Toledo's historical engagement with glass enable or support its leadership in photovoltaic research and development is to make a point that simplifies and elides the human labor that makes that transition possible. Automotive glass, residential and commercial glass, fiberglass as building material and as insulation: each of these contributes a face in the faceted identity of glass city, the city of Toledo, that sits below Michigan and its industrial car design and manufacturing cluster.

Sitting at the crossroads of automotive glass research, residential and commercial structural glass, advanced materials and manufacturing, Toledo and northwest Ohio have a bright future because glass is a necessary component not only of future homes and smart devices but the next generation of clean energy production. Whether manufactured in Toledo, the East Midwest, the greater American industrial heartland, or globally as Gorilla Glass has found a home in Japan or Taiwan, the knowledge base of advanced glass research remains in the eponymously named Glass City. To be a technical communicator means knowing and understanding the major products and industrial history of the city. Knowledge opens up metaphors, processes, and predecessors for writers, local landmarks and significance that help those trying to understand its culture, its present pride, as well as prospects for the future. It is also necessary to understand failures and current predicaments. Such knowledge helps innovations find purchase in existing networks. And it helps ease fears of the unknown.

Returning to Moretti's work in geographic networks, to live and work in Toledo both opens opportunities and closes others down. As a hub in the wheel of glass, "A growing body of research suggests that cities are not just a collection of individuals but complex, interrelated environments that foster the generation of new ideas and new ways of doing business" (Moretti, 15). Innovations in glass research, in any of the realms in which glass plays a part, whether automotive, photovoltaic, construction, and so on, to be innovative in glass in Toledo is to be recognizable as globally innovative. But innovation takes many forms, as I have gestured here, toward innovation in photovoltaic cells, which takes the form of research and development at Xunlight, as well as in building materials and commercialization as they spin off residential and commercial building products divisions. Or, by combining the knowledge base of advanced automotive manufacturing with solar energy production, creating more efficient methods of installing and maintaining medium- and large-scale photovoltaic arrays. And each requires communication experts to move information from one expert to another with precision to allow transfer of high-level expertise; technical communication specialists are needed in Ohio's glass and automotive engineering corridor as much as they are needed in Silicon Valley's hardware design, software invention, aftermarket support, and customer communication. Yet there has been less attention to emplacing rhetorically trained experts in advanced manufacturing, research and development, and photovoltaic research. As a field, rhetoricians have expressed interest in these laboratories as sites for research, and opportunities to study the epistemological making of scientific knowledge. We have not immersed ourselves as partners and players in the laboratories and manufacturing spaces as professional writers, as participants and employees, as potentially contributing to the establishment, dissemination, and recording of the knowledge created in the varieties of workplaces that make up Toledo's less eponymously but more provocative nickname, Frog City.

Rather than preparing anonymous students for an equally generic high-tech workplace writing software documentation and endlessly replicating web best practices, the aim can and should be to emplace programs in local high-technology work culture. Information technologies may still be the focus, but they will be jobs networking research offices for computers supporting research in next-generation polymer-infused glass, or, like George Jansen, manager of Hub, problem solving with unique but industry-specific technology and research needs. These are the jobs that students with rhetorical and technological preparation can and should be competing for, and they will land them once their attention to local histories and traditions are supported in our curricula and classrooms. Gerald Savage, tracing metis, asserted a vision of the techno-rhetor as sophistic tactician versus the strategist philosopher, and that definition will serve rhetorically trained technical communicators far into the postindustrial future (Kynell-Hunt and Savage, 2003, 2004).

Each of these four professionals—operations manager, education administrator, entrepreneur, and research scientist—spend a significant part of their day writing and communicating in a variety of media. While none of them think of themselves primarily as a professional or technical communicator (see Selzer, 1983, establishing this line of thinking for TPC research), their expertise is multiplied through awareness of cultural extensions of their message: awareness of stakeholders and the necessity of arguments working in multiple ways for their constituents. The operations manager, already working long days, balances each internal communication with issues of morale and logistics. Representations of these communications are shared to the host institution as well as to the administrators and community partners that control short- and long-term funding decisions. This position is similar to the plant manager in the previous chapter who innovated by bringing arguments derived from economic, public relations, and cultural trends to bear on decision making. The education administrator makes pitches to prospective students and concerned family members who are equally invested in the viability of each student's future. As representatives, politicians are implicated in the success or failure of these educational futures, the working futures these curricula represent. But educators are responsible to a host of internal stakeholders as well. The entrepreneur is constantly reminded of his responsibilities to his investors; in turn, investors are interested in profitmaking and less so in the changing manufacturing environment. They want to see return on their investment. The responsibilities of the plant manager and chief executive officer are multiple and complex enough. Add to them responsibility for employees and making weekly payroll to the entrepreneur's responsibilities. And while the research scientist's chief concern is for science and scientific research, many additional jobs and even entire businesses rely on Kampinelli's ability to usefully transfer knowledge from the laboratory space to the manufacturing floor, from the realm of moving theoretical findings to scientific accuracy but then to viable product. There are numerous and continual reminders of the work of communication at the heart of the work of professionals in high-technology industries.

Each of these four postindustrial workers represent a rich site where further investigation and articulation of workplace writing and scientific communication can be conducted. The research Hub requires regular written reports from its research associates. Administration writes reports assessing the effectiveness of new programs. Entrepreneurs pitch their products to angel investors. Xunlight has marketing specialists commercially promoting their products. Yet none of these professionals knew about technical writing as a specialty field of study: a scientific communicator with understanding of journalism could issue powerful press releases about breakthrough research and translation happening at the Hub, administration could tout the effectiveness of pioneering professional programs, entrepreneurial pitches could be improved with research conducted on previous failures the angel investors backed—just to know how the new project differs from the old. And Xunlight could support technocultural agents into discussions of benefits of structural photovoltaic glass at the local level of demonstrating both the power of the science and its viability as an element in creating and maintaining manufacturing strength in the region. The contributions of the TPC are powerful and instructive because of the additive capacity of effective communication: a culture that (1) understands promising scientific breakthroughs, (2) participates in and feels like beneficiaries of investment in commercializing these changes, and (3) lobbies powerful state and national interests on behalf of these projects.

The chorus asks: what is Toledo if not a node in the automotive network? It reevaluates and recycles its natural resources in silica, used as a raw material for industrial glass, turned into technologies and products in automotive glass, transformed into fiberglass for lightweight construction and insulation. Agility allows these industrial breakthroughs to be rearticulated as photovoltaic products and durable advanced glass for digital device screens. Maneuverability reveals the region's skill in navigating change: its collective metis. More importantly, perhaps, are the ways in which metis are revealed in technology transfer, from laboratory to manufacturing to mundane products being installed by robot modules attached to farm equipment. The chorus is satisfied with Toledo's innovation and the rearticulation of its regional core competencies.

Next-generation glass technologies represent one future for Toledo. The city's traditional strength in commercial glass, both fiberglass and automotive glass, make it well-positioned to continue to take advantage of the need for high-technology glass in a variety of new applications. Yes, automotive glass remains an important base, and Toledo's physical emplacement within the 20th-century automotive network centered on Detroit continues to benefit the Queen City. These assets yield deep knowledge bases with industrial process and logistics, research and development, clean rooms, and medical knowledge, all of which come together in new and interesting ways, where glass research is conducted in laboratories kept as free of contaminants as an operating theater and global logistics networks inform the production of nano-impregnated glass for device manufacture. Postindustrial hybrids and deep recycling of skillsets mark Toledo's future as different from but reliant upon its past.

Notes

1 www.utoledo.edu/research/pvic/.
2 www.cleveland.com/metro/index.ssf/2013/01/sun-catching_solar_farm_to_pow.html.
3 www.nytimes.com/2013/05/29/business/energy-environment/solar-powers-dark-side.html.
4 See Krug (2010).
5 See Ratcliffe (2006).
6 http://rgp.org/.
7 www.nrel.gov.
8 www.nored.org.
9 www.toledobiz.com/Files/SCOUT_articles/scout1206isofoton.html.
10 http://jfs.ohio.gov/owd/wia/DislocatedWorker-home.stm.
11 http://catalog.owens.edu/preview_program.php?catoid=9&poid=2166&returnto=3508.
12 www.alexproducts.cc.
13 http://xunlight.com.
14 www.truenorthpower.com.
15 www.nrel.gov/buildings/pdfs/48295.pdf.
16 www.treehugger.com/sustainable-product-design/lighting-the-future-walmart-converting-hundreds-of-stores-lot-lighting-to-leds.html.
17 www.altenerg.com/back_issues/index.php-content_id=41.htm.
18 http://news.walmart.com/news-archive/2012/07/30/walmart-unveils-100th-solar-installation-in-california.
19 Interview.
20 See PowerSouth Energy Cooperative website for more on the Macintosh CAE (COmpressed Air Storage) Facility: http://www.powersouth.com/mcintosh_power_plant/compressed_air_energy.

5 Ludington, Michigan, Pumped Storage as quasi-object

Michigan's lower peninsula is surrounded by water on the west, north, and east. Ask Michiganders where they are from, and they will likely hold up a hand and point, locating their hometown on the Lower Peninsula's "mitten" of their hand. Toledo, Ohio, is on the southeast edge by the wrist bone. Detroit is at the thumb's first joint. Bay City is where the thumb rejoins the hand. The Mackinac Bridge is at the tip of the middle finger, connecting the lower to upper peninsulas. Traverse City is where the pinky rejoins the hand. Muskegon, Grand Rapids, Lansing, and Flint are the knuckles. Ludington is north of Muskegon on the western coast on Lake Michigan, a ferry ride from Manitowoc, Wisconsin. Ludington is a beautiful, peaceful, wooded summer playground. But it wasn't always that way.

Ludington, Michigan, an industrial-age town built on the shores of Lake Michigan, was recently the subject of an National Public Radio (NPR) story[1] that described its coal-powered ferry. The follow-up story announced that the ferry was ordered to stop dumping coal ash into Lake Michigan; together, the ferry company and the Environmental Protection Agency (EPA) came up with a solution:[2]

> After decades of letting the Badger pollute the lake, the Environmental Protection Agency issued an ultimatum: Stop dumping or be grounded. Finally, this off-season, the boat's owner installed a $2 million solution: a set of blue pipes that collect ash each trip, about 500 tons per year. Once a week, that ash gets trucked to Charlevoix, Mich., for use in making cement products.
>
> (ibid)

A legacy of the coal and steam age, the ferry was first threatened with mothballing, and then new regulation gave the ferry a new lease on life. No longer able to directly dump coal ash into the lake, the shipping company instead collaborated with the EPA and invented a solution relying on new technology that turns waste ash into input, eventually utilizing 500 tons of coal ash that turned a pollution stream into an ingredient. Coal ash gets made into cementitious products and finds a new life.

The coal-powered ferry and the link between northwest Michigan and northeast Wisconsin could be the subject of another book-length study about networks of withering industrial connections this coal-fired floating bridge reveals in its coming-to-end. For the purposes of this chapter, however, the ferry becomes a sidelight and explanatory feature for understanding Ludington Pumped Storage as a thing, a place, an outcome: historically significant—an object in its own light and a place that removes this shoreline from the obscure undefined space of northwest Michigan to Ludington, ferry landing, connection point between Michigan and Wisconsin, representative of a long-gone era of lumber and related sawmills, and the discovery of salt deposits under coniferous forest. With these resources, Ludington served as a resource collection point and minor manufacturing center in its own right in the late 19th century. The pumped storage plant maintains Ludington as a site of interest in the postindustrial age. For a hundred years, Ludington was a bustling town supplying raw materials—lumber and salt—and finished products, among them the parlor game Skittles that was originally manufactured from lumber mill scraps, the Fitch Four Drive Tractor Company, FloraCraft, and Great Lakes Castings. A local history articulates this industrial to postindustrial development, and today the major industries are tourism and energy production at the Ludington Pumped Water Storage facility.[3]

Born in the nuclear age, Ludington Pumped Storage was designed to capture the energy produced at peak capacity when demand was low. Pumped storage facilities were imagined where nuclear-generated electricity was abundant and practically free. Nuclear power plants, at least those designed in the middle of the 20th century, were either on or off with little variation in production capacity. So overnight, when Michiganders slept and summer temperatures backed off their daytime highs and cool breezes blew off lakes Michigan, Huron, and Superior, electricity demand plummeted. No more air conditioning, hot water for showering and laundry, few dishwashers, and little industrial activity left huge electricity capacity unused, and because there was no easy way to store the energy produced, prices plummeted. Today, peak rates in summer can reach over a hundred dollars a megawatt while nighttime rates plummet to near zero.

The solution was, in the middle 20th century, to capture the excess energy produced by pumping water uphill into a gigantic storage reservoir. At peak demand, the water would run downhill through generators, producing electricity to meet demand at peak hours. Overall, it reduced the cost of electricity produced at peak demand hours and made it unnecessary to build extra nuclear, conventional coal, gas, or petroleum production capacity just to meet the need during those crucial high-demand moments in the dog days of a hazy, hot, humid Midwestern summer.

Ironically—at least in technological terms—close to 30% of the electric power produced was lost to inefficiency. Even today and in the near future when rare-earth magnets, superconducting wires, and ultra-efficient turbines will increase effectiveness of the plant, nearly 20% of the electricity produced will be lost. It is no surprise, of course: there is no perfect system, and pumping water uphill is a costly endeavor. Even when new technologies like next-generation lubricants, nanotechnologies, and other efficiency creators come online, the gains in efficiency will be marginal and modest. Economic and network analysis can show where peak electricity cost compared to overnight excess production can yield additional gains, but this process maximizes output of the system. The technology displaces electricity production in space and time, in effect transferring production from the dead of night to the heat of the day, making the power originally produced at 2:00 a.m. available to sweaty citizens who want the electricity to maintain a comfortable temperature with air conditioning systems while washing dishes, running the refrigerator, and heating water for washing and bathing. It is only an effective technology insofar as production and usage are time-shifted from high capacity and low demand to peak demand. Time-shifting electricity production costs 20% of the electricity produced, even utilizing today's ultra-high technological high-efficiency, advanced materials, and rationalized design. But without this innovation, *all* the electricity produced overnight would be lost—100% versus 20%. Additionally, new power plants would need to be built and brought online to meet the peak demand, commanding a premium price, and producing electricity on-demand is more expensive, and often more polluting.

After learning about the Ludington Pumped Storage facility, I had to see it, and made some calls to Citizens' Energy in Michigan. Eventually, I received a call from a man named Mitch who seemed reluctant to help. A few weeks later, I coincidentally received a call from another Mitch. The previous call had come from Citizen's PR man. This call came from an engineer. I was convinced he was going to ask me for my paperwork, my 27B-6, but thankfully this was not a Terry Gilliam movie. "Yes." I imagine the *kairos* of that call, and how this connection might not have been made without a little serendipity.

It was a peculiar half-hour conversation. After the first 20 minutes, in which I was asked about my security clearance, my interest in the site, and what I understood about the technology, Mitch said this sentence, "Thank you, Professor Salvo. I wanted to be sure that you weren't wasting my time and that I wouldn't be wasting yours." Just like an engineer: all social niceties stripped away. He tried to persuade me that the site was not innovative. "That site utilizes hundred-year-old technology." Yes, I understood that. "The wind turbines don't directly provide energy to the pumps." Yes, the energy is sold to the main grid, and while some of it may end up in use at the pumps, there's no way to trace which electrons were produced where. I would later find out that indirect power was Mitch's concern, and why he didn't think much of the technology at the pumped storage facility. "It's not a battery."

Wasted time is the engineers' lowest, most venal sin. Work or play. It's what has elevated automation to near sainthood, sanctifying the logarithms that lead to subroutines that become computer languages that save workers from having to physically repeat steps, and now automate thinking steps as well. Don't waste time, and an engineer will spend a month as an individual to save everyone 14 seconds, as a contribution to the collective. And together, those 14 seconds times 2 billion internet denizens equals the minutes and hours we contribute as the crowd, as our collective *Cognitive Surplus* (Shirky, 2011). Shirky's argument about the internet's gift economy convinces, yet few tasks are as routinized as this vision of work asserts. As the industrial age replaced human labor with mechanical engines, so now thinking and repetition are replaced by the power of thought-engines. And right there the MBAs and the engineers have their battlefield: the gift of automation becomes the scourge of unemployment and displacement, the source of postindustrial wealth and of its misery and disproportionate flows of power. Quietly, capital is in control of the means of production (again) as in the gilded age.

So mid-November, the week before Thanksgiving, I head north to Ludington, hoping it doesn't snow, considering side-trips to Traverse City, possible stops along the postindustrial path to what started as a lumber and fur-trading outpost that has become a summertime beach and ice cream, fall hunting, and spring salmon destination. I told Mitch I was interested in the sights, the smells, and the context of the battery. It reminds me of the Hoover Dam tour in Nevada, only I'll be alone and there is no paid tour. Cool. I have special access.

The major mathematical breakthrough is, according to Mitch, Scottish. The original 20th-century design uses straight fins in the turbine design; new design innovations introduce curved blades and incrementally increase efficiency.[4] Mitch also mentions moving from fixed to louvered blades (Göde, 2009). At different water flow rates, the louvers can be maneuvered to produce the most electricity (Brunes, 2009). The blade design of the next generation of hydro-electric turbines improves the efficiency of the Francis Turbine design. A modified and refined (and enormous) Francis runner is installed in the Chinese Three Rivers Gorge dam project. Chinese engineers visited Ludington in the 1990s, as the Three Gorges Dam was being designed, and later revisited as the hydro-electric turbines were installed in China. The pressures on hydroelectricity production create networks of informed experts that transcend physical limitations, and dispersed networks have points at sites of hydroelectricity production around the globe. Chinese and Japanese electrical and construction engineers, their legal teams, and technical consultants, traveled thousands of miles to see the turbines installed onsite in Michigan to learn important unspoken, expert-level details. The opportunity to see the technology in use, emplaced in its environment, could not be avoided. Otherwise, video and other real-time telepresence technologies would have satisfied with images and recordings. Visiting in the flesh, in real life, in time and space, continues to reward the cost in both fuel and time because there is an advantage to traveling to a place rather than relying only on virtual telepresence. A conglomerate organization consisting of Japanese and Chinese partners now manufactures these turbines; the pairing hybridizes Japanese capacity in engineering, logistics, and management with Chinese labor costs, materials procurement, and cost cutting. There was already some collaboration and trading, and the group that manufactured the turbines for the Three Rivers Gorge project is manufacturing the new advanced turbines being fitted at Ludington.

Fences, freedom: nature, protection

A five-point buck proudly, loudly trumpeted his location behind the razor-wire fence at the pumped storage plant. More than the geese or the beaver family at the Subaru Indiana Assembly (SIA) campus, which are more nuisance than symbol, this white-tailed alpha male seemed aware that he was safe. The animal trumpeted its dominance from the peak of a man-made hill, an earthen dam that held millions upon millions of cubic feet of water in standing reserve, waiting to be turned back into electricity.

Mitch O'Brien, former military officer, power plant representative, and energy company manager represents the counterpoint to the Spinuzzian critique of the designer-hero.[5] He's a former US Department of Defense employee who worked on declassifying and commercializing military technology, the original source of technology transfer. A self-described policy nerd, he said he was surprised after graduating with his political-science undergraduate degree that "I had a talent for explaining highly complex technologies and processes to citizens." And he is right. Our conversation was wide-ranging and rich, deep, and diverse.

The fog was thick at the bottom of the man-made hill, and then the wind started and howled fiercely as we ascended, and I am happy I followed Mitch' advice and prepared for inclement weather, including gloves, a warm hat, and wind-proof winter coat. Our relationship began with an email, followed by a phone conversation where he paused after 20 minutes to let me know he had decided I would not waste his time. Now it was blossoming into a forced uphill march in fog that was starting to disperse in a bitter wind, just a few degrees above freezing, to an unprotected lookout overlooking the reservoir blanketed, invisible, under fog. I had passed another test: winded, sucking air, and shivering, I managed to ask three quick questions in succession about the pumped storage facility. Mitch, only a few years older but in much better physical shape—like he could run a super-marathon, or a serious iron-man event *right now*—seemed surprised that, red-faced and breathing heavily, I managed to stay focused on the work that had compelled me to drive 6 hours, 300 miles, north to incongruous Ludington in November.

It was on the walk down from that disappointingly grey vantage that the five-point buck emerged from the mist. It was, to say the very least, a moment. I mentioned to Mitch that the animal was what all the hunters in camouflage and orange I had seen around town were after. Mitch quipped, "Certainly. But they won't shoot him." Well, yes, as he was behind 10 feet of fence topped by razor wire. Then Mitch let something of himself slip through, "If a hunter ever joked like that, I would tell him he was perfectly free to shoot that beautiful deer. But he would forfeit quite a lot of freedom from that point forward." Consequences. He smiled. I took him to mean that there was potential for prosecution for shooting that deer after pulling the trigger. It was a curt rule-of-law assertion. Point taken. But it's cold. Let's get out of the wind.

Upon reaching the footbridge over the country road that takes pedestrians from the upper to the lower part of the facility, six penstocks—28-foot wide pipes that transfer water up and down—became visible through the lifting fog. So there is the moment: the buck in the foreground, trumpeting, the penstocks emerging from the fog behind, and the electric carrier lines that transfer power to the plant while pumping and those taking power from the plant when producing. All that was visible, my introduction to the site and justification for traveling all those miles, confirming the importance of being "on site" while Mitch jokes about hunting on posted land.

Mitch seemed set on getting his point across that wind turbines and solar energy will not replace all the fossil fuel–generated electricity. While wind and other alternatives are important transitional and stopgap technologies, they cannot replace traditional systems. At his argument's core lies the assertion that Ludington is not a producer of electricity. Rather, it is an energy storage scheme. Indeed, Ludington Pumped Storage was originally designed as an ancillary technology for a nuclear tomorrow that never arrived, and another pumped storage facility was planned farther north. After billions were invested, nuclear power plants were never built in the numbers forecast for a number of interrelated reasons, including Chernobyl's meltdown. Numerous potential pumped water sites ring the upper Great Lakes, frigid deindustrialized lakefront awaiting a new generation of postindustrial participation.

Ludington operated at approximately 70% efficiency before its recent upgrade. Even after investing nearly a billion dollars, that rate of efficiency only marginally shifts. Current upgrades in design and technology along with refurbishments at the site will result in a 9% improvement, but it isn't clear to me whether that means efficiency is added to the 70% number, perhaps improving to 79% efficiency overall. That would be impressive, although hardly game changing. Technical measures of efficiency reflect persnickety scientific principles, like friction, and there's no such thing as a perpetual motion machine. Something gets lost in the transfer. Consumers Energy can only recapture 70%, or nearly 80% after a billion-dollar upgrade, of the expended energy that moves the water from lake to reservoir level. That is, at its current 1,872 megawatts of production, it took approximately 560 megawatts to move the water uphill. Those megawatts are lost, produced at night when demand is low, but it remains a staggering number. In the future, the 2,172 megawatts output will require approximately 650 megawatts invested. Or will it take somewhere between those numbers? "If you torture the data long enough, it will confess to anything," asserts Darrell Huff (1954).

In either case, there is a net loss of power. Why is this still a useful and viable plant?

It is *economically* valuable, and it allows energy created during off-peak times to be used during high-peak times, which is why Ludington has been referred to as a battery. But Mitch doesn't like "battery," which he alludes to when discussing the wind turbines off to the northwest and southeast. Those turbines supply electricity to the grid and not directly to the Ludington pumps, and so Mitch would not be comfortable calling Ludington a battery unless they were supplying the electricity directly to the Ludington pumps. (The pumps are also generators.)

The Ludington pumped-water storage facility is economically viable because of its ability to time-shift energy production from the lowest-cost-per-megawatt time of day to the most expensive. Economic analysis yields technical improvement. Time shifting is particularly attractive for nuclear-generated electricity—nuclear generators are binary, on or off, at full capacity or offline. At night, or during cool spells during summer or warm spells during winter, they continue spooling electricity off onto the grid that is wasted unless it can be put to use. Hence the pumped storage: at night, or otherwise low demand times, water is pumped with excess capacity and the water is used to create electricity during high-demand times. Then, Ludington is worth its water pumped while 70° at 2 a.m., even at 70% efficiency. First, it relieves the pressure of extra demand at peak times. There is an economic advantage. Moreover, time shifting is a form of power storage—moving power from when it is produced to when it is needed. Wind and solar are only viable when the wind cooperates and the sun is shining, and so Ludington's time-shifting ability becomes valuable again in a new context, capable of capturing solar and wind energy when available and storing it until it is called upon.

At peak times, lower-efficiency natural gas–fired turbines provide stopgap electrical energy. When available, wind-generated electricity would also be directly available on the grid to relieve the pressure on capacity. But on-demand gas turbines are expensive—over a hundred dollars per megawatt—compared to the $25–$50 per megawatt for electricity produced by coal, similar price ranges for nuclear, and even at 70% of efficiency, 130% of $25–$50 is a lot better in comparison to 100% of $100–$300 per megawatt. The relative economic advantage of time shifting is what makes Ludington viable. But the electricity is valuable precisely because of the workings of the market: value is accrued in context, in real time, based on supply and demand.

Worrying Ludington: institutional identity

Ludington provides an excellent example where regulation requires clear communication with stakeholders—specifically with end users. Documents published on company websites and intended for public access reveal organizational values. Regulation, already a preoccupation, emerges as source for much of the effective producer-to-consumer communication.

Basic information, available online, allows the casual user to find out more about his or her local utility company.[6] There is a revealing aerial picture, statistics, environmental impact overview, and recreational statement, as well as some technical information explaining how the site works and how the technologies of pumped storage operate. Part of my method has been to determine how much could be learned about the place through the web resources. In comparison, SIA is completely opaque to this perspective.[7] In many ways, Subaru is invisible to the web except for its marketing,[8] and the car manufacturer relies on advertising subcontractors to represent its identity, while Consumers Energy aims for transparency in its operations and responsibility to its constituents. As an energy utility being publicly traded, Consumers Energy strives for clarity, and many of its web pages have been designed as pedagogical spaces intended to teach their customers where their energy comes from. The pages also explain why energy is expensive and seems to increase in cost over time, and they address the needs of investors while also portraying the company as corporate citizens, effective environmental stewards, and community partners.

For contrast, compare Consumers Energy's pages to those of my local utility company, Duke Energy.[9] Duke is larger than Consumers, covering more states and more end users. But more importantly, it is regulated differently, and its communication strategy differs greatly from Consumers. Duke offers no equivalent to Consumers' site: no technical descriptions and little information is provided about local production. Clearly there are different ideological reasons for the practice, as well as different communities of participation and address.

When looking at Duke Energy's website, I chose the landfill gas page specifically because of the overall similarity to the Ludington site—the page describes a facility that squeezes efficiencies out of existing resources and recycles wastes as new inputs by generating electricity by burning the gasses emanating from a landfill. However, Duke's web space provides a completely different experience, and it treats its audience differently. Numerous examples of facilities that capture landfill outgas and burn effluent to produce electricity are described. But these examples, all in North Carolina, are left without links and without accompanying diagrams or explanations of how the process works. The website presents examples and references to success, efficiency gains, and responsible stewardship, but there is no attempt at education, at outreach; no attempt is made to inform the reader. The web pages are an extension of Duke's public relations campaign, a representation and face of the company, but ultimately the site does not treat the reader as a partner. Where the Consumers website encourages further inquiry and connection, the Duke site is an endpoint. It presents only what Duke is willing to reveal. And that is the point. We aren't, as readers, invited to understand the site's information within a larger context of energy production nor to understand the energy consumer's place, my house's place, or my meter's place, within the network. It is, in the broadest sense, generic while Consumers' website is strongly local and tied to place. On the map at Consumers Energy, Ludington is clearly visible as the pinky tip on the west side of the Michigan Mitten with the Tippy and Hodenpyl hydro plants visible on the Manistee River.[10] Duke offers no equivalent, and it is difficult to find similar information online for the State of Indiana. As a consumer, I am simply left without resources or references.

Two web pages, one from Duke Energy[11] and the other from Consumers Energy,[12] are the most directly comparable, and they demonstrate the different attitudes each organization takes communicating with customers. Duke offers legalese: descriptions of how to meet requirements to become a net energy producer and sell energy back to the grid. The site offers links to forms, and to required standards that end users must meet. Consumers Energy, on the other hand, offers explanations: how end users might produce excess electricity, how the grid would utilize user-produced power, and what it means for the grid to become a two-way conduit accepting excess electricity as well as distributing centrally produced electricity. Consumers Energy uses an important informating strategy and takes a step toward next-generation smart-grid technology. Rather than a one-way relationship from producer to consumer, back-to-grid production turns the utility from an electricity supplier to an electricity broker, negotiating the terms of the electricity market. It is a brave new world, indeed, and Consumers Energy makes the outlines of these new kinds of relationships clear while Duke keeps the whys, whens, and contexts more darkly mysterious.

This change from energy delivery to energy management replicates the cultural change in the internet age from broadcast technology to peer-to-peer networking. As Rifkin articulates in the *Third Industrial*

Revolution,[13] it represents a transformation in cultural attitudes toward energy and electricity. Like the workplace changes wrought by information technology, a two-way electricity grid promises great change and reconfiguration both for how electrical power is supplied as well as for how cultural power is distributed. It is this latter disruption—a reconfiguration of cultural power with potential for energy independence—that parallels unfettered access to information to unmetered access to clean electricity, or at least a meter that measures contribution to the grid as well as consumption of electricity taken from the grid.

Why pumped storage is not a battery

If energy was directly transferred from windmill to pump, moving the water uphill where it awaited use as electricity generation, Mitch would have accepted the label *battery* for Ludington Pumped Storage. Instead, because the electricity flows to the general grid, and then from the grid to the pumps (or from the pumps in generation mode back to the general grid), he resisted calling it a battery. But the public might better understand the concept of pumped storage through use of the term *battery*. This distinction remains an important technical point for this stakeholder, Mitch, one I would not cross as a technical communicator. And it is these small-seeming decisions that keep numerous technical matters too complex for general consumption. I won't offer a solution but rather point to this instance of deciding *what to name the system* as an important technocultural moment, one that has the power to obfuscate or make accessible the technical knowledge of the Ludington Pumped Storage station. I am confident in my understanding of the technologies, and I accept the technical rationale for resisting simplification of naming the site. Yet why not *Ludington Battery?*

My impression on that day was that my research participant drew a distinction between a closed and an open system. A closed system might accurately be called storage, and referred to as a battery in shorthand, where wind and/or solar energy pumped water uphill as conditions and supply allowed. Because the pumped storage currently operated as an open system taking energy from and then supplying energy to the general electricity grid, it was irresponsible to call the system a battery, even if it resulted in widespread understanding of the facility in the electricity supply and distribution system.

Dissonance reveals an important role for the technical and professional communicator (TPC) in relaying public information and educating about both the technology as well as the institution of the utility. The technical communicator can communicate with the public about the service their utility provides in precisely this hyper-regulated space. The TPC, acting as the user/consumer advocate, is uniquely placed in the network to deliver information to the utility. That is, just as electricity will need to flow from household production in times of surplus, so too information will need to flow from the homestead back to the offices and energy production sites of the utility. Such flows back across the user/producer boundary are familiar to TPCs, reflecting the completion of the cultural circuit created by usability and user information: informing decision making with consumer information. Also, this change in the relationship between utility and consumer illustrates the power of regulation in identifying the demands of multiple stakeholders to account for environmental, statewide, and local community concerns. How are all these competing demands taken into account? One way of accounting for the variable needs of stakeholders is through regulation that requires the engineers and scientists to consider not just scientific or supply motivation, but to hear the voices of these citizen concerns as valid sources of information in the production and distribution of energy: usable utility.

Ludington as quasi-object

First, the hum, the hum of electricity over the high-voltage wires, pulsing, bringing Michigan to life. I hear the water rushing through the pipes, up and down. Then, the deafening squeal of the turbines spinning, the pumps pumping. Water pumping up, water rushing down, turbines spinning, lubricants in the pumps creating an acrid smell, the ozone crackling as electricity juices up the wires, sending human-instantiated lightning arcing through the woods to the cities where the electrons illuminate the night, cool hot houses, heat cold water, turn pumps, move things, hammer, roll, slam, clang, bam, and boom. A vast heaving network of people, houses, domestic technologies, infrastructural equipment knit together, noisily *doing* rather than becoming. Ludington is a place where energy generation happens. It remains useful and usable, a key component in producing electricity beyond normal capacity, and is a nonreductive place for seeing the upper reaches of Lake Michigan as standing reserve.

Latour's *Aramis* brings a technocultural Frankenstein to life in order to teach the postindustrial parable of loving our monsters, not accidentally taking part in a new environmental movement that argues for a love and re-engagement with (advanced) nuclear generation of electrical energy. Here, a well-off Frenchman (here an *ad hominem* reference to Latour-the-man, son of a wine merchant) whose nationalist interests would favor the heavily nuclear-dependent French—exporting nuclear technology expertise to an electricity-hungry world. Electricite de France (EdF) operates 58 reactors, exporting energy "principally to Switzerland and Italy, as well as to Germany, Belgium, Spain, and UK."[14] Areva, a large nuclear concern, shares with EdF the desire to spread French technologies to Asia, the Americas, Africa, resulting in the formation of Agence France Nucleaire International (AFNI). I am not accusing anyone of anything, but tracing the networks of connection that emerge through analysis that moves extra-textually, from the helpless closing off through critique (a steamless inquiry)[15] to the outside concerns that recognize issues like national sovereignty, globalization of advanced energy technology (which, together with Danish development of wind power through Vestas, German solar resources in BSW-Solar, Chinese manufacturing of solar panels at scale) gesture toward a cleaner energy future that omits North American expertise more allied to fracturing shale to gain access to gas trapped in the permeable layers of rock. These are the important extra-textual connections necessary to understanding the meaning, the network, the connections between people, discourse, and things that generate a viable flow of power much more important than the steamless drive of discourse alone. And it is perhaps the necessity of bringing discourse, artifacts, and people back together that defines Latour's emergent attention to matters of concern. The facts do not offer ways forward, do not offer insight. However, insight also does not, cannot, emerge through attention to discourses alone.

Yet Latour, the agent willing, allows Latour, the author-function and brand, to associate, to give name and tacit approval to *The Breakthrough Institute*.[16] The name of the network/organization follows closely the meta-argument being made throughout this chapter: that not any particular breakthrough (though nuclear energy is particularly delicious in its politico-social connections vis-à-vis Latour, as author-, brand-, and self-/identity formation) but the act of breaking through entrenched rent-seeking discursive institutions, like "critical" academic attention-formulations, runs without their own steam.

Technoculture drives my reading practice and articulation of writing practice as productive technology. Texts whose sole input is other texts—discourse derived of discourse only—are impotent, powerless, without import. They have no means of reproduction in culture, and are sequestered. Latour's own texts have consistently warned of these isolations, (variously) of minds-in-vats, of unloved technologies, of factish gods, and steamless theoretical engines. On its face, then, Latour may be indicating that there is a reality, some extant phenomenon of science, an extant universe beyond our discourse about that universe. While discourse alone has no power, phenomena without discourse (both literally and figuratively) have no meaning: meaning is created through discourse. And it is through articulation that phenomena enter the network of people and things and retain potent parts of the network so long as they are given attention and cultural engagement that Latour names *froth*. Returning to the *Pasteurization of France* (1988), then, we might assert that there has been a consistent Latourian concern with the froth, with the bother of culture, the friction, that reminds us from where significance comes. Latour reminds us that, on one hand, microscopic animals are our enemy—eliminated through pasteurization. But in other contexts, microbes are our partners, as in bread making and fermentation. Without microbes there are no partnerships and no allies (Latour, 1988, p. 162–176). All are co-creations, phenomena emerging as network players because of sustained attention, because of the indifferent phenomena sustained discourse brings forth in significance, and because we are surrounded by the black boxes—artifacts—that house histories of discursive relations, microbes, previous plans that yielded results, and all the froth and ferment of minds in constant and continued engagement with these phenomenon outside their vats, outside their textual streams of isolated discourse.

But if there is a safe nuclear technology and a green atomic revolution, Ludington comes back into focus. This extender of electrical efficiency would roar back as a working design awaiting deployment across the upper Midwest, pumping unimaginable millions of gallons of water uphill during the underutilized midnight hours waiting to be brought online during the demanding summer days. Ludington not only becomes interesting but lovable again, and perhaps even reproducible as pumped storage facilities might be built along Lakes Michigan, Superior, and Huron, returning jobs and industry back to the far upper Midwest, returning design, engineering, architecture work, and a second generation of construction, high-tech manufacturing and secondary light industrial work to the region, as well as all the services those industries consume and enable. The impoverished populace awaits the opportunities such a shift would support, a population spurned from their first industrial love and hoping a new suitor returns to drive a postindustrial rebirth.

Whether thorium replaces uranium as a fuel for nuclear reactors is beyond this analysis, and really beside the point being argued. Truly, I am agnostic on this point (and many others); yet I watch interestedly, waiting to see if some of the promises of thorium-salt alloys result in increased safety and reduced pollution than uranium-based nuclear electricity generation. One telling prophecy that remains to either froth or flatten is the accused connection between American military-industrial need and (dirty) nuclear discussion. As *Wired*[17] put it:

> Uranium is currently the actinide of choice for the industry, used (sometimes with a little plutonium) in 100 percent of the world's commercial reactors. But it's a problematic fuel. In most reactors, sustaining a chain reaction requires extremely rare uranium-235, which must be purified, or enriched, from far more common U-238. The reactors also leave behind plutonium-239, itself radioactive (and useful to technologically sophisticated organizations bent on making bombs).
> (*Wired*)

It all sounds too good to be true: a clean alternative to uranium, and a narrative and reasonable argument about what happened to the thorium-fluoride salt technology, which has, again according to *Wired*, "zero risk of meltdown":

> In 1965, Weinberg and his team built a working reactor, one that suspended the byproducts of thorium in a molten salt bath, and he spent the rest of his 18-year tenure trying to make thorium the heart of the nation's atomic power effort. He failed. Uranium reactors had already been established, and Hyman Rickover, de facto head of the US nuclear program, wanted the plutonium from uranium-powered nuclear plants to make bombs. Increasingly shunted aside, Weinberg was finally forced out in 1973.
>
> (ibid)

Talk about learning to love the bomb, Dr. Strangelove style! It begins to sound oddly and suspiciously like a conspiracy theory, a set of accusations meant to prop up a failed technology. Thorium-fluoride failed and lost out to uranium and plutonium, artifacts of a technology that the military fell in love with, and we may as well get reasonably priced electricity from the deal. But in the wake of Fukushima, the Japanese and, it seems, the rest of the world spurn the love the island nation once had for fission. While we wait to master fusion, thorium seems to provide a promising alternative, a new object of desire, a new potential partner:

> In France, which already generates more than 75% of its electricity from nuclear power, the Laboratoire de Physique Subatomique et de Cosmologie has been building models of variations of Weinberg's design for molten salt reactors to see if they can be made to work efficiently. The real action, though, is in India and China, both of which need to satisfy an immense and growing demand for electricity. The world's largest source of thorium, India, doesn't have any commercial thorium reactors yet. But it has announced plans to increase its nuclear power capacity...
>
> (ibid)

But like any new love, each infatuation can be blinding. If only *Wired*, or only this single author in a single issue of *Wired*, is in love with thorium nuclear energy, there is little hope. *Wired* is promiscuous with its affections, falling in love each month with ever-new, always unlikely technocultural scenarios. Again, Latour asserts, helpfully:

> The difference between the old rhetoric and the new is not that the first makes use of external allies which the second refrains from using; the difference is that the first uses only *a few* of them and the second *very many*.
>
> (Latour, 1988, p. 61)

Wired takes on new external allies in each issue of the magazine, as every chapter of this book takes on new external allies in each chapter, multiplying places, networks, technologies, and discourses, adding so very many people as allies that readers' heads may be spinning trying to keep up with who appears at which site, and what the overall picture might be. By making so many predictions, some of them simply have to hit, and statistics require unlikely outcomes to happen. There are as many reasons to stay out of thorium futures as the Institute for Energy and Environmental Resources (IEER) states:

> Proponents claim that thorium fuel significantly reduces the volume, weight, and long-term radiotoxicity of spent fuel. Using thorium in a nuclear reactor creates radioactive waste that proponents claim would only have to be isolated from the environment for 500 years, as opposed to the irradiated uranium-only fuel that remains dangerous for hundreds of thousands of years. This claim is wrong. The fission of thorium creates long-lived fission products like technetium-99 (half-life over 200,000 years). While the mix of fission products is somewhat different than with uranium fuel, the same range of fission products is created. With or without reprocessing, these fission products have to be disposed of in a geologic repository.
>
> (IEER factsheet[18])

Hardly a panacea.[19] Yet, the comparison of what we have now with uranium-fueled nuclear power compared with the wastes of thorium, with the added benefit of avoiding the catastrophe of a Chernobyl-style meltdown, seems more favorable than IEER is willing to credit to the technology. IEER seems to be comparing development of thorium not just to existing uranium-fueled electric generation, but to comparisons of non-nuclear versus nuclear power, which is not a fair comparison. Fossil fuel electricity generation, and especially coal-fired conventional generation, has created nonsustainable levels of carbon emissions and global warming, and the creation of tons of radioactive waste, while problematic, would be a new problem. In the late age of automobility, we might romanticize horses and the age of the beast of burden, yet it hardly makes sense to return to horses and oxcarts to transport our Chinese-made iPhones. It is like looking back at pre-automotive transportation and forgetting that dense downtown areas were once fouled with tons of horse manure, riddled with pests, and rampant with disease.[20] Fortunately, and *not* unfortunately, we cannot go back to an earlier, filthier, odiferous age either of horses or of wood burning. A fairer comparison would make measured contrast between thorium and uranium fuel.

A very real problem occurs when comparing an existing technology and its attendant drawbacks, in the case of uranium fuel, with an as-yet unrealized technology in the form of thorium. For proponents, thorium retains the luster of the yet-to-be, and while it has technological hurdles still to jump, the benefits can be idealized. Thorium still can be imagined as a solution for a host of drawbacks of existing nuclear technologies. Meanwhile, detractors of as-yet unrealized technologies can create numerous phantom challenges, as the IEER has. The current creation of weapons-grade plutonium as a by-product seems reason enough to seriously consider the switch. But it does throw the utopian cheerleading of the *Wired* article into better context: Thorium isn't perfect, and it does not solve some of the basic problems of using fissionable nuclear material as fuel. There is no magic solution, but the prospect of converting weapons-grade plutonium as a *cleaner* atomic fuel is an increasingly hard argument to ignore in an age of terror in which rogue nongovernmental anarchists want to build dirty nuclear weapons and purposely contaminate population centers. It is also an age of nuclear stockpile build-down in which thousands of tons of weapons-grade material can be put to good, clean energy–creating use. And while we have some time to make decisions, stockpiles remain targeted. The materials, both plutonium and thorium, have half-lives of thousands upon thousands of years: geological time—posthuman eons. But other networks desire to put these same materials to nefarious use.

The exchange, from *Wired* to IEER and beyond, reveals the very froth Latour was then and is now interested in articulating. Uranium-fueled nuclear generation of electricity is a formidable foe, or suitor, because some artifacts exist. Like an engagement ring given as proof of commitment—at least on the financial end of courtship—the reactors, mines, and geological internment repositories are real insofar as they exist in the word, as is the political discourse that surrounds these technologies and the decision-making process that must inevitably become politicized. Tellingly, the IEER fact sheet ends with a concern for inhaled thorium versus uranium, and shifts discussion to worker safety: "This makes worker protection more difficult and expensive for a given level of annual dose." It seems unlikely that much tolerance for inhaled uranium exists, and so this seems a red herring of an argument. I start to wonder if the military interest in producing weapons-grade plutonium wasn't a deciding factor in mid-20th-century nuclear power decision making.[21] The promise of this quasi-object is compelling, compelling enough to investigate and consider the unknown to replace the status quo.

Falling in love with the quasi-object

Whether thorium, uranium, coal, wind, or natural gas powers electric generation is less a matter of concern for this chapter than for culture at large. Latour's attention to the quasi-object makes *Aramis* and other mid-1990s Latourian projects so powerfully compelling. Latour's interest is always the cultural discussion at hand, and his stated desire is to return to helpfulness in the realm of nuclear energy. His role is that of a global French intellectual, convincing the world to employ French nuclear technology that would result in more French engineers employed, more global regard for French design, and more income for French engineering concerns.

But Latour's curiosity here does not in any way disqualify his participation in the discourse. Rather, it defines another motivation, a reason for his interest. Due diligence uncovers conflicting webs of influence that inform his and others' decision making. This is no smoking gun, that somehow mid-20th-century military interests cast a superior technology—thorium-fluoride salts—as inferior for access to weapons-grade plutonium. Instead, the discourse that excluded all but the most powerful military and political voices determined that, given these circumstances, uranium-fueled nuclear-generated electricity made the most sense—was lovable by more interest groups—than thorium. Today, with different stakeholders represented at the decision-making table, and all too much awareness of the cost of another meltdown, not to mention the prospect of keeping weapons-grade material manufacturing to a minimum, thorium as quasi-object has a fighting chance against the uranium-object-in-fact.

The quasi-object is a fantasy and a phantom, an unrequited love and a desire for more than the status quo. The quasi-object is speculative and theoretical, not yet here. And yet, the potential for its existence is strong. It is *potentially* viable, rather than completely speculative, and nothing has yet prevented its existence. It may not yet exist, but its existence would not contradict any known laws of the universe.

Smart grid technology; Michigan and Citizens power and light; smart metering; report on using energy; shifting usage; washing dishes, running laundry late at night to take advantage of better electricity rates—all these methods are means of making usage visible to end users, and are a form of end-user documentation. The power of showing, of accurately representing what electricity load looks like, can have a profound impact on how people interact with their technologies. Waking up, turning down the thermostat that starts up the air conditioner, putting on the electric kettle, putting bread in the toaster, and running a hot shower, represent high-draw electricity-intensive comforts whose spike in demand can be significantly reduced simply by spreading them out over a longer period of time each morning. Have the air conditioning come on after showering, or before getting out of bed, make toast and tea after the air conditioning has shut down. None of these behavioral changes alters the overall electricity demand but it does smooth out the spike, and coupled with thousands of waking citizens can result in a different morning electricity demand spike profile. Such is the vision behind sequestered electricity in the form of a whole-home battery from Tesla that charges overnight when electricity is cheapest and can be used on demand.[22]

Each example offered above is part of a vanguard of modest steps toward smart grid technology. The change from a monolithic modernist faceless utility that always provides clean water and cheap electricity shifts to a gaming of the system: to understand when rates are lower and when they are higher allows individuals incentives to create and use technologies that allow them to pivot. It allows participation and decision making at the individual level: deciding to run the dishwasher overnight, or regenerate a water softener or other devices when electricity costs are reduced. To consider timing one's working day differently, to wake before peak demand, or get a later start. Something as modest as a programmable thermostat can be used creatively to run multiple timed programs, dividing the day into cooler and warmer segments requiring less cooling and heating. Or, the thermostats can cool the house for the last hour of cheap electricity, a lower 7 a.m. setting being cheaper than changing the setting at 11 a.m. These static programmable technologies allow for modest savings. But more agile technologies like the Nest[23] allow for even greater control. The Nest re-programs itself based on previous behavior, allowing the temperature to climb or fall without restraint during times of slack usage, changing behavior when humans interact with it. In effect, the thermostat is pushing toward greatest efficiency and only relents when its human partners direct it to provide more cooling. Its behavior is not based on the thermostat's understanding of comfort or programming the device with thresholds of human comfort. Rather, the device is seeking to expend as little energy as possible. It turns on and off heating and cooling mechanisms according to programmed algorithms rather than arbitrary temperature measurements. This is a retroactive technology with potential to find marginal savings that, if used in great numbers, could produce huge saving in the aggregate.

What other technologies, like those of time-shifting electricity demand load, might be developed if entrepreneurs are given the challenge? If given the data of peak electricity demand, the constraints of daily routines and schedules, and the desires of users for comfort and convenience at reasonable cost, what new realms of economic development and invention can be unleashed?

Imagine an electric-run climate control system that stores coolness during low-demand overnight hours. That system, coupled with passive solar design technologies, results in a model that requires manufacture, remanufacture, and retrofitting of existing buildings. It introduces whole new economies of efficiency while requiring locally produced expertise and jobs that are not mobile. So too would a variety of technologies become possible: battery storage of electricity, heat and coolness stored in water or other advanced coolants, light displaced to hours of darkness. LED light bulbs seem to be on the verge of replacing CFL florescent bulbs, which themselves had been meant as replacements for incandescent bulbs. The hue and cry that accompanied the discussion of CFL technology is an excellent example of the kind of context, a discussion ably captured in two books, Freeberg's *Age of Edison* (2014) and Jonnes' *Empires of Light* (2003), as well as the PBS television series *Tesla: Master of Lightning* (2004). We are in the infancy of our relationship with electricity as well as with digital technology, which is so dependent upon electricity. A recent report announced news that Portugal ran for 4 days on renewable energy alone with zero carbon emissions.[24] Similar announcements accompany benchmark accomplishments in Germany,[25] Scotland,[26] and elsewhere in the European Union.[27] The reporting of countries and regions meeting low and no carbon emission benchmarks and for other clean energy production goals are reminiscent of the announcements and celebrations of bringing electricity and light to cities in the Freeberg and Jonnes' narratives referenced above.

The chorus grows restive; electricity has transformed so much. Yet culture demands impossibilities. Among the demands are clean energy without sacrifice, without pollution, unlimited electricity on demand, and power far beyond the capacity of the original grid's limits. How does technology move from infrastructure built to support coal-generated electricity to temperamental (and temporal) sources like wind, hydro, and solar energy? Ludington's pumped storage was an important component of the never-realized nuclear future, but it is compatible with intermittent clean sources of electricity. Meeting impossible demands of culture requires finding new energy sources to increase efficiency as well as improve the carbon footprint of production. New technologies and techniques meld advanced materials with design to eke out marginal improvements in new context: metis, technê, kairos.

Here, the technical communicator is responsible not for the design of the storage system or for the engineering of electricity or design of electronics. Rather, with an understanding of technological history, the techno-rhetor is able to speak with people and make texts that balance creatively and responsibly a narrative of the situation, within constraints both legal and social, addressing solutions that can be coupled to realize locally articulated goals. Communication remains key, and standards and regulations represent social, political, and cultural constraints, and are not unfortunate hindrances to be eliminated but exemplify boundaries that would keep any potential solutions from flourishing either in the marketplace or in practice. These advances in application, design, and efficiency are not based on scientific research but on technocultural design and responsible negotiation of regulation—that is, of invention within cultural and social constraint.

Notes

1 www.npr.org/2013/03/04/172954678/steamship-anchors-a-community-but-its-days-may-be-numbered.
2 www.npr.org/2015/05/31/410903693/on-lake-michigan-a-cleaner-coal-powered-ship-ferries-on.
3 See Peterson, Paul S. *The Story of Ludington: Born of logs, nurtured by carferries, forged by resilience.* Heritage Publishers, Phoenix, AZ. 2011.
4 https://en.wikipedia.org/wiki/Francis_turbine.
5 See Spinuzzi (2005) "Lost in the Translation."
6 http://consumersenergy.com/content.aspx?id=1830.
7 www.subaru-sia.com.
8 www.subaru.com/.
9 www.duke-energy.com/environment/landfillgas.asp.
10 www.consumersenergy.com/content.aspx?id=2021.
11 www.duke-energy.com/indiana/renewable-energy.asp.
12 www.consumersenergy.com/content.aspx?ID=1799.
13 See Chapter 1.
14 www.world-nuclear.org/info/inf40.html.
15 See Latour (2004) "Why has Critique Run Out of Steam?".
16 http://thebreakthrough.org.
17 www.wired.com/magazine/2009/12/ff_new_nukes/all/.
18 http://ieer.org/resource/factsheets/thorium-fuel-panacea-nuclear-power/.
19 The back and forth, what Latour called "froth" in Pasteurization of France (1987), between proponents of two different nuclear fuels demonstrates the role of rhetoric in many guises. http://energyfromthorium.com/ieer-rebuttal/.
20 See Vanderbilt's *Traffic* (2009) for an accessible history of the problems of horse-driven transport from Roman times through the early 20th century.
21 www.motherjones.com/mojo/2013/01/nuclear-energy-china-thorium.
22 www.tesla.com/powerwall.
23 https://nest.com/thermostat/meet-nest-thermostat/.
24 www.theguardian.com/environment/2016/may/18/portugal-runs-for-four-days-straight-on-renewable-energy-alone (Accessed May 27, 2016).
25 www.bloomberg.com/news/articles/2016-05-16/germany-just-got-almost-all-of-its-power-from-renewable-energy (Accessed May 27, 2016).
26 www.gov.scot/Resource/0046/00469235.pdf (Accessed May 27, 2016). http://thescienceexplorer.com/nature/scotland-now-generates-more-50-its-electricity-renewable-energy-sources (Accessed May 27, 2016).
27 https://ec.europa.eu/energy/en/topics/markets-and-consumers/single-market-progress-report (Accessed May 27, 2016).

6 Homegrown innovation
Indiana

Lafayette/West Lafayette, Indiana, is emerging as a new materials and processes cluster, centered at the Morrill Land, Sea, Air, and Space Grant main campus of Purdue University. It feeds innovations and technologies into three medical-biological clusters in northeast, central, and southwest regions of Indiana. The steel and metals refining cluster in the northwest part of the state benefits, as does the automotive cluster that stretches from Indiana across Ohio and Michigan to Toledo and Detroit. The globally competitive benefits of this complex high-technology cluster are expressed in everyday, mundane relationships, collaborations, and artifacts. Nowhere is this relationship revealed more clearly than in West Lafayette's wastewater treatment plant alongside the Wabash River, located at the southern end of campus where Purdue's physical plant, its electricity and air conditioning systems, meet the Wabash. It's where the *other* end of Purdue interfaces with its host community. There is a utility road directly across from the wastewater plant. The plant was built in 1958, and since 1998, the university and the local municipal government of West Lafayette have collaborated to create innovative techniques and technologies in the name of environmental stewardship expressed through cleanup of the Wabash river and its waterfront.

Flowing generally south by southwest, the Wabash River defines the western border of the state bordering Illinois. Illinois, in turn, is bordered on its west by the Mississippi. The Wabash joins the Ohio River, which empties into the Mississippi. These three rivers delineate a great deal of the East-Midwest region, the grain and corn belts, the postindustrial heartland. These rivers flow through industrial areas and collect agricultural wastes, and contribute to the hypoxic "dead zone" in the Gulf of Mexico.[1] Water treatment at the source of contamination, at each of the thousands of municipalities along the river system, collectively is thought to provide the best potential relief for the runoff. By starting at upriver communities, the hope is that immediate downstream neighbors will benefit from improved water quality. It is a strategy that contains cultural rhetorical elements: Greater Lafayette residents, having experienced a return on their investment, will advocate for downstream water intervention. Local investment in the form of increased water bills cannot be undone by downstream neighbors acting as free riders and polluting with impunity. It is a far-sighted, powerful rhetoric for willing cooperation, and Purdue and West Lafayette together have worked to utilize the internet to share their news, science, and quality of life information. Already, across the river in Lafayette, there have been moves to improve water treatment and invest in advanced water reclamation technologies.

It is important to remember how tied this community is to its river. Named for Gilbert Du Motier, Marquis de Lafayette, the city is fabled to be the northernmost point reachable by paddle steamboats. Although today it is 2 hours north by automobile by interstate, the city of Chicago was an arduous journey overland and via boat across southern Lake Michigan. Barges transported agricultural products and manufactured goods south, linking Lafayette to Southern Illinois river towns, to St. Louis, Memphis, and on through New Orleans. Naming these Francophone municipalities calls attention to contested colonial ground, a transportation link from Quebec and Montréal and maritime Canada into the warm Gulf of Mexico and Caribbean. There are historical and cultural connections to these long-gone river ancestors and to the power of the rivers beyond their destructive floods. Tying into this river transportation and trade history places Lafayette not just in geography but also in time, and serves to remind downstream neighbors of their responsibilities for river stewardship.

The West Lafayette municipal government maintains a web presence aimed at making its efforts at wastewater treatment and green initiatives visible.[2] It also provides a historical page that records major developments in the wastewater facility.[3] Purdue University includes its local engagement as part of its land grant mission, going so far as to reward faculty with advancement, while also publishing frequent news releases about collaboration with local government.[4] Purdue's food waste and other refuse are turned into electricity at the West Lafayette wastewater plant.[5] Together, the university is working with the host city closely enough to include the city's digester and wastewater treatment in the university's master plan as well as a key component of the university's sustainability and green initiatives. The electricity generated by food scraps is used throughout campus and in the city, increasing overall efficiency and decreasing costs. A published report reveals that electricity produced traditionally and taken from the grid (and paid for by local utility users) peaked and then began to decline, even though a larger mass of waste and water was being treated at the facility, reportedly saving West Lafayette taxpayers over $40,000 annually (and for which I am grateful, even if my share is a few pennies annually).

This is where accountability and transparency are important elements of democratic self-government, and local residents have a say in the continued efforts of greening the processes, even if it means paying more in the short run for long-term returns. Looking closely at the electricity consumption charts provided by the city's Go Greener Commission, a government committee, producing electricity on site is only the first stage of savings realized by reducing transportation costs of the food scraps, which in turn saves Purdue money in the form of diesel that would have been used to cart the refuse and in not having to dump material—up to 5 tons daily—into municipal landfill, or paying to ship the material to offsite landfills at considerable cost. I think about the relationship between Subaru's Kaizen strategies of continuous improvement and iterative design as an increasingly valuable concept that brings increased efficiencies. Toyota recently offered an in-kind contribution to a soup kitchen[6] by using Kaizen to make recommendations for improvements. No one seemed to quibble whether or not service improved at the church facility; it quite clearly had. But the need for real and not symbolic capitol ruined what would have been a public relations coup. Instead of a check in X amount *plus* a corporate intervention, the idea and resulting intervention was seen as less than adequate, especially in the *New York Times* report. The power of cash is difficult to argue with, which is why the savings at the wastewater facilities and through other green initiatives are turned into dollar equivalents.

Innovation remains an important long-term goal. Kaizen and iterative design, always improving, always changing for the better, may confound traditional short-term planning and thinking. However, it is necessary to redefine and take control of the challenges of environmental stewardship and balance with the need or growing the economy, which is itself dependent on the invention, utilization, and deployment, of advanced technologies that increase the efficacy and productivity of fossil fuels. We have to be sure to wring every kilowatt out of coal, out of our waste food, and out of our water if we are to sustain our standard of living. The local wastewater utility has demonstrated that environmentally responsible interventions turn out to be fiscally responsible, although they are costly to purchase at the front end. This is not a new conclusion and is well documented in the field of environmental economics, but the realm of technical communicators and professionals trained in cultural rhetorics exists in communicating the fiscal benefits and economic reach by creating clean-energy jobs. From research and development to installation and maintenance of digesters and mini-turbines, why do we not get a constant drumbeat of the benefits of responsible environmental benefits? And how can that oversight be turned in favor of the communities already reaping these benefits, like my adopted hometown and its electricity-producing water treatment plant and biofuel-creating waste digester?

After a decade of living and researching in Indiana, I understand its relationship to technology, innovation, and change differently. The corn, soybeans, limestone, lumber, and labor the state provides are all raw materials of an advanced postindustrial economy. The universities spread across the state research innovative and next-generation use of these materials, as well as the effective use of labor, of human mind and muscle. With Eli Lilly and Company headquarters and research and development in Indianapolis, Mead Johnson Nutritionals in Evansville, and the Warsaw medical instruments cluster, the state boasts an unusual concentration of advanced medical, biomedical, bioengineering, and genetics expertise. The region from Gary to Calumet boasts the largest steel production area in the United States, as well as a concentration of petroleum refineries. In the southern part of the state, coal is mined and used to produce electricity. Lafayette hosts Subaru, the automaker that is the focus of its own chapter; Caterpillar, Large Engine Division; Wabash National, world's largest semi-truck manufacturer; Alcoa, aluminum extrusion research, aerospace, and drilling products; Nanshan, aluminum recycling and ingots; Evonik Tippecanoe Lab for pharmaceutical manufacture research; Tate and Lyle, agricultural products and sweeteners; TRW, commercial steering systems; Landis+Gyr, electric meters; and Cargill, soybean oil mill. Purdue supports a research park, with *12 pages* of company names listed as participants, located at four different research campuses.

Although they do not produce digital equipment or the software to run them, these are unmistakably high-technology businesses, and each requires the skill sets of effective communication, research, and organizational history. Each of these concerns, spread throughout Indiana, makes products and produces wastes and effluents. Subaru leads them all in limiting their wastes, reducing the toxic effluents, and reducing energy consumption. While only Subaru explicitly names their process Kaizen, part of a lean manufacturing regime, all these high-technology sites employ versions of quality management and process analysis that allow for process innovation and redeployment of resources in order to capture efficiencies that emerge from expertise clustering, innovation, and iterative design. These firms, their processes, and their leading-edge applications of technology gesture toward a promising future for globally competitive organizations to emerge from what was originally thought an unlikely location: the corn and grain belt of the industrial Midwest. Anchored by practical research programs at land grant institutions and effective technology transfer programs, skills clusters translate meaningfully to the challenges of today's global economy.

Nanshan and Alcoa

Does comparison of Nanshan and Alcoa belong here? I think it does. Alcoa, like US Steel, is pursuing high-value, high-investment, hugely capital- and resource-intensive cutting-edge technology. They employ Purdue's (and the world's) great engineering graduates and metallurgical experts. Most daily applications of steel do not need US Steel's highest quality products. So too, Alcoa's high-end aluminum-based research produces materials inappropriate for the mass market. This plant in Lafayette does not produce aluminum cans. Alcoa is in Lafayette because of a long history of industrial metallurgy that began in the 19th century, and contributed to Purdue's identity as Boilermakers at the dawn of the locomotive age.

At the same time, food storage and home canning also contributed to Ball Canning's success and its visibility. The Ball Family chased resource advantages in moving from New York to Indiana, contributing to the persistence of the city of Muncie by supporting the establishment of Indiana Teacher's College and then its expansion and widening scope as Ball State University. The company history describes their itinerant company, following its fortune and growing its brand:

> The brothers—Edmund, Frank, George, Lucius and William—moved the company from Buffalo, New York, to Muncie, Indiana, in 1887 to take advantage of abundant natural gas reserves essential to making glass.[7]

Ball was an early industrial-agricultural hybrid, establishing first the home-based glass jar canning at its center. Packaging remains a huge industry, and connects networks of products and manufacturing, marketing, and logistical distribution.

While it remains a privately held company, Ball no longer manufactures the glass jars that display the family name. Successive generations have remained restless and continued to follow developments and innovations. In their own words,

> Ball no longer manufactures the ubiquitous canning jars, but we've expanded and grown into a worldwide metal packaging company that makes billions of recyclable metal containers, and a *unique aerospace business that designs one-of-a-kind solutions to answer scientific and technical challenges.*
>
> (emphasis added)

Ball is synonymous with home canning and agriculture. But they are also known for commercial innovation, and according to Ball Canning's website, 95% of canned craft beer uses a Ball branded can.[8] The company is trying to equate cultural "cool" with their brand, but the Ball family has moved on, beyond Indiana and canning, to Colorado and high-technology aerospace metallurgy. The persistence of Ball in Indiana reinforces skills clustering while the new business of aerospace research and development is a form of deep recycling, albeit outside the focused region of this study, adding value to aluminum by producing space-age metals.

Nanshan is a Chinese company that, like Subaru arriving in the 1980s, saw a market American corporations had neglected: low-quality aluminum for canning, bottling, routine casting, and rough metallurgy. The (literal) recycling economy depends on the ability to recycle! And Nanshan is promising to produce many low-cost aluminum ingots both through recycling as well as through smelting lower-quality ores still available in the Great Lakes region. Nanshan, rather than competing with Alcoa, will likely supply a great deal of its raw product, providing a low-cost, local source of aluminum that Alcoa will remanufacture into high-quality exportable next-generation materials, some of which may end up in Subaru cars, in the electricity-generating steam turbines at the ADM campus, the windmills on the plains, or the turbines on call at Ludington. They may hold the photovoltaics arrays in place in Ohio. Or they may become a humble can.

Nanshan promises low-cost commodity aluminum by maximizing production per unit of heat or electric energy. Like Subaru, they are considering time-shifting energy-intensive production to early morning, evening, or even overnight hours to access the cheapest electricity and gas rates. Nanshan proudly describes the layers of automation, minimizing their labor costs. Centrally located within easy reach of major highways and railroad lines, the rhetoric of efficiency extends to transportation and delivery networks, proximity to major manufacturing facilities, as well as to closeness to customers: both consumers of end-products as well as consumers of middle-level business-to-business transactions. Nanshan is committed to reducing costs as their primary principle of comparative advantage, and therefore seeks to deliver the aluminum to regional, national, and international markets at competitive cost. As petroleum fuel expenditures increase, worldwide shipping of commodity materials becomes prohibitive, and the entire network of aluminum consumers will benefit from a materials manufacturer committed to producing low-cost commodity ingots. What might be perceived as a competitor, Alcoa is actually a partner and customer whose success will buoy the fortunes of the new manufacturing facility. Chinese attention to cost-cutting and experience with low-margin commodities provides an opportunity for Alcoa to concentrate on manufacturing its high-tech, high-research, thought- and labor-intensive innovations. Everyone, from Alcoa's corporate customers to Ball canning to Ft. Wayne Metals, will benefit from better and more affordable consumer goods, from an aluminum trinket made in the United States to small-batch aluminum cans containing unique microbrewed product distributed to craft beer consumers around the world. I await a Nanshan-Subaru collaboration where economic efficiency and iterative design meet. Late in 2016, ALCOA formally spun off its Lafayette research and development facility. It has been renamed Arconic.

Fort Wayne Metals

The City of Fort Wayne is located in northeast Indiana, the hub of a wheel nearly equidistant from Chicago, Illinois, and Gary, Indiana, in the northwest; Lansing and Detroit, Michigan; Toledo, Columbus, and (a little further to the south) Cincinnati, Ohio; and finally to the southwest, Indianapolis and Lafayette, Indiana. Fort Wayne has important ties to the automobile manufacturing network clustered in and around Detroit and Toledo, a network that has now dispersed and spread across the middle West. The city is also about halfway between Cleveland and Chicago, making it part of the iron and steel network emanating from the Great Lakes northern ore fields to smelters and foundries historically in Cleveland, Pittsburgh, and Gary. It is no surprise to find advanced materials research and engineering in the medium-sized city, with a stable population of approximately a quarter million people.

Warsaw, Indiana, about 40 miles west northwest of Fort Wayne, serves as the center of another specialized high-technology industry cluster, as described by Peter Marsh in *The New Industrial Revolution* (2012):

> Warsaw contains about 100 orthopaedics-related enterprises, including device makers, suppliers, and service businesses. Between them, they account for about 6,000 jobs within a radius of a few kilometers of the town centre.
>
> (165, British spelling in original)

Fort Wayne Metals, lying as it does within strategic supply distances of automobile, metals, and now orthopedics, sought to supply Warsaw's surgical and medical manufacturing with their high-end metals. First, surgical steel was utilized, forming and shaping US Steel products smelted in Gary and Pittsburgh that met the needs of the 20th-century medical industry. Coupled with metal products supplied to automobile supply chains, Fort Wayne Metals diversified its businesses and began supplying a variety of materials throughout the web of manufacturing centers surrounding Fort Wayne. Later, Fort Wayne Metals began a research arm of its own, becoming more specialized in its materials production but more diversified in its global production. In effect, Fort Wayne Metals defines the eastern edge of the Warsaw cluster:

> Warsaw's orthopaedic businesses constitute a manufacturing cluster. A cluster is a group of companies in the same industry, located in a small area.
>
> (ibid)

Fort Wayne Metals supplies specialty metals to the Warsaw cluster, where many of its customers are located. The metals company also competes with some of its customers by manufacturing specialty parts and equipment, but much of its business is derived through supplying other companies with the research-intensive materials that this cluster of medical device manufacturers need.

One such material is ultra-high strength, flexible metal strands. During my visit to Fort Wayne Metals a sample of a strand of steel alloy made of 13 braided metal threads was shared with me. It was tiny: all 13 strands together were thinner than a human hair, and the braid was stronger than a single piece of steel alloy. I was warned to be careful as it could easily cut my skin if I put too much pressure on the braided strand. Later, at home, I did cut myself showing the sample to amazed colleagues. It is an impressive advanced outcome of a once-humble steel distribution and supply chain aimed at light manufacturing metal products for the automobile industry.

Another material seems more science fiction than reality, but indeed not only does this material exist, it is more widely used in medicine than I would ever have guessed. It is called a bistable alloy or a piezoelectric alloy. These metals have shape memory, and the sample I was given constituted a spring that, after I had flattened and straitened the corkscrew, returned to its spring shape in about a minute. It looks like a parlor trick that, once contextualized, gives greater depth to understanding its value in medical context. Bistability allows the alloy to retain its shape at two distinct temperature points, say at room temperature and body temperature.

The last sample, which I was allowed to hold but unfortunately had to return to my tour guide, was a stent that was flat and roughly the thickness of a hair at room temperature but expanded to become an 8-inch wire cylinder at 90°. In this formation, at body temperature, it becomes a stent capable of maintaining structural integrity inside a blood vessel, strengthening a damaged vessel, allowing the human being it is implanted within to continue pumping blood through the cylinder. The significance of being thread-thin at room temperature will be readily apparent to anyone who has had keyhole surgery or, even less invasively, catheter-entry surgery. Fort Wayne Metals manufactures the stents, implants, and instruments with which these advanced medical procedures are performed.

Beyond manufacturing metals, Fort Wayne Metals also conducts medical-device research that has begun to yield results. The first generations of stents and implants were failing, not just those manufactured here, but all metal parts used in medical implants. The devices were getting rejected by patients' bodies at unacceptable rates, requiring either additional rounds of surgery or removal of the medical appliances. In response, the company collaborated with medical researchers and developed patented strategies for bonding anti-rejection medicines directly to the devices. This breakthrough hybrid provided a high-technology, high-intellectual value solution—of impregnating medical devices with medicine and using implants as medication delivering systems. The resulting innovation adds value and justifies high salaries and high prices.[9] In addition, patients need not be quarantined for their health because the small amounts of localized anti-rejection medication does not suppress the individual's entire immune system—a requirement of systemic rejection reduction that simply is not necessary with the new designed and advanced materials (Abizaid and Costa, 2010).

In addition to seeing the instruments and the implants, part of my tour consisted of a room of disassembly tables where the instrument packages for robotic surgery were being deconstructed and prepared for new instrument packages.[10] Before the tour, I had never thought about the tiny scalpels, forceps, clamps, and miniaturized instruments necessary for robotic surgery. Here at Fort Wayne Metals, custom surgical packages were planned, assembled, packaged, and shipped, and then received after use, disassembled, sterilized or discarded as appropriate, and prepared for another surgery. The process seemed one cause of the long backlog for routine surgery. But it was also reassuring that the surgical robot's equipment package was being custom assembled based on each patient's needs, each surgeon's preferences, and the local practices of each operating theater. I just would not have expected to learn that the robotic surgical instrument packages were being assembled and made ready for deployment at an industrial park in Fort Wayne, Indiana.

The disassembly stations did not exist in clean rooms, although they were meticulously clean spaces. Clean rooms—sterile rooms—existed elsewhere where tours, and guests of any kind, would not be permitted. I was assured that they looked much like the disassembly stations, with additional layers of cleaning and disinfecting capacity. Positive air pressure supplied conditioned, sterilized air, and ensured that air escaped outward when any doors were opened, and the spaces met the stringent regulations set by appropriate medical regulators.

In addition to the medical devices being researched, designed, assembled, and distributed, Fort Wayne Metals' core business remains in designing, inventing, and marketing innovative alloys and advanced new metal hybrid materials for a variety of medical, industrial, and even photovoltaic use. The company has built a microforge in one of its buildings on campus, which was designed to imitate one at US Steel, but was an order of magnitude, 100 times, smaller. The microforge enables Fort Wayne Metals to locally make small batches of advanced alloys. Thirteen threads woven together that are still thinner than a human hair do not require huge, industrial quantities of raw materials. Indeed, a batch of the size US Steel was accustomed to producing would prove economically unfeasible, and Fort Wayne Metals would only utilize a small fraction of what the large foundry would need to produce in order to realize economies of scale. By producing the alloys it needed locally on site, Fort Wayne Metals was quickly set to see a return on its investment.

On my tour, we discussed how quickly innovations were being made in advanced materials, and how each different medical company whose instruments and metal parts were supplied by Fort Wayne Metals earned patents and trademarks based on miniscule metallurgical and design differentiations. The microforge was central to Fort Wayne Metal's success as a supplier to this medical cluster. It could deliver custom metal alloys in a timely manner in small amounts at profit while allowing their partner businesses to remain both regionally and globally competitive in both price and schedule. Purdue advanced materials engineering faculty are regular collaborators with Fort Wayne Metals, both performing consulting research as well as participating in industrial (postindustrial, really) metallurgical production. In fact, I met my contact at Fort Wayne Metals on Purdue's campus during the Materials X Conference: the Advanced Materials Summit where local businesses discuss shared challenges and consult with university faculty, reaching more mutual opportunities for basic and applied research while creating sites for student internships and eventual employment.

At this point, my contact began to ask me about the undergraduate students in the professional writing program at Purdue. He was racking his brain trying to figure out how I intended to use our newly formed relationship to place writing students at Fort Wayne Metals. As we continued to talk, I began asking him about the challenges he faced as the personnel manager. He was rightly proud of having put together a functioning team—more than functioning or competent, they are outstanding, really—and full of optimism, high morale, and a can-do attitude. They were enthusiastic and dedicated, at times, however, too willing to gut it out when they should be smarter about their work. Eventually, after singing all the praises he could imagine, his face darkened. "I've got one for you, "he said, and I knew that he was starting to trust, at least so far as he was willing to admit to me that his team, although outstanding, was not perfect.

Slowly he began to explain that he had recently, about 4 months earlier, hired a new engineer. The engineer had a young family: a spouse who stayed home with two children. The engineer, the personnel manager asserted, had a great work ethic and understood what it meant to hold a job. When I asked what that meant, he praised the Purdue graduates— farm kids, he called them—who arrived early and stayed until the job was done. Working hours were suggestions, and if it meant coming in an hour earlier or staying later, or eating lunch at a workbench rather than going out to the local country club, they did it. "Some of these other new kids, they expect to work from 10 to 4, and aren't willing to get dirty or stay until the job is done," he said. He mentioned some other colleges and universities, but well, he was also feeling me out, trying to see if I was Boilermaker proud, willing to praise my own students and institution. "Farm kids, they know what it's like to get up with the sun and stay out working until the job is done, they understand there are busy seasons and waiting seasons, and that nobody sleeps at harvest." It's an interesting narrative of work and definition of teamwork.

The new engineer was pushing, trying to impress this demanding personnel director, and had gotten into the habit of staying late on Tuesday nights, often staying until 8:00 or 9:00 in the evening, 3, 4, 5 hours later than others. Eventually, the administrator had figured out that the technicians were completing almost everything they were asked to do during their regular workweek. However, there was a highly technical step that the technicians were routinely failing to accomplish. The engineer and this manager both knew that the process was sensitive and the manager appreciated the effort to keep the process rolling, yet knew this was an unsustainable arrangement. It turns out Tuesday wasn't a random day. On Monday and Tuesday, the technicians completed the process through about the halfway point. Staying late Tuesday, the process was usually completed Wednesday and Thursday, with quality review, meetings, new software training, or planning taking place on Friday. The cycle started again each Monday. Eventually, the personnel manager feared, the young engineer would burn out, unable to maintain an extra day's work each week, perhaps even leave for another position. And the manager was well aware that the engineer earned substantially more than the technicians. Indeed, they were employed precisely to keep the engineer occupied with higher-level challenges for which higher pay was appropriate. Something had to be done.

> "Is this the only such challenge at the workplace?" I asked.
> "Well, it's representative. We've got a few places where processes bog down. Some of the engineers stay and get the problems worked out. Others get upset and storm about the place. Others just allow some setups [a reference to the complex assemblies of metal components] to fail quality control."

The metaphor that stuck with my tour guide, who was also in charge of hiring, was himself a retired military officer. Soldiers look for advantages both in battle and in preparation for battle, from improved tactics to asymmetrical warfare to bombers equipped with smart bombs and laser-guided weaponry that decrease the overall numbers of sorties. Morale has been a force multiplier as long as there has been warfare: Napoleon believed it increased fighting effectiveness "three to one" (Englund, 102). V. Mary Abraham in aboveandbeyondKM.com, a knowledge management blog, applies the force multiplier metaphor to knowledge management, listing training and education, reputation, strategy and tactics, and terrain as important force multipliers with morale.[11] And, as a sophist, I was willing to extend the metaphor to keep my audience engaged.

Force multiplication in the workplace also has implications in morale. The young engineer and others who were failing to effectively teach the technicians how to complete complex tasks were harming morale. That was clear in the manager's discussion of the engineer and in the engineer's own descriptions. I asked if the technicians' morale was deteriorating. At first, both the manager and engineer described perceived conflict. The technicians had come to expect the engineer to fix any problems they had with the manufacturing and assembly process. I suspected that they had also begun taking advantage of the situation because any faults during quality control were apparently being blamed on the engineer. And it was resulting in a lack of unit cohesion, another military metaphor. The engineer was not being perceived or treated as an authority. I asked about training: how had the technicians been taught to complete the technical assembly process? The young engineer verbally described the steps to me. I asked him to show me.

Rather than ask the engineer to train the technicians directly, I asked if there was someone in-house who was maintaining the website. There was. They had a staff writer who maintained the website text, wrote documentation, and kept the company history. That person, I suggested, should watch the engineer and record the steps, and only when the historian had effectively duplicated the entire process, including passing quality control without the reviewers knowing who had assembled it, should the technicians be trained. And they should be trained not by the engineer but by the company historian.

I asked them to try the change, and that I wanted an intern to work alongside the historian. Unfortunately, it proved impossible to place an intern at the site, but I do know that they created a new position in technical communication and training, someone who answers directly to the personnel manager, and works both with training technicians in new assembly processes and in regulatory and research writing. In a follow-up phone call, it was reported that morale has improved, but it isn't yet satisfactory. And that is, ultimately, the point. Small improvements made over time put an institution on a better trajectory toward larger improvement and change.

While some might accuse me of misplaced heroism, I instead assert that it is an example of workplace analysis where, through the process of observation, a chokepoint in communication is observed. I have written about this as *information architecture*, although the phrase has come to mean something quite distinct in database design, and so I have pretty much abandoned that moniker for *experience architecture* (see Salvo, 2014 for more). However, *force multiplication* is imbued with too much military connotation, and I hesitate to propose using it among my academic colleagues. But with this military-trained personnel administrator, the term worked quite effectively. I will leave naming this expertise to others, preferring to think of it as one among many systemic observation methods technical rhetors will need at their disposal. The conclusion invokes Gerald Savage's articulation of metis, to sailing, and through his research to the sophists. It is not heroism but the application of rhetorical analysis to intervene in the workplace and bring about constructive change. It perhaps moves beyond methods of institutional critique to enroll in a process of institutional engagement, but becoming productive is not something for which I feel any particular need to apologize.

Fort Wayne Metals participates in numerous metallurgical, research, manufacturing, automotive, surgical, and medical instrument networks, but it is also part of a global network of advanced design:

> It might appear that clusters fit poorly into a global manufacturing sector that is becoming more fragmented and dispersed. The two concepts are, however, compatible. Clusters and 'networked manufacturing' are mirror images of each other, one looking inwards to small communities of businesses squeezed into a small area, the other looking outwards to a dispersed value chain with nodal points in many countries.
>
> (165–6)

The Fort Wayne Metals campus, which comprises parcels of land along the regional airport frontage road, supplying advanced alloys in small batches suitable for use in Warsaw, Indiana's medical equipment cluster, while supplying robotic surgical suite prescriptions to hospitals dispersed nationally, and competing globally by providing advanced materials and advanced materials research through a collaboration with Purdue University. At the end of the tour, with my bistable alloy samples in hand and all these thoughts jumbled in my head, Marsh's analysis rings true: Fort Wayne Metals is looking inward to participating most closely with Warsaw's surgical equipment cluster. More broadly, it participates in and contributes to Indiana's reputation as a medical research center. Globally, it looks outward to Europe, Asia, and South America as markets for its most advanced, specialized, and expensive alloys and metal/medicine hybrids.

Cook Biotech

Cook Biotech forms a cornerstone of Purdue's Research Park. The site reverses the accustomed roles between writers and researchers/engineers: the US Food and Drug Administration (FDA) consults closely with their communicators, who deliver design specifications and regulatory limitations to the project managers, who work closely with biomedical engineers to design within the structured limitations of FDA regulation. This is a far cry from the documentation role described in system-centered design (Johnson) and from what is reported in numerous technical communication sources where the writer is forgotten and debased, uninitiated or unconnected to the overall project and brought in at the end to clean up documentation. Tomlin (2008) describes the way in which FDA regulators flip accustomed power relationships between subject matter experts and documentation specialists. Cook Biotech also represents recycling, as well as boundary-crossing hybridity, and is a little disquieting. They recycle pig flesh, reutilizing specific parts of the animal and preparing it through much processing to become an inert input, a raw material, in medical implants used in human healthcare. They develop products such as artificial skin for accidents and burns, artificial cartilage and connective tissues, even barriers used besides internal organs in hernia repairs. These products are judged superior to artificial skin, connective tissues, and supportive fascia, in part because they have the irreproducible ability to flex and stretch like human skin and membranes due to their natural origin as porcine viscera. Yet this is exactly where the need for cultural engagement arises.

Somehow, Americans are more willing to accept a manufactured implant, whether metal, plastic, or hybrid, that is wholly inorganic compared to an organically sourced surgical implant. Overcoming this cultural factor is an important part of the business challenge facing this startup company. It cannot rely on people's acceptance of the power of medical intervention to accept its products. It is also crossing into forbidden territory. Swine, as common farm animals, present a challenge to the sense of taboo of some patients whose religious and cultural traditions forbid consumption of pork, pig meat. The miraculous power of medical intervention arises from its connections to science and technology and not to the barnyard, and so acceptance of these products may be slower than for other interventions that arise from the lab. There is a cultural-rhetorical challenge in getting people to accept the sourcing of a safer and more effective but taboo material in order to save lives and improve quality of life for patients receiving the surgical intervention. Since 1975, pig heart valves have been used as replacements in damaged human hearts.

Culture plays an important part in the acceptance of such porcine biomedical applications. An artificial valve, or 3D printed organ (see Ledford, 2015) is one thing; it is quite another to accept a pig's heart valve as a replacement for one's own faulty anatomy, and so, too, with porcine corneas and knee joint ligaments. Taboos over pork's uncleanliness, its impurity and offensiveness to religious sensibilities, cannot be ignored. Scientific research takes predictable approaches, such as surveying attitudes (Easterbrook and Maddern, 2008) and appealing to religious authority (Goyal et al., 2013), to weigh in on the issue. But both scientistic approaches miss the larger cultural issues at stake. The question of implantation differs significantly from Levitican purity for consumption, prior to understanding germ theory and basic food safety, which is not to mention lack of understanding of nanotechnology and molecular engineering. There simply is no ethical precedence for emerging technoculture and the many ways cultural taboos are transgressed by what is possible in technoculture and biomedicine. The history of biomedical pigs through the 1990s is available in Roher et al. (1996) and Schook et al. (2013), and the research is fascinating, but the lag in cultural accommodation is palpable.

The problems surrounding abdominal plastic mesh inserts are a case in point. No problems have ever been associated with Cook's naturally sourced product. Indeed, the company believes its products are the solution to the problem described in the FDA's warnings. Beginning shortly after the artificial plastic meshes were being implanted, women began reporting problems and complaints with bleeding and pain. The problems may have stemmed from the plastic mesh being too rigid and unable to give and stretch like natural tissues resulting in "over 1,000 adverse event reports about mesh" the FDA has recognized and reported, although it concludes: "the exact cause of these adverse events hasn't been identified, they're likely to be the result of multiple factors. Further investigation is needed."[12] Research continues, although a variety of products have demonstrated some capacity to replace the artificial plastic mesh (Mangera et al., 2013; Culligan et al., 2013; Karlovsky et al., 2005). Both the list of references and the ongoing discussion highlight the role of writing, technical, scientific, and research report writing, in the process of knowledge-making. It is no less political than pain medicine as traced in Scott Graham's recent work (2015) that articulates the interconnected networks of medicine, treatment, providers, and patients.

Andrew Feenberg's work in alternative modernity (1995) first called my attention to the difficult kairotic work of speaking up at the moment when activist impact would be greatest. Feenberg writes of AIDS activists summoning the will to put themselves at risk and reject a paternalistic patient protection. What good is safeguarding an individual who is dying mysteriously when he (and most early deaths from AIDS were men) is willing to be given experimental treatment, even if death was proof of ineffectiveness? Similarly, women changed medicalized birthing practices and enabled partners, midwives, and doulas to attend the birth and put medical treatment to the side until when/if necessary (p. 105). The moment of action is always brought to mind: women, in labor, refusing to enter delivery rooms until significant others or attendant specialists are invited to participate. Participants exercising their rights, expressing their preferences, and insisting on transformation can bring change to the most reluctant institutions, with reverberating repercussions transmitted. To be sensitive to these waves, these murmurs of dissatisfaction, that is the source of a rhetorician's power and relies upon *attunement.*

The conversation of 20th-century development of technical communication orbited around challenges of legitimacy. Bernadette Longo's

Spurious Coin (1998) meaningfully articulated the concern with the metaphor of coinage: science, and then the business and technological development it supported, relied upon writing to turn thought into action, planning into artifact, and to share this practical knowledge. In 1998, Grabill and Simmons defined a new focus of power by describing a critical rhetoric of risk, then Beverly Sauer's book with a similar title appeared in 2003, *The Rhetoric of Risk*, and developed a parallel thesis in three mining locations in the United States, South Africa, and Australia. And I want to acknowledge Sauer's analysis that in part inspired the methodology of this volume. Discussion of risk, power, and authority spilled over into the early 21st century, skillfully tackled in a two-volume collection of essays edited by Gerald Savage and the late Teresa Kynell-Hunt. *Power and Legitimacy*, they proclaimed, was the central issue of the workplace practice of technical communication. It all, according to Longo, goes back to Agricola and the distinction between the science of metallurgy and the hopeful nonscientific practices of alchemy.

By returning the question of legitimacy to its historical roots, Grabill and Simmons' assertion of a public role in risk assessment asserted both a new method as well as new opportunities for technical and scientific communication that this book is moving beyond risk into new postindustrial workplaces. Perhaps its value rests in recognition that questions of legitimacy are perennial; more pointedly, too, that these questions change within each configuration. These power relationships change not just because of the variables at each workplace but also in each kind of workplace. After an early 20th century of unquestioned authority granted through military and postwar hierarchies, the later 20th century in posthierarchical flattening, coupled with innovation-driven digital workplaces, left technical communicators seeking to understand their relative fall from grace, or at least from empowerment. As I have traveled across the Midwest and encountered a variety of workplaces with a staggering array of power and authority configurations, in hindsight the obsession with workplace authority seems misplaced if not occasionally indulgent, particularly when compared with the configurations of authority that exist in medical equipment design and manufacturing.

I first learned of Cook Biotech's work when my colleague mentioned them to me. Professor Jennifer Bay runs the professional writing internship program, and she received a call asking for a professional writing student intern who would know the scientific method and who was familiar with high-technology research settings. It seemed like a strong fit, and we went together to tour the facility and learn more about the work being undertaken at Purdue's research park.

During the tour and conversation (and on subsequent visits), it became clear that Cook operated very differently than I had come to expect. The bioengineers and medical designers were waiting on their communication attachés to return from meetings with the FDA, under which implants and a wide range of medical devices are regulated. After numerous redesign cycles, the federal agency had concerns— understandable given the history of a range of devices that had raised prospects of failures, bleeding, rejection, additional invasive operations, and interventions with patients. Cook was the quintessential high-risk environment, and here the company's medical writers, anatomical illustrators, and regulatory communicators were in direct contact with the federal agencies regulating the designs and ultimately in control of the marketplace's acceptance and success of these highly designed but ultimately naturally sourced xenograft materials. It was an exciting opportunity for an internship unlike any other I had experienced, and we placed a wonderful student in the position who has gone on to interesting professional work. But Cook Biotech, like Fort Wayne Metals, reverses the relationships between engineer and designer and the communication specialist from a traditional one that places the technical communicator under the engineer or designer in the organizational hierarchy.

Slack et al. (1993) emphasized the importance of the authorship of the communicator, yet so much of the field's development relies on an unequal power relationship between so-called subject matter experts (SMEs) such as the engineers and programmers with whom technical writers work (see, for example, Lee and Melenbacher, 2000). While researchers like Davis et al. (2007) and Tomlin (2008) emphasize the regulatory requirements of medical and technical data, the practice at Cook illustrates the way in which the communicators were tasked with gathering experts together and explaining, contextually as well as technically, what the design provided as well as how the design responded to the concerns expressed by the FDA. The federal regulators communicated mostly in writing with some phone interaction for clarity, but it was the communicators who were moving information from regulators to designers. The ultimate success or failure of specific designs depends on the communicator's ability to effectively inform engineers of the contextualized concerns of the organization, the federal regulators who represent the needs of citizens for whom (and quite literally into whom) these devices are implanted. The technical communicator is revealed to be the contact point in a complex technocultural web. The firm wants to create and distribute effective devices, and through that to develop an identity as a purveyor of quality, durable, effective devices. The FDA wishes to protect citizens from poorly designed, fragile, ineffective designs and to minimize suffering and unnecessary medical procedures. And citizens want to be able to trust both government regulation and the device designs to alleviate the conditions the implants are designed to solve, at reasonable cost and minimal risk. Positioned as communicators, moving technical and medical data across thresholds of cultural difference and differentials of power, the distinction between a documentation specialist and emergent forms of medical, risk, and cultural information becomes more starkly clear.

Widespread employment of technical communicators in hardware and software industries in computer design, manufacturing, and programming has led technical communication to overlook a variety of emergent practices in high-risk metallurgy, medical design, surgical equipment, as well as other emerging fields. Not only is the accustomed underappreciation expressed by our partners of the digital world gone—engineering, scientific, and programming subject matter experts—the site and practices of Cook Biotech demonstrate the important and empowered roles available for well-prepared, highly motivated technical rhetors.

While Fort Wayne Metals defines a step away from the engineering autonomy enjoyed by software and hardware engineers, Cook Biotech represents a site of even more authority on the part of regulatory, medical, and science writers who transfer data and demands from governmental regulatory bodies to the engineering workbench. In large part, these interinstitutional communication specialists define the design trajectory for medical products. Their authority and professionalism flip the relationship between institutionally powerful engineer and relatively powerless communicator, particularly in this realm of high-risk communication.

Braun automotive

It's with some trepidation that I revisit the site that kicked off this study: Braun Corporation of Winamac, Indiana. I wrote about it with Meredith (Zoetewey) Johnson and Kate Agena in *Technical Communication* (2007). In hindsight, this site became the nexus of thinking about globalization amid the cornfields. But then I started tracing out the networks, and they cohere, like anything does once you come to understand the nodes, the connectors, the attractors strange and mundane, and the local resources that lead to local conditions that serve as advantages. What makes this place different from another, and how has history and circumstance conspired to create a node at a place that, at first glance, seems to be outside the realm of connection, or at least disconnected? Winamac is the tail end of the medical network that runs through northeastern Indiana centered at Warsaw. A fearful and ironic relationship exists between the digital workplace—the creation workshops of the tools of the digital age—and the industrial manufacturing site utilizing the "work" but not the "play" aspects of the digital technology.

I was invited to visit the Braun Corporation in Winamac, Indiana. Braun exemplified solidity and permanence—the place-based immovability and presence I had lacked in Texas, and again in Boston—and which still struck me as so different here in the postindustrial Midwest.

As my visits to SIA were teaching me, however, integrating digital technology in automobile manufacture was no less sophisticated or challenging as using digital technology for the production of more digital technology (hardware, software, networking, web-based environments, apps, social media, etc). Rather, it differed in the measurement of success. Engineering required dependability in the world: cars that started, followed roads, and worked predictably and reliably. Curiously, the demand for timely updates and innovation in the digital world has come at the expense of stability and reliability, with crashes and failures becoming part of the online experience—planning for failure rather than avoiding it. The App Store has shoddy merchandise in comparison to the predictable, stable, and reliable automobile rolling off assembly lines.

Striking contrasts illustrate the difference between Braun and Subaru, gesturing toward the gap between the two firms. Where Subaru was dominated by its robotic assembly lines and massive next-generation parts presses, Braun had two flat linear assembly lines that could have been part of mid-20th-century manufacturing or could just as easily have been assembling high-end automobiles. Braun's lines were dominated by people at work rather than machines in action. In an early description of Braun, I made the observation that workers brought with them an outmoded sense of what work was, that one had to sweat and toil and feel exhausted at the end of the day. That article recounts the history of the company and its leader, Ralph Braun, among other details about the work done at the plant. Their interface was analog, and few screens stood between their manipulation of tools and parts. People were assembling and making Entervans, Braun's leading product at the time.

The Entervan is an interesting postindustrial hybrid. Early in the company's history, Ralph Braun had his engineers working on making vehicles from the ground up. However, as illustrated by the extreme high-tech and huge capital investment at cutting-edge automotive plants like Subaru, the kind of exacting and flexible manufacturing—heavy on robotics, computers, and thought-work—exemplifies late 20th-century prognostications about postindustrial work, where marketing and design are as important as nationalistic claims to being home-grown or American made or manufactured. Ralph Braun and his team recognized that minivans designed for the domestic US and world market and assembled in Detroit, Michigan, would have everything and more that a similar vehicle designed and built in Winamac would have. Moreover, it would be produced more efficiently. Buying complete minivans and shipping them from Detroit to Winamac was more cost effective and produced a better product than if Braun had attempted to build its own vehicles from scratch.

Interestingly, the finished product at one site—a Dodge minivan—is used as input, as a component, of another, further product that is the result of customization and addresses the needs of a group of differently abled users. Entervans allow for different driving interfaces: all-hand-controlled throttle and braking, wheelchair entry, foot-enabled steering. These are all user-specific design alterations made possible by the tradition of van conversions, and reference a tinkerer tradition of customization in which a finished product is altered to fit specific need. That Braun created a business out of customization specifically for accessibility applications testifies both to the limits of mass production and traditional modern industrial production methods as well as its strengths. Braun could not and decided it would not attempt to compete with Dodge/Chrysler as a producer of automobiles. Instead, they partnered with the automotive corporation in order to negotiate the best possible pricing on large orders of vans. Focused on producing the most units at the lowest cost for the largest number of users, and making them happy with a standard design within limits of factory-installed options, Dodge/Chrysler becomes a partner with Braun as well, enabling the small rural company to specialize and provide its Entervan.

Without dwelling on too much redesign detail, Entervans have their floors lowered and their ceilings lifted to accommodate wheelchair conveyance into and out of the van. Motorized ramps extend from the side of the van at the driver's command. Utilizing Dodge/Chrysler's design and manufacturing muscle, materials procurement, and safety and engineering expertise, Braun is able to concentrate on its core mission of accessibility and independence for its drivers. Dodge/Chrysler gains its own public relations advantage by providing access to those for whom a standard driving interface is insufficient without being distracted into another business model, where Dodge/Chrysler may not have the focus or commitment like Braun. Interestingly, much of the underlying Dodge/Chrysler minivan is changed in the transformation, and it is amazing that the economics continue to favor the customization and conversion model of re-engineering rather than scratch-building.

The Entervan remains Braun's most popular product after two decades, but interestingly Braun has new partnerships with two Japanese automakers. Braun has begun offering models based on Honda and Toyota minivans, as the Japanese car manufacturers have gained market share in the US market, like Subaru. Important here is the realization that Braun was seeking Purdue's advice in next-generation materials and manufacturing processes in order to create lighter, stronger ramps that required less powerful motors to extend and retract, which resulted in better battery life and safer use. Again, Braun finds itself in partnership with another regional institution—a state-supported Carnegie Category Research 1 University, Purdue, which itself becomes a node in the manufacturing network, supplying research expertise. Innovation emerges amid the interplay nodes interacting by establishing the regional network of suppliers as well as research, exemplified in this brief exchange among nodes of the network: Braun, Chrysler/Dodge, and Purdue. New materials engineering research from campus is put to work through technology extension—which is becoming an increasingly common function of the engagement mission of research centers like university campuses.

Braun relies on industrial efficiencies, existing investments, styling and design of Dodge/Chrysler, and it produces a noncompetitive product that meets the needs of a specialized audience. That the small Indiana-based firm does this using another finished industrial product is what makes Braun postindustrial. It could not exist—its products, its business model, its innovation—without the underlying success of its partners. Like in previous chapters that describe 21st-century electricity production that is built atop 19th-century steam technology—and older gravity-driven moving water and wind—so much of the emerging next-generation technology in a variety of fields is built atop older technologies and practices. Innovation is often about mixing varieties of existing solutions together in new and innovative ways.

Though postindustrial in its remanufacturing model, Braun's management philosophy was decidedly industrial in its structure and practice. While the engineering core had access to high-end workstations running the latest versions of CAD/CAM software, communication—the life-blood of the networked economy—was actively discouraged. The web, personal email, and social networking were all explicitly banned and the ban rigidly enforced through network tracking. There was legitimate concern regarding industrial espionage, but more so a distrust of the power of networks made for a closed-access shop that tried to maintain a "business is for working" atmosphere and actively dissuaded any blending of work and play.

Braun is exemplary both in its commitment to its niche market, its relationship to research and development, and its partnership with classic industrial manufacturing. Its engagement with a network of informated high-tech industries and its insistence on separating work and play, public and private, also reveal its transitional postindustrial identity: managers clinging to traditional structures because they "work, and work hard," just as workers cling to values of physical exertion, sweat, and respect for muscle-weariness as proof of the worthiness of one's work efforts. Valuing hard work: the phrase certainly is not meant as criticism, and reflects the organization's values. Yet working hard without clearly articulated goals can be counter-productive and expensive. Although not intended as criticism, valuing toil above productivity reveals the postindustrial experience of workplaces seeking advantage among their competitors by putting new technologies, techniques, and management styles to work for them to take advantage of existing opportunities. The goal throughout this text is to trace these emerging opportunities, to recount the stories of organizations that have taken advantage of them, and to articulate the means of learning unique formations of local culture and technology so that more people can be put meaningfully to work.

Bolter and Grusin have called this layering of technologies remediation. Radio did not eliminate or eradicate newspapers, nor did television make radio cease to be. Rather, newspapers, radio, and television have all been changed—remediated—by the World Wide Web. So, too, technologies of energy and communication have been remediated, or reformulated, by the advent of new technologies. Even nuclear power plants rely on underlying steam technologies to generate electricity. However, those underlying technologies—their design, use, and sustainability—need to be investigated and closely evaluated in this time of remediation. Some additional efficiencies may be realized employing next-generation materials and processes, and some of the challenges are institutional and organizational—removing human inertia and hidebound ideas. Braun is transitional and retains elements of industrial management and structure, yet fulfills so many elements of the postindustrial. In its hybridity it is perhaps the best representation of a postindustrial organization. It strives to realize the promises of the dawning new age, while so many elements of its working traditions are still carried over from the earlier industrial age. Braun is a hybrid of what has worked and what will work into the future. Its challenge is to remain viable until that future arrives.

Postindustrial hybrids: loving our monsters, throwing away categories

These questions are well addressed by communication specialists who understand technology at the cultural level of granularity and magnification, who can better articulate their professional place within the configuration of culture, technology, and legality. The technologies of coal gasification, of pumped storage, and of iterative design seem almost harmless when compared to the challenges of communicating the advantages and challenges (let alone unforeseen consequences) of nanotechnology, genetic engineering, and clean energy research.

Data-mining is a case in point. It can be empowering when citizens are using data in the aggregate to analyze and solve problems caused by mass access to the power grid. It can be disempowering when data are used to correct or discipline individuals who are out of the norm—norm defined and established by the same data analysis, and abnormality called out by statistical variation. Once the desire for changing behavior is made clear, potential for coercion is introduced. The ongoing fight over copyright makes two points clear: first, once data can be collected and analyzed, it can be quickly shifted from descriptive to prescriptive application, and from there to disciplinary application; second, it is very difficult to separate the power of the state in understanding what is happening to shifting to the power of the corporation in manipulating and marketing what is happening to their advantage.

Subaru's consideration of time-shifting production to the cooler pre-dawn and early morning hours will certainly redefine the notion of the carbon footprint, perhaps cutting peak demand modestly, at most 5%–10%. But that may result in one fewer electricity production/generation facility. One fewer nuclear generator. One fewer windmill. Again, this kind of approach is marginal and incremental. Modest. But in the aggregate, again, there is perceptible shift and significant gain in over-all efficiency. What gains can be made in deferred building? Restraint connects back to the Illinois site at ADM and the role of the technical communicator as marshaling available means of persuasion: when to save, when to spend—when to invest, and being able to articulate the investment so its logic can be revealed to stakeholders.

Design, redesign, and the power of iterative design: materials innovations and remanufacturing allow Ludington Pumped Storage to wring every bit of power through efficiency. Yes, the billion-dollar investment realizes a modest 9% gain in efficiency of the existing turbines, but it comes with no additional investment in the physical plant and a relatively modest cost in replacing the pump/generators, which in terms of the overall plant are considered consumables as well. They will need to be replaced eventually; why not increase their effectiveness?

Environmentalism drives my contact Mitch mad. He told one funny story about a single dead salmon. He pointed up at the millions of gallons of water and laughed/blurted, "How many dead salmon do you think are floating around in all that water?" I guessed there were a few. He went on to tell the story. Biking and hiking trails as well as disc golf were available on the land surrounding the Ludington Pumped Storage facility. An environmental group was on a tour of the park that Ludington makes available—trading recreational space for goodwill to keep the local people satisfied with their power-producing neighbors. These folks were horrified when, as the reservoir emptied in the process of producing electricity on a warm summer afternoon, a large adult Chinook salmon floated beyond the swimmer's safety buoys at the base of the generators. The dead fish created an uproar among these environmentally minded citizens. At first, my contact told the story as if he was incensed—that a dozen people seeing one dead fish had been able to impact the plant to the point of requiring an expensive fish net and change in policy and procedure at the plant. Perhaps noticing my horrified expression, or realizing that there were other more flattering narratives to tell me, he shifted to talk about how it was a good thing, after all, that procedures have changed and the plant now takes pains to keep fish and birds safe during the production of electricity. In my mind it is a powerful reminder of the important role for both sanctioned and unsanctioned citizen input, as described in Simmons (2008) and elsewhere, although I do not think my opinion was shared. I do agree that one salmon is certainly not reason enough to reduce reliance on Ludington or the electricity it stores. Any attempt to replace its low-cost, low-impact electricity would result in far higher environmental damage and degradation. Indeed, it is unclear if the fish was harmed in any way by the pumped storage facility. It could have been a dead fish swept upstream by the pumps that reappeared after some time in the upper reservoir. It could have been sucked upstream alive earlier in its life, lived its life span in the upper reservoir, only to be ejected at death into the great lake itself. Or it could have been either sick or healthy and killed by the process. Either way, the question then must be asked: is a single fish—even a number of salmon—an entire school of salmon, perhaps?—a sufficient cost to derail the plant and the benefits it provides? What is that threshold? Particularly as hydro-electric facilities are dismantled across the West, what are the relative costs of halting production, and what other displaced costs are reintroduced that hydroelectric production better accomplishes? In the relatively healthy upper reaches of Lake Michigan, does it make sense to protect a species teeming in numbers in the inland freshwater oceans?

Are there resources available to build additional Ludington-like pumped storage plants across the upper Great Lakes? Mitch mentioned there were numerous additional sites that were approved for pumped storage in Michigan, Minnesota, and Wisconsin, with the potential for similar plants on Canadian shores. Will Michigan, will the upper Midwest realize savings of resources and pollution promised by these potential sites? There are multiple sites along the upper Midwest and Great Lakes that are awaiting the potential to be tied in to a new era of nuclear electricity production, if it again becomes feasible to build nuclear power plants, a doubtful proposition post-Fukushima, and in the short term, but perhaps necessary in the long term. Perhaps these sites will store electricity produced by a new, as yet unrealized power production network that will come to be.

The challenge is in negotiating the relationship of massive power concentration in the megaproject without giving up long-term dialogue. How does the postmodern shift from the modern in its relationship of concentrated capital and power to the stakeholders? At one level, important change lies in recognition that there are multiple stakeholders. Articulating a role for regulation, in addressing the concerns of these stakeholders, is important, and in not giving up regulation as somehow un-American, but instead describing regulation as an important part of energy management, and the cultural drive for elimination of regulation as somehow, maddeningly, un-American or somehow anti-democratic. Regulation, with the consent of stakeholders, is by definition a democratic process of self-regulation and an extension of self-government into the technocratic realm. Recalling Flyvbjerg's (2003) megaprojects, friction emerges through due process, regulation, and the expression of citizen concerns that makes democracy an ethical political system. It puts the lie to "frictionless" capitalism, puts the lie to the Gates-funded myth of laissez-faire global capitalism, and really puts the lie to the latter-day Randians who would welcome an unfettered, untaxed, unregulated laissez-faire form of totalitarianism overseen by corporate oligarchs. Each presents challenging decisions with long-ranging impacts on the environment, on the distribution of power and authority, and on the very configuration of society. It is a fork in the road, and the Obama administration's all-of-the-above strategy had left open the potential utilization of nuclear resources, reopening the potential for a Latourian love affair with the atom, either splitting or uniting them—fission or fusion—that will influence the ways in which energy production technologies and fuels are articulated in this century.

Complicating this decision making is the abundance of cheap coal, the increasing costs of moving massive resources like rocks across the globe, and the fracking technologies that have created a contemporary rush to promote cheap natural gas. But its cheapness is itself a political choice, borne of libertarian policies toward resource rights and the lack of enforcement of environmental regulations. And without refocusing this text's argument on hydraulic fracturing, or fracking, and its cultural and social impacts, I simply want to point out that it has an artificially low price tag while environmental and safety regulations catch up with the technology. Better put, when the political will is exercised to enforce laws on new and emerging means of exploiting natural resources, as if lawmakers should somehow be forgiven for not being able to marshal the wherewithal to create timely regulatory language to account for shale-sequestered methane. Elsewhere, also being investigated are new and recycled sources of natural gases like the outgassing wastes produced by landfills as well as powerfully inventive technologies like algae-based biofuels and plasma burning of unrecyclable wastes. Regulation of these can prove difficult as regulators don't want to burden new and promising technologies with onerous and stifling regulations, but new sources of fossil fuels like that produced by fracking for gas seem like a difference without a distinction—it should be taxed equally with other forms of natural gas.

Judgments need to be identified and represented in the noisy public, the agora, using the technologies at our disposal, the social and online media by which information is disseminated in culture. And those representations are necessarily partisan and value laden, and create a rich playing field of technorhetoricians with a variety of their own values and interests to participate as they see fit in these ongoing and emerging spaces of debate, whether large-scale like the renegotiation of our relationship to nuclear technology and fossil fuels, or increasing capacity for green energy sources in smaller ways, like negotiating the regulations for communities, power companies, local governments, and other stakeholders to collaborate on building and maintaining wind farms and reusing sites like old slaughterhouses and contaminated but centrally located obsolete industrial brown sites like the one in Cleveland.

With metallurgy and Kaizen as in Fort Wayne Metals, the discussion centers on putting in a design to not only replace what has been worn out, but a new upgraded design that increases efficiency, improves usability, and advances the viability and life span because of design, advanced materials, and the way physical materials breakthroughs increase, incrementally, the human and pure technical effectiveness of these existing systems. It requires new economics and a deeper and richer understanding what is a "good" investment, and each of these changes in design, practice, materials, and cultural impact are rhetorical and cultural communication problems rather than technical or management problems. In an age of information we have myriad potential solutions, and the problem is in the multiplication of alternatives that remain undifferentiated as they vie for control of the marketplace. Fort Wayne Metals makes sense at the crossroads of the implant and prosthetics center that exists around Warsaw, Indiana. So too does the placement of Ludington at the wet and underpopulated northern extremes of the Great Lakes make sense as a place, although it is simultaneously important to remember that these northern stretches of coastline along the inland freshwater seas were the most highly industrialized in the 19th century. So while some resources are persistent, like the promise of cheap over-water transport on the Great Lakes, they are not eternal, as canals, railroads, highways, and eventually airplanes displaced this natural place-based advantage. Design can seek to reinvigorate these natural place-based advantages, but design alone cannot create advantages.

The shift from labor-intensive agriculture to an industrial economy was not as revolutionary, perhaps, as our historical narrative asserts. Rather, these changes are incremental, and there will be vast differences and diversities among these different sites for new energy extraction. So for instance, we have technologies developed in Iceland being applied to sites in Nevada where mountain formation creates pockets of exploitable geothermal energy akin to Iceland's volcanic action. Scotland's Lochs, Norwegian Fjords, and the northern Great Lakes share family resemblances that knit them together into a global network of shared learning and common technologies, *Together with Technology* (2008) as Swarts identifies elements of the human and nonhuman network.

Haraway reminds the reader that too often humans and nonhumans working together is seen not as augmentation or technoculture, but as monstrous, unnatural hybrids that erase our humanity rather than extend our grasp beyond animal limits. Susan Leigh Star (2010) reminds us that soft technologies, like documentation and classification systems, archival sorting and retrieval methods, even our institutions themselves are extensions of the human technological drive, and subject to human engagement—indeed, as human creations, they can only be impacted by concerted human effort. But as such, they also are subject not only to narrative interventions but to layering of mythological meaning and status.

The critical approach, which Latour declared to have lost its steam in 2003, has largely remained inert—an analytical cross-referencing and impotent companion literature—rather than representing an engaged action-oriented reformation engine. Latour's postcritical assertion is that we love our technologies, come to terms with our monsters, and create an engagement born of recognition of family resemblance. Rickert (2013) does not require filial engagement, but rather attunement, which—related to the Greek chôrus—cinches connection to ancient rhetorical concepts which move them into the brave new world of the postindustrial. The chôrus witnesses the actions of the players and is the judgement of society upon the actors. For Rickert, love—filial or otherwise—is not the point, but the postcritical stance is marked by sustained engagement.

Rhetoric and workplace writing have sustained their relationship at least since Agricola, which as part of the transition from magical lore to metallurgy and, eventually, science, is the epoch of interest to the postindustrial study. Ong's contention in *Orality and Literacy*, going back to the invention of the alphabet, is that literacy and the incantations contained in the symbols of alphabetic texts were often connected to magic, his evidence being the connection of the word grammar in Middle English to glamour, or spell-casting (Ong, 1991, pp. 85–93). Postindustrial workplace managers seem to still be enthralled by the glamour of an old spell, that of efficiency.

Steven Katz connected the ethic of efficacy to Nazi rhetoric, but did not stop there. Through tracing the mundane documents of the Shoah, Katz asserts that the drive for quick results, for efficacy, allowed Nazis to dehumanize their victims. While many users of Katz' work broadly implicate efficiency as complicit in genocide, rereading Katz shows that it is efficacy and dehumanization that create the problem—and where articulating citizen need and stakeholders in a dialogic ethic can counteract the dehumanization of silencing. It is true that efficiency unbound is problematic, yet in the realm of the environment and postindustrial innovation, efficiency used to eke out the most power possible from each unit of carbon-emitting fuel is imperative to both remaining competitive with other firms and offering the best chance for environmental sustainability. The potential to unyoke culture from its fantasies of infinite efficiency would end the idea of "modern" culture. But this would be an epochal shift: it may not be possible for quite some time—but we will keep our eye fixed on it as a possibility. Moving away from fossil fuel dependency would move us away from industrial culture, at least as it has been widely understood as harnessing work from steam power, from extracting excess mechanical energy from burning fossil fuels.

Yet so many postindustrial technologies have at their core some version of the steam engine. Photovoltaic technology is the exception, and the electrons that spill over from sun-capturing technologies are as close to mimesis of photosynthesis that human beings have yet ever attained. Even renewables are implicated as relying on industrial-age technology: take California's Ivanpah's sun-driven boiler as an example.[13] Set in the Mojave Desert, Ivanpah's mirrors concentrate sunlight onto collectors that in turn drive turbines and generate electricity from the resulting steam. This clean-energy project relies on old steam engine tech, using pistons and heat to turn physical work into energy.

Even though the transition has begun, there remains a strong need for obsolete technologies. The boilers, whether static in the desert and used to generate electricity, or mobile on locomotives—driven by coal or diesel hybrid—the technologies of the postindustrial rely on the technologies of the industrial, asserting why no new moniker has emerged. We remain "post-." Hanging. Waiting. The mascot remains operative; Purdue's Boilermakers remain relevant. Indeed, micro-brewing and micro-distilling, hipster culture—the microbrewery—has resulted in many new jobs. While social media networking and guerilla advertising are new kinds of work, welders, machinists, and brewmasters have been resurrected as important returning workers, their skill sets returning as their expertise is once again valued as part of an artisanal culture. While undeniably a niche market, these skill sets are persistent. Jeff Rice (2016) traces taxonomies and terminologies of "crafty" and "revolutionary," capturing the reemergence of expertise in microbrewing, representing a deep recycling of technical expertise that brings emergent practices appropriate for the cultural context driven by social media and new experience, what Judd (2006) names a global commodity chain putting new experiences at the heart of tourism and leisure. Home-grown energy production, agricultural hybrid production, and new manufacturing all move toward this form of "revolutionary" activity that distinguishes local place from mass experience.

Organizations with expectations for change represent an emergent intelligence—dependent upon a convergence of technologies and discourses. Postindustrial change is ushering in a new mode of knowledge-making. While reliant on science, experimentation and factuality are insufficient. Every workplace is engaged in high-technology work, from plows and threshers equipped with global positioning systems to smelters playing global markets for ore to clean-energy generation that relies on balancing supply from fickle sources like wind and solar. All rely on organizational and cultural communication modes invented in the steam age that were digitized at the end of the 20th century. Questions remain about which are set to be remediated and which will fall by the wayside.

Notes

1 http://water.usgs.gov/nawqa/sparrow/gulf_findings/index.html (Accessed May 6, 2016).
2 www.westlafayette.in.gov/department/index.php?structureid=19 (Accessed May 6, 2016).
3 www.westlafayette.in.gov/department/division.php?structureid=183 (Accessed May 6, 2016).
4 https://news.uns.purdue.edu/x/2009b/090923ZarateWaste.html (Accessed May 6, 2016).
5 www.purdue.edu/sustainability/initiatives/waste_recycling/foodwaste.html.
6 www.nytimes.com/2013/07/27/nyregion/in-lieu-of-money-toyota-donates-efficiency-to-new-york-charity.html?_r=0 (Accessed May 6, 2016).
7 www.ball.com/na/about-ball/overview/history-timeline.
8 www.ball.com/na/solutions/markets-capabilities/capabilities/beverage-cans/specialty-cans.
9 See patents # US8333801 B2, # US5873904 A, and # US6616617 B1 for examples.
10 See patents # US7762825 B2, # US7763015 B2, and # US9271799 B2 for additional examples.
11 http://aboveandbeyondkm.com/2011/09/are-you-a-force-multiplier.html (Accessed May 6, 2016).
12 www.fda.gov/MedicalDevices/Safety/AlertsandNotices/TipsandArticleson DeviceSafety/ucm169802.htm.
13 www.nytimes.com/2014/02/14/business/energy-environment/a-big-solar-plant-opens-facing-doubts-about-its-future.html.

7 Postindustrial Midwest

Mesh, network, place

The postindustrial is not about ending industry. Rather, the postindustrial age is defined by the removal of human labor from industrial production. Simultaneously, the postindustrial age recognizes the limits of the planet's ability to either provide endless virgin raw materials or accept endless streams of waste from industrial or biological processes. The term postindustrial and the use of the prefix *post-* recognizes that, although things have changed and the epoch is no longer comfortably industrial and industrializing, civilization around the world continues to depend on industrial processes to meet basic needs for the production of goods, for infrastructure, and food production. While recognizing the limits of industrialization, and searching for alternatives and for next-generation technologies, reliance and dependence continue to define our relationship to industrialized technologies and the industrial networks of resource procurement, logistics, expertise, and distribution. We remain industrial while seeing glimpses of and striving for a post-industrial, post-carbon future.

Such is the postindustrial present. Solutions remain elusive, yet the global communication networks that we rely upon for mundane communication of information pertaining to international trade also provide conduits to share solutions. While these solutions will be challenging and expensive to articulate, research, and apply, global communications networks make them easy to distribute. What has not changed is the challenge of rhetoric, of finding an audience willing and able to turn ideas and research into practices. This challenge falls to the rhetor today as much as in Agricola's or Ned Ludd's time with the added challenge of communicating technologically-imbued, organizationally situated solutions. It is a time of technorhetors.

What employment means, what work means, what fair remuneration mean: all these definitions are up for discussion. In the 1970s, Bell and others were able to see beyond the initial stirrings and articulated coming changes. The service industry and, later, personal computing machines changed both the face and the interfaces of business and industry. In the 21st century the limits of the biosphere and the physical limits of the planet are being recognized as limits to human achievement and civilization.

Therefore, what it means to work and to produce, to write, in the postindustrial Midwest will impact and participate in articulating what these things come to mean globally. This study, this book, has been designed to offer glimpses of partial answers from a next generation automobile assembly plant in north-central Indiana, to an agricultural manufacturing site in Illinois, to photovoltaic technology manufacturing in Ohio, to pumped storage in Michigan. Each of these sites offers a facet, one face, of the change that characterizes not just how we will produce the goods, devices, services, and energy we need without depleting the plant's resources, but how we can communicate and share the innovations, efficiencies, and designs that together represent sustainable best practices that will define the next generation of work and play.

In the Midwest, there are many things to count amongst our assets. First, geography is an asset in that knowledge and knowhow are embedded in communities and cities, clustering advantages as Marsh argues and Moretti build on as a geography of future work. As the study maps sites and places—specific organizations where practices are emerging—the wisdom of postmodern mapping as a metaphor but more importantly as a visual and intellectual mode of inquiry, as a method and methodology for meaning-making, crystalizes. The work of Patricia Sullivan and James Porter (1997) is no more evident as here, where the clusters around Fort Wayne and Toledo, Winamac and Ludington, Decatur and Lafayette become discernible—visible centers of practice and innovation.

Discussions in Technical and Professional Communication seem to imply that technorhetorical inquiry should be limited or focused onto one field or one mode of inquiry, to transfer attention from software and hardware, from internetworking computers, to healthcare communication. The very variety and boundary-crossing nature of knowledge in the postindustrial is what necessitates the dispersed approach, concentrating not on individual sites but taking in many sites of innovation separately, Latour's *very many* allies of the new rhetoric (Science in Action, p. 61). There is much to learn from intense, sustained, longitudinal inquiry at particular sites. Yet there remain other payoffs comparing numerous sites in succession, as in this study, designed to highlight commonalities and similar challenges that appear repeatedly in different guise at numerous worksites. Knowledge and technique, data and technology, change as they transfer from site to site, value revealed mapping these concepts as they move from worksite to worksite, and from one industry to another.

The interface technologies that appear at each site—the many similar faces of the infinitely plastic communications machine—the computer that becomes a telecommunications device that becomes socialization as well as broadcast medium. The computing devices act as communication conduit at each site, and this is not unimportant. It becomes a new center as everything else becomes a form of the communication of data and symbolic analysis and symbol manipulation rather than the movement of atoms becomes ever clearer our task, our work. Nicolas Negroponte's *Being Digital* (1995) first gestured towards this emergent experience but the outlines are becoming far less blurry and poetic and rather are more clearly distinct—some even say "real."

Bernadette Longo ends her history of science, management, and technical writing with an optimistic hope for the field's contribution to contributing to human knowledge:

> We are in a position to combine the liberal arts and sciences in a system of teaching and communicating that draws on the strengths of both traditions, from scientific induction to rhetorical invention, from mechanical design to artistic visualization, from empirical observation to literary critique. Like our first-cousin composition studies, technical and professional communication share an openness to combining disparate research approaches to form alloyed knowledge that is more robust than it could possibly be using one research approach alone.
>
> (Longo, 164)

Almost two decades into the 21st century, the outlines of a newly resonant hybrid knowledge, neither purely scientific nor humanistic, is emerging. Longo uses the metallurgical term *alloy* which resonates both as hybridity which this study employs throughout and its related concept of hybrid vigor, where the offspring displays strengths neither parent exhibits. The metallurgical term also resonates historically with the tradition Longo links with Agricola and the then-emergent knowledge-making practices of alchemy. It is important to recall that alchemy before the enlightenment was to our understanding of science as the as-yet unnamed emergent network knowledge is to this techno-rhetorical-cultural mashup. Ascendant but mysterious, powerful but mistrusted. The very moniker postindustrial, in insisting on the "post" prefix, draws attention to itself as incomplete and underway: new knowledge, new processes, new ways of working all are incipient, yet no widely-accepted narrative for understanding its outlines, values, or practices has coalesced. Throughout this study, the combination of seemingly disparate elements create both alloyed knowledge and alloyed practices that emerge both better equipped for contemporary context and the challenges of global postindustrial culture. Whether one adheres to Rifkin's (2011) or Marsh's (2012) version of a "third" or "new" industrial revolution in an age of post-carbon clean energy and automation, or a new emplacement for employment and employment clusters as in Moretti (2012), or even if Bell's (1973) vision of the arriving but not yet ascendant postindustrial culture remains one's touchstone, the power of emerging hybrid constructions is striking. Digital technology, advanced and lightweight materials engineering, clean energy technology, and emergent management techniques have created new contexts in which old skills at first appear obsolete. Upon closer investigation, these hard-won capacities give localized communities advantages in global production networks. The challenge remains articulating and rearticulating local advantages in the context of these global networks, in language and in visual representations and media that make sense to decision-makers and stakeholders within and beyond their organizations. Advantage also accrues, and continues to accumulate, within organizations that recognize that these new rules define the field of contest.

Whether one's metaphor is gameplay or warfare or cooperation, the underlying process and concepts remain similar. One can "fight" for advantage, or "play" to win, or "collaborate" with allies who may have originally been constructed as adversaries. Science and humanities may seem an oil-and-water mix, but consider the hybrids that energize the sites catalogued in this volume. At Subaru, perhaps the most striking practice is the peace struck between labor and management. Perhaps it could be written off as an odd one-off, or a victory of management over organized labor and that would be a powerful critique if not for a comparable configuration and similar conclusion described in Cassano (2011) and then in an extended study, Cutcher-Gershenfeld et al. (2015). *Inside the Ford-UAW Transformation* describes the hard work and, yes, bravery necessary to reorient both sides, management and labor, to see the firm in its global context in which Ford's existence was challenged by its international competitors that had evolved into very different institutions. Ford did not take government bailout money after the recession of 2007–2009, and seems to be competing effectively in the global automotive market, but the challenge remains to create a new approach at Ford and other American automobile manufacturers.

Have Ford, General Motors, and Chevrolet become learning institutions, committed to iterative change, or will this be another in a line of replacement-thinking, "revolutionary" disruptive thinking, that threatens current reconfigurations like the shuttered Budd plant in Michigan? Or has indigenous American automobile manufacturing learned from its transplanted Japanese and European competitors? Allegations at Mercedes Benz, Honda, Mazda,[1] Mitsubishi,[2] Suzuki, Hyundai,[3] Kia,[4] BMW,[5] and Nissan[6] have followed Volkswagen's admission that it cheated on EPA fuel efficiency and emissions testing. While falsified at numerous manufacturers,[7] Ford and others managed to post impressive improvements in effluent measurements and gain market share both as effective providers of efficient, well-designed automobiles but as fair dealers in the marketplace. Yet Ford also settled claims that it misrepresented its hybrid cars' fuel efficiency.[8] While heeding the assertion by Bloomberg News[9] that "cheating on emissions is almost as old as pollution tests," the same article goes on to quote the executive director for the center for Auto Safety that Volkwagen took cheating to a new level of "sophisticated deception." While the results of emissions testing have often been questioned by consumers and the EPA, lax self-reporting standards create environments ripe for abuse, often losing the faith of the very people the standards are designed to protect.[10] While the cheating damages the environment, perhaps more important is the damage such cheating does to the expectations of citizens who want to make informed decisions about a major purchase, like an automobile, and the impact its use will have on the environment. The impact of meaningless efficiency ratings on the cars they (we!) purchase leaves consumers without any informed choice. While the distinction between rating a car at 29 and 31 miles per gallon is negligible over the lifetime of the vehicle, a search criteria that only includes those rated at 30 mpg efficiency eliminates a design with honest reporting from the consumer's consideration. It implicates the citizen as well as the manufacturer in the interplay of data, information, and design. Simple, quick, and simplified information leads to equally shallow decision-making.

Subaru is committed to realizing its long-term goal of carbon neutrality, a stretch goal by any analysis. Yet, in attaining zero-landfill ahead of projected schedule, and becoming a regional leader in sustainability and advanced manufacturing, the goal seems attainable. Further, it helps Subaru continue to market itself as an environmentally responsible corporate citizen—allowing it to pressure its rivals to compete on its terms. Subaru has successfully shifted its business model to market institutional change. It sells environmental stewardship and clean manufacturing as much as the comfort, ride, and reliability of its automobile products. Has Ford transformed itself into an equivalent innovation engine and environmental steward, or has it replaced an older model of industrial production for a new postindustrial norm? Meanwhile, the long-term impact of cheating on German, Japanese, and Korean car makers has yet to be determined.

In Illinois, ADM continues to lead globally. It recognized late last century that any boundaries between industrial and agricultural production are illusory, and are at the least fluid if not fictional. Agricultural products are simply raw materials, and corn, soybeans, and other crops grown across the Midwest region are used to create vitamins, alcohol, industrial gasses, and animal feeds. Central to the efficiencies are decision-making based on the prices of these products on an ever-changing market. If soy-based vitamin E products are in high demand in the Mediterranean, production of ingredients for emollients will be produced, sold on the appropriate markets, and logistics networks utilized to ship the product to the appropriate facility. Another day, production may shift to extracting alcohols from corn to produce both ethanol fuel ingredients (from the tailings) and bourbon for a growing international market. In both scenarios, the spent grains—the part of the physical seed left after extracting alcohol and vitamin E—is used to feed tilapia in the aquaponics production facility or mixed with coal and ethanol to create electricity.

Central to these operations and the decision-making is information. Previously, decision-making would be made as guesswork and estimates. This year's production would be based on last year's numbers, how much vitamin E will the market demand, how many tons of corn for food, how many gallons of ethanol? Global markets and trends now are observable and the data reaches decision-makers almost instantaneously. As grain trucks enter the facility, the station is capable of recording multiple points of data. These data points already include the moisture content of the grain, the seed source and its geographical origination point, fertilizers and insecticides used, the handling methods and the identity of the carriers transporting the grain to market. Most importantly, the information can be used to support a range of decisions about the ultimate utilization of the materials, and inform subsequent decisions to best direct the grains to their best uses depending on the market. That is, the information about the produce coupled with the current market together creates a new information point suggesting one or more applications over others. In order to reach this point, however, much work has to be done in order to match potential to product. That work—mechanical, scientific, data-driven, information manipulation as well as rhetorical analysis—needs to be recognized and paid for. No other moment captures the relationship between matching opportunity to context than the operations manager who effectively pitched reuse rather than waste for the excess heat generated in the process of electricity generation that made the aquaponics facility and its organic herbs, vegetables, and fish possible. Like Subaru, ADM is a flexible learning organization. Imagination in the form of the ability to recognize the fiction of the boundaries between the farm and the factory, to see the potential for soy-based plastics and fish shipped live, and electricity production beyond simple coal-burning. To imagine possibilities is a necessary first step. But then to marshal groups of people together with techniques— the technologies—both within organizations as well as to those outside its boundaries, to the general public, as valuable innovations and not as dangerous aberrations, postindustrial monsters, but instead as valuable partners: such is the contemporary face of an ancient challenge. Technê is both about technology and technique, as Pender (2011) argues.

Fluidity of identity and the deep recycling of skills together define the challenge facing northwestern Ohio and Toledo. From two narrow sites in Subaru in Indiana and ADM Illinois, Toledo supports a cluster of interrelated industries that contribute to the development and mass production of photovoltaic technologies. The photovoltaic future—a clean energy future—has to become palpable for a community and a network of people and institutions to become committed to its realization. By leveraging local networks of expertise and experience, northwest Ohio has become both a center for research and education, from everything from basic research to the creation of commercialization and manufacturing techniques, to innovative installations and community commitments to producing solar energy. Postindustrial Toledo is built on its industrial former self, on its unique knowledge and experience, and is a site of technology transfer (see Ockwell and Mallett, 2012; Baird and Dilger, 2017[11]). Baird and Dilger provide an especially interesting study as educators, like those who designed the Corning Community College green technologies associates degree, who create programs that prepare students for promising next-generation work where the opportunities are growing but perhaps not as robustly in place as they will shortly become. What will be the legacy costs and maintenance needs for the wind turbines that have been installed across the postindustrial Midwest? Such are acts of faith and projection. Students and institutions both take risks to first articulate and then take advantage of opportunities whose outlines are just now discernable.

Past to future, tense networks

There are important advantages some places have over others for indigenous strengths and knowledge bases and skills traditions. It brings back the importance of history and uniqueness to reveal why places exist, why they endure, and how these places become not only geographically but also culturally important. The region of the American Midwest that is the focus of this study lies at the confluence North America's largest river system, bounded on the south by the Ohio River and West by the Mississippi. The enormous Great Lakes bound the region to the north, and represent the world's largest surface supply of fresh water. The Great Lakes also provide a low-cost transportation network that knits together ore fields in the north to smelters in the south, from which raw materials can be shipped to manufacturing plants and manufactured goods can be shipped to local and global markets. By sea, by land carriage, and by multimodal logistics: trucks on highways, railroad networks, and the growing importance of just-in-time component, web-based retail, and fresh food deliveries mediated by air travel through major airports. The largest air carrier at Indianapolis International Airport is Federal Express.

So in an attempt to describe the importance of place, this study has discussed numerous workplace sites in the American Midwest in the postindustrial age. That age emerged with the use of coal to produce steam power. Burning coal for power dramatically changed human work and created both new ways of collecting communities together as well as new traditions for creating human identity. The factory and the cities that grew up around them changed the landscape, and even created new ways of understanding people's sense of self. Identity formation is evident in the names communities give to their heroes: evident in the traditions of naming. The Boilermakers, Purdue's nickname, reveals the local tradition of supplying the intertwined railroad, industrial, and agricultural networks from the 19th century its steam boilers to drive railroad locomotives—an evocative name for a technology—as well as early steam plows that shared many design elements, to the driving force behind the working wheels that drove steam hammers and industrial presses. These interwoven technologies support networks of people, making places where they settle, interleaving their skills and abilities with the communities they form and the intuitions they create. Indiana's overlapping automobile and life sciences networks leave an enduring mesh of expertise and ability that is expressible as local advantage for a global market.

Yet the postindustrial has not broken free of its industrial origins. England and Scotland are rightly considered the creation point of the steam engine, and the free-thinking modern engineers utilized technologies in new and frightening ways that ended up giving shape to the emergent industrial revolution that coupled coal with the piston-driven engine that produced physical work from heat. My goal is to keep the discussion short and focused on salient details that illustrate relationships I want to highlight. For an accessible historical treatment of the industrial revolution, I recommend Roger Osborne's *Iron, Steam, and Money* (2013) that describes this era and place in strikingly clear terms.

Osborne in *Iron, Steam and Money* (2013) asserts a network of people, thinking, and technologies that reflect relationships between people and their artifacts that, if not techno-determinist, then reveal the ways in which people displace their agencies into their technologies. I use Latour's term quasi-object to describe the Ludington Pumped storage system as an element in the network of people and objects that make Citizens' Energy in Michigan an important player in clean energy research—a cultural space of interaction as much as it is a showcase of emergent and reutilized technology. Places like Ludington exist first because of their proximity to natural resources. Places, at first, are dependent on resources, and built upon a resource-determinist argument along the lines of Jared Diamond's wildly popular *Guns, Germs and Steel* (2005). But once people are emplaced, places are further entrenched and reinforced by what those citizens put into their local communities. Ludington began as a port from which nearby salt was shipped, over which grew substantial lumber reserves, astride a navigable port. These advantages then became expertise in mining, generalizable as engineering, leading to recognition of potential for damming water for hydroelectricity, eventually leading to recognition of the bluffs the lake as a suitable site for building the dams, conduits, and Francis turbines that that make pumped storage possible.

Ludington exists because of continued investment and reinvestment by citizens. It is a durable place because people with skills and knowledge have remained long after the salt was mined and old-growth forests cut down. So too were the cities of the early Industrial Revolution created. According to Osborne:

> Manchester became a hotbed of Chartism, trade unionism, and so-cialism, and it provided a radical alternative voice in the country against the established powers of the capital; at the same time the city's merchants and middle classes formed an influential force, lead-ing the campaign for repeal of the Corn Laws and in favor of free trade, while opposing imperialism adventurism, thereby expressing a brand of liberalism that became known as the Manchester School.
> (Osborne, 224)

Osbourne continues:

> Manchester's subsequent history has also reflected a key element of the Industrial Revolution, for the city has retained a culture of con-tinuous innovation; far from being a museum piece, Manchester has entered the so-called post-industrial age with its spirit of practical ingenuity intact. It has remained a commercial city with manufac-turing its servant rather than the master of its industrial power.
> (Osbourne, 225)

Osborne represents the city of Manchester in northern England as an outcome of the commitment its citizens show for the place they have together created, a "culture of continuous innovation." The city is driven by "practical ingenuity," which is as good a description of the driving force that made the Industrial Revolution possible. Osbourne condenses the challenge of the postindustrial age in a capsule text on the "energy equation" which is at the heart of the coal-fired industrial revolution. It is this equation that make fossil fuels so immensely valuable and such a pressing challenge to overcome. It also gestures towards why steam en-ergy remains at the heart of most fuel-to-work engines, and why the term (post)industrial remains the most accurate descriptor for the current age. We rely on ever-better refinements of basic technologies developed at the dawn of the modern industrial age, and so while we look towards (post)modern, (post)industrial futures, we remain largely modern and industrial in our reliance on fossil fuels, cultivation of annual plants for food production, and factory mass-production. I switch to the awkward parenthetical construction of these terms surrounding post, as (post), to emphasize that as much as we have been looking beyond the borders, categories, and limitations of the industrial age, we continue to rely upon technologies and social institutions created at its dawning moments, and those social networks are reliant upon the freedoms granted by labor-saving energy production techniques. Indeed, the steam engine is the origin technology from which all other technologies depend, if not directly than because of the free time and leisure the work of the piston enabled human beings broadly to enjoy and then to put back to work in education, research, science, social institutions, and civil society. It is worth quoting Osbourne here at length:

> In a wholly organic economy the number of people that can be fed, given shelter, clothed and kept warm is limited by the amount of material that can be produced by the land; and while this can be increased, it will inevitably reach a limit leading to a stagnant economy. The energy input into agriculture in the form of machinery, fertilizers, transport and so on, therefore becomes crucial: in the industrial countries of the 21st century such external energy input allows the population to be fed by the labor of just 2% of the workforce.
>
> At an individual level the fundamental change brought by external energy is just as stark. If a coal miner in the late 18th century consumed around 3,500 calories a day mining around 200 kilos of coal, the coal contains 500 times as much energy as the food he has consumed. And if the fuel is used in an engine with even 1% efficiency he is delivery many times the mechanical energy he is expending. This mechanical energy is then available to the mill worker in a steam-powered factory who is able to expand the work he can perform by a factor of ten or a hundred because of the energy that the miner has placed at his elbow. Calculations for other industrializing countries reveal that by the 19th century coal derived energy produced the equivalent of a workforce increased by 250%. In contrast, people in subsistence economies where there is no ready supply of energy in the form of fossil fuel are at a huge disadvantage. As it takes about three calories of fuel to cook one calorie of food, the fuel that is required in the form of timber takes up space needed for crops and diminishes the overall amount of calorific energy that can be gained from the land. Having coal-derived energy is therefore a double bonus.
>
> (Osbourne, 68–69)

Coal provided huge advantages to the British midlands, to Scotland, and drove the engine of the British Empire; in that ancient fuel ripe for exploitation waited the seeds of social enlightenment brought about from the free time for thinking and dreaming up alternatives to the then current status quo. It allowed the miners opportunity to talk together to realize their emplacement at the chokepoint of the literal fuel of the expansion of the global empire, the first global age that ended with the First World War. For Osborne, the history of Manchester's social innovation and unique intellectual development can be ultimately traced back to harnessing coal, and then working to maintain the benefits of that natural resource among the people in the city: Chartism, trade unionism, socialism, middle classes, free trade. Eighty miles to the south, the city of Birmingham is on a substantial if smaller coal reserve. It is here the Birmingham School of Cultural Studies was founded in 1964 and operated until 2002.

The takeaway is the persistence of resources. Manchester and Birmingham, Wales and Scotland produced working cultures and values different from those of the dominant government and seat of power in London. Those traditions were built on the lives made possible by indigenous resources, here, coal. Mapping those resources returns the analysis to the cities. Urban centers were supported by, then sustained and innovated, and generations of skill, knowledge, and lore passed from generation to generation to become the foundations of identities and traditions, communities. From the ancient geographical features that produced confluences, gathering people and resources, that made one place better suited to organization and urbanization than others. Atop these natural resources are human-made transportation networks of steel rails and poured asphalt, airborne transportation, and political movements leading to emigration and immigration. In broad strokes, it made recognizable features of a world new to vast numbers of immigrants first arriving on American shores from many European countries (Ward, 1981).

Immigration provides the bridge back to the American Midwest, relinquishing the British and Scottish focus of the last few paragraphs. As I obsess about maps, mapping, and place, historical antecedents abound. Ward's book offers a map where he locates an area comprising Michigan, Illinois, Indiana, and Ohio together as the "East Midwest" offering both antecedent in localization as well as source for some historical and regional mappings. As the introduction alludes, the region Ward names the "East Midwest" is bound to the north by the Great Lakes and Canada, with oceangoing vessels either arriving through the St Laurence Seaway through Québec and Montreal and into the Great Lakes, or up the Hudson River and across New York. Looking at any geographical map, it is stunning to realize that New York City overcame the natural advantages of New Orleans to become the preeminent American City. New Orleans, situated at the mouth of the Mississippi with access to the Gulf of México, through its (relatively) calm and protected waters, to the world's great harbors and maritime ports, the Crescent City should have been the largest and most important urban site and population center.

But the story of the great Erie Canal, catapulting New York ahead of all other American cities, waits for another techno rhetorical volume. Until then, Anderson's *Course of Empire* (1984) and Bernstein's *Wedding of the Waters* (2006) offer the closest in theme to what is described above that enabled the American Midwest to take advantage of its natural resources and emplace populations of citizens capable of innovating and contributing to the search for a new postindustrial configuration of social interaction, civil institutions, and meaningful identity formation in sustainable new work and communities. However, competing discourses surround the many sites and communities impacted by the emergence of postindustrial change; it offers few solutions. It may provide orientation for understanding the problems, to begin to imagine what solutions in this time of constant and relentless change might need to address, and suggest methods for engaging the often contradictory demands of ever-growing populations of individuals that often seem at odds with each other as well as often harboring contradictions within themselves. But solutions?

Hearing the voice of culture

This study opens with Rickert's articulation of the chôra, the voice of culture, as a player on the stage in ancient Greek drama. Rickert's expression is not scientific, but it is useful in its representation of a singular voice, a multiplicity made one. The chorus is a single entity made of many voices. Stakeholders rarely share a message for decision-makers, and the chorus does not sing as one. Yet the chord—the voices together—can form harmony. An effective answer to addressing a wicked problem speaks to the needs of many competing voices simultaneously, to greater and lesser degree, somehow responsive to multiple demands put simultaneously to the rhetor, the technical communicator, responsible for disseminating information.

Yet Rickert disputes the notion of harmony:

> There is no easy harmony here, but there is a certain sense of ecology in that human being becomes attuned to how it is gathered across things so that things must matter beyond their direct use-value for human pursuits.
>
> (Rickert, 34)

Here, I take it that Rickert identifies a mode of understanding Heidegger's "standing reserve," where the German bemoaned the engineer's inability to see the Rhine as anything other than potential to drive the turbines to make electricity, much like this analysis sees Lake Michigan as standing reserve waiting to be put to use by excess electricity and pumped uphill during times of abundance and low demand. The entire system requires seeing through a lens of standing-reserve, *gestell*. That is, I see with techno-cultural eyes. To move post-critically, Rickert allows me to see anew, and my own enframing does not require resistance or critique. Instead, it allows a different vision.

Let pumped storage be seen as standing reserve; Ludington as quasi-object. The site is not only the pump-generators, the impoundment dam, and the reservoir but it is the collection of all these things as well as the system of which these elements are part. Further, the power stored and the electricity (re)produced there at the site are bridges to an earlier vision of the future, an unrealized nuclear future. Discussion, resolution left for another time, includes investigation of Thorium rather than Plutonium as a nuclear fuel, a new nuclear future championed by some but suspect, dangerous, untrustworthy to others. All these attributes make the Ludington pumped storage facility simultaneously an object of cultural interest and somehow representative of more than the agglomeration of technologies gathered at the site along the northwestern coast of Michigan. It is a portal back to a different vision, a nuclear vision, of clean electric energy. And simultaneously, the site is a portal ahead to a new clean energy future. The site, for a variety of reasons of culture, regulation, and transparency is not likely to be a direct circuit in which wind is used when abundant to create electricity to directly run the pumps that propel the water uphill for storage. Ludington will never accurately be described as a battery. Yet the appeal of the description is culturally powerful. As we consider the varieties of clean-energy, post-carbon futures, Ludington remains a compelling site, awaiting the right communicator, and a fitting and convincing narrative, to gather all its attendant elements together and integrate the pumps, cement, fins, transfer pipes, and electricity infrastructure into a new future clean energy system. Whether driven by efficient clean renewables, or a cleaner, safer new nuclear fission utilizing thorium or another fuel, or an even further-off future fusion technology, this place, this salt and lumber transportation point, retains an important place in a clean energy network that is not yet realized yet remains tantalizingly suggestive of an emergent clean-energy future.

Attunement to rhetorical being opens possibilities. Ludington is, to human eyes, potential clean energy storage. It is also, however, spawning ground for salmon and in turn, hunting ground for osprey. The fenced areas protecting the mechanical infrastructure also become harem-ground for gathering rutting deer (recall that a trophy buck appeared trumpeting on the human-created hillside under which water was being elevated for later electricity re-generation). No human had argued for the creation of salmon spawning, osprey-hunting, white-tailed deer mating grounds. Yet numerous agents—animal, technological, human—are attuned to the ways in which the site can be renegotiated and rearticulated.

Steven Katz, offering perhaps some level of antidote to mention of Heidegger above, criticizes the efficiency drive at the heart of both modernity and western thought generally. His work "Rhetoric of Expediency" (1992) is widely read and cited. The essay title emphasizes expediency. However, the argument is often broadened into an ethic of *efficiency*, both because of the slide of one term into the other and the author's own oscillating use of the terms and of the cultural significance placed on *increasing* efficiency. Expedience brings to mind the dismissive lumping together of all the cheating on the EPA's fuel standards. Cheating provides an expedient solution to a thorny problem. Cheating is expedient, and expedience cannot be used to dismiss the importance of either regulation or engagement with stakeholders. Efficiency, however, is not an identical synonym. The efficiencies gained by attention to electricity markets on a hot summer afternoon versus excess capacity available for pennies on the dollar during cooler nighttime hours will maintain the Ludington pumped storage station as a viable clean energy assemblage. Whereas expedience in covering up a dead salmon will not further the rhetorical aims of Citizens Energy and their attempts to create widespread buy-in for the technology. Openness, transparency, and engagement with citizens and their concerns for the environment: dealing with the public presents inefficiencies with which Citizens Energy has to contend. It would be expedient not to have to deal with the voices of culture, loud, confusing and contradictory. Yet these concerns must be dealt with and provided honest assessments of potential damages to fish stocks, and clear communication about what healthy numbers of spawning salmon look like, for instance, a single dead fish is never a problem whereas mass die-off and/or chemical contaminants are serious issues. While inefficient, democratic engagement requires engagement with the public, with the chôra, with the agora. To avoid such interaction is unethical: expedient, clean, and easy, but unethical nonetheless.

Katz's attention to expediency offers an important post-critical as well as post-human measure. Efficiency is not only about minimizing costs to produce electricity, or automobiles, or food. Instead, efficiency is reinterpreted as getting the most out of raw materials, having the lightest impact possible on the environment, and providing the greatest productivity possible using the supply of fossil fuels that are recognized as finite and destructive. The problem really has not been with *efficiency*, which is a preoccupation of this study throughout, with wringing efficiencies out of existing process and creating new processes, utilizing the effluence of one process as the raw materials of the next and so forth. Rather, expedience brought about by silencing stakeholders' voices and alternative visions is the problem. Here again, Simmons (2008) study *Participation and Power: Civic Discourse in Environmental Policy Decisions* testifies to the importance of inefficiencies in communication supporting efficient use of environmental resources. It is an unethical expedience that would erase engagement with dissenting voices.

Again, Rickert (2013) goes on to describe a different way to understand rhetorical agency. Classical through modern rhetorical theory assesses the rhetor on conscious intent, on how well one realizes what one set out to do, that when done well, "intent equals result." (34–5). Calling this "built in retroactivity" (35), rhetoric is limited to being human-centered. Postindustrial technorhetoric needs Rickert's rhetorical attunement to recognize the technocultural assemblages that distinguish it from modern and pre-modern rhetorical action, if not relinquishing the desire for matching intent with outcome. Remember the hillside was not built for the salmon, stag, or the osprey but all dwell there quite sustainably:

> We are already so engaged with the world, wedded to it through an infinite array of perceptual, discursive, and material assemblages. We are not in a rhetorical situation so much as in a rhetorical lifeworld. We are jointed through the world's latticework; we are not just the builders rearranging its stage. This notion of materiality opens us to the way the world reveals itself as a complex stitchwork of relationships, shaped and conditioned by elements that lie beyond what humans can do or say.
>
> (213)

Rickert's use of "jointed" returns discussion to a word I use too much. I struggle to limit the times it appears in this study: the word *articulation*. Jointed assemblage invoked the idea of articulation, and articulation theory—how things come together and how they move in relationship to one another—is central to cultural studies as defined by Slack et al. (1993, 2006). Articulation runs contrary to either translation or transmission models of rhetoric:

> To send out technical communicators with this kind of knowledge is to send them out armed. It is impossible for technical communicators to take full responsibility for their work until they understand their role from an articulation view.
>
> (44 in Scott, Longo and Wills, reprint 2006 of 1993 essay)

Rickert's perspective might quip that no preparation prepares anyone or anything to take full responsibility, yet the meaning of Slack, Miller and Doak's assertion is clear. Without a sense of articulation and rearticulation, technical and professional communicators would be insufficiently prepared to face the complex networks of expertise they intend to join. Postindustrial writing requires a comfort with hybridity and new ways of doing things and new definitions of work. Writing in an age of automation and roboticization—in an new wave of the industrial revolution—also requires that we embrace what Haraway called our monsters (1992), whether they be institutional structures that blur comfortable, re-naturalized borders between industrial and agricultural production, between labor and management, between objects and systems, between human and non-human agency. Rickert, more recently grown accustomed to the hybrid company we keep in the postindustrial, is happy with stitchwork as a metaphor. Both representations rely upon communication and engagement, with recognizing the value of stakeholders and their input, not to change things entirely from one iteration to the next but to slowly change things over time for the better, not radically change (or disrupt) for change's sake. We then can see our role not as control or even persuasion, but of management of change, consistent with Faber's analyses of discursive (2007) and organizational (2002) change.

Professional and technical communication can be imbued with rhetorical attunement not to reduce their power but to understand how work done in a variety of contexts informs and enriches other agencies in the network, in the assemblage. Here, new materials manufacturing, in agriculture, and clean energy are discussed but the conclusions apply to a wide range of fields because postindustrial work is moving towards high technology symbolic analytical work in all work contexts.

Notes

1 www.theguardian.com/environment/2015/oct/09/mercedes-honda-mazda-mitsubishi-diesel-emissions-row.
2 www.nytimes.com/2016/05/12/business/international/mitsubishi-cheating-scandal-expands-to-more-models.html.
3 www.japantoday.com/category/business/view/suzuki-shares-dive-on-reports-of-improper-fuel-testing.
4 www.wsj.com/articles/u-s-fines-hyundai-kia-for-overstating-fuel-economy-1415028646.
5 https://yosemite.epa.gov/opa/admpress.nsf/596e17d7cac720848525781f0043 629e/fd585d03bae8df0585257d79004e428d!OpenDocument.
6 www.nytimes.com/2016/05/17/business/south-korea-nissan-emissions-cheating.html.
7 www.nytimes.com/2015/09/25/business/international/volkswagen-emissions-pollution-regulations.html.
8 www.nytimes.com/2014/06/13/business/ford-lowers-fuel-economy-ratings-on-some-of-its-cars.html.
9 www.bloomberg.com/news/articles/2015-09-23/carmaker-cheating-on-emissions-almost-as-old-as-pollution-tests.
10 www.thedailybeast.com/articles/2015/09/25/vw-isn-t-even-the-worst-polluter-tests-are-made-to-be-fooled.html.
11 Neil Baird and Bradley Dilger, "How Students Perceive Transitions: Dispositions and Transfer in Internships," *College Composition and Communication*, 2017.

Conclusion
TPC futures

To paraphrase William Gibson, the future of technical and professional communication (TPC) is already here, it just isn't evenly distributed. That is, it has not yet become clear which varieties or hybrids of the dozens of versions already operative will remain unpruned. This is why I am skeptical of the vision of pruning back experimental and wide-ranging rhetorical approaches and trying, as St. Amant and Melançon (2016) suggest, to allow commonality to drive a consensus definition:

> In this way, commonality brings not only legitimacy but also power. By getting together behind a shared idea of concept, individuals can exercise change as a unit. They can do so by having the members of the body undertake a systematic, focused and continuous approach to address topics of shared interest to the whole. Thus, commonality engenders legitimacy in the eyes of others and power in terms of the attention outsiders give to the group and its interests. Such ideas are central to shaping approaches to power and legitimacy in TPC today.
> (Incommensurability, 2)

Oh, if only it were true! Do these things, and power and legitimacy will be construed upon practitioners and academics, our work and our research! Change does not happen by command and control in the postindustrial age, if it has ever happened that way, and many things are easier said than done. Rather, it seems that in perfect hindsight we can declare, only descriptively, how and where dominant modes of action earned their primacy of practice. Descriptive historical perspective is privileged because time has already passed, futures defined and determined. The energy expended to determine what the set of "systematic, focused and continuous approach to address topics of shared interest to the whole" (St. Amant and Melançon, 2016) would eliminate potentially fruitful varieties of TPC research before being cultivated, and would also redirect time and attention away from generating research and investigating research sites. Development, investigation, experimentation, and description would be abandoned and replaced instead by a destructive battle for supremacy. Besides, the time for that kind of work has passed.

To illustrate the mesh of interests that inform this study, in addition to the postindustrial Midwestern manufacturing, agricultural, and energy sites, there are references to the tradition of hardware and software development in Silicon Valley as well as in Boston's internet companies, the coal fields of Britain and Scotland, environmental and nuclear cleanup activists, telecommunications workers, and emergent healthcare sites, robotics, maker culture and 3D printing, microbrewing, regulatory writing, clean energy, photovoltaics, mobile computing interface, and assembly. With a shorter sense of history, like the 20th-century perspective offered by Connors (1982) of the rise of technical writing instruction in the United States, the culmination of technical writing with usable interfaces and mobile computing may just be a rational ending to the field. However, following a longer historical trajectory, like Longo's (2000) work that looks further back to the transition from alchemy to metallurgy in Agricola, or like Kimball's forward-looking "golden age" (2016), this study asserts that the field is just beginning—and is poised to emerge as a global interest in the human-constructed and designed world. Modernity was, in part, a displacement of rhetoric as the primary mode of knowledge production and dissemination. Latour (1993) calls this condition the *amodern* in *We Have Never Been Modern*, in contrast to the postmodern. Similarly, Beverly Sauer, in *The Rhetoric of Risk* (2002), investigates mining and safety practices at three sites around the globe. Her approach has inspired its own thread of research, including J. Blake Scott's (2014) study of AIDS, activism, and the expert/lay audience divide. *Risky Rhetoric* influenced Graham's (2015) study of pain medication that influences the direction and reach of this study. From mining to risk to medicine, who can foretell the "commonality" of these texts? Their commonality is a shared grounding in rhetoric, present in communication among agents, and impossible to predetermine.

Jerry Savage convincingly argues that the trickster is the postindustrial technical communicator. The modern age was the age of the professional while the postindustrial favors the consultant. Mêtis the ability to organize disparate skills into smooth and successful action as in sailing; technê understood as beyond knack or technology and instead understood as improvisation like a Jazz musician; and kairos understood not simply as context but as the opportune moment in which numerous variables come to fortuitous alignment—these rhetorical concepts illustrate the articulation necessary for a rhetor to act meaningfully in a technocultural context.

Knowledge and action are contingent, unbound categories become ironic, and power is built through temporary solidarities rather than enduring bonds. This version of the postindustrial is consistent with Richard Rorty's late-20th-century prognostications (Rorty, 1989). Rorty clings to hope for the future, even if it remains broadly liberal in its reliance upon reason and dialogue, Buber's I-thou relationship between people (2010, 1937). Rorty is perhaps most direct in *Philosophy and Social Hope* (1999), but he remains relativistic in expressing an anticipative vision of a future that moves toward less cruelty by design and measured action.

As Rickert observes, the one-to-one relationship between intention and outcome may be less clear, and the focus taken off persuasion. Persuasion, coercion, is replaced by a dwelling in the moment, an engagement that results not in quick victories but in sustained emplacement through time. This study has identified successful rhetorical engagement at a variety of sites across the postindustrial Midwest, each a version of an emergent truth and none capturing the whole picture. It remains a daunting project, naïve perhaps in its own way, but optimistic insofar as it insists on an expansive understanding of workplace communication grounded in sophisticated (and sophistical) rhetoric that can engage and impact the development of work and an emergent definition of expertise:

> Naïve cynicism is absolutist; its practitioners assume that anything you don't deplore you wholeheartedly endorse. But denouncing anything less than perfection as morally compromising means pursuing aggrandizement of the self, not engagement with a place or a system or community, as the highest priority.
>
> (Solnit, 2016)

In cynical times, it is a challenge to work productively. Impurity is the mark of capitulation, or of appeasement. Professional and technical communication is dirty insofar as it accepts that its workplace embroilments are necessary, impure. The studies offered here engage communities, places and systems, in order to understand the outlines and possibilities for meaningful literate work. These hybrid configurations, networks and meshes, of humans and their technological and cultural artifacts (and technocultural artifacts) are monsters that threaten the neat categories of the industrial and modern age. Engagement—filial sustained interaction—with these assemblages offers a means of maintaining places from which merge local advantage. In other words, people together with the institutions, memories, and technologies create places worth inhabiting and sustaining. Our work at these places gives our existence meaning, and our time structure, and it is cynical to imagine that there is any detachment from others that is ultimately possible, or even desirable.

Fordist factory work enabled the American working class to emerge as a middle class with reasonable pay and humane benefits. But factory work, the very jobs celebrated for supporting stability and communities throughout the American Midwest, ravaged the environment by dumping unsustainable levels of pollutants without accounting for those indirect costs. The work itself, caricatured by Raymond Scott's "Powerhouse" (1937), was repetitive, dirty, dangerous, and frightfully boring, even dehumanizing. I catch the look of abject horror when I recommend that a student, who has stated they are pursuing social media as a career area, consider a working life in advanced manufacturing. That flicker of revulsion stems from an older industrial dehumanization of the factory assembly line, equally well lampooned in DEVO's version of "Working in the Coal Mine." But the postmodern assembly plant, at least in the postindustrial Midwest, is relatively quiet, safe, and well regulated. The values of Subaru are those of their customers: safety, environmental responsibility, and advanced technology. The postindustrial assembly floor is strangely quiet, and while challenges remain in safety, environmental goals, and stimulating work (at least on the assembly floor), Subaru represents a new standard of automobile assembly—the new, robotically partnered, dynamic-press factory now widely adopted by Ford, GM, and others. In Illinois, farming takes place 11 months of the year in a heated greenhouse, and planting and harvesting are done from ergonomic chairs. In Ohio and Michigan, glimpses of the clean-energy future are discernable as wind, photovoltaics, and pumped storage are woven into a new mesh of low-carbon electricity generation.

Absolutes are hard to find in the monstrous postindustrial era. Successes are partial, localized, and temporary. Better put, the postindustrial era recognizes that successes have always been partial, localized, and temporary. In contrast to a totalizing modern industrial vision, these local accomplishments are easily dismissed. Such cynical appraisal misses the important need for work as part of human identity formation as well as economic development, not to mention the agglomeration of expertise, history, ideas, and wealth in geographical space—what we have learned to call *places*. Silicon Valley's promise of connectivity and frictionless digital culture ignores the need for electricity to power the sleekly designed devices. They rely upon but make invisible research in advanced materials like shatterproof Gorilla Glass and photovoltaic glass; like advanced aluminum alloys; like the sophisticated production facilities and manufacturing processes that wed processes, institutions, and technologies; and research and development organizations that make these devices possible. I have traveled to numerous sites and studied the interwoven networks and meshes of expertise in order to articulate the local advantages existing in particular places. These clusters of expertise are valuable and in need of articulation to, first, accrue value that is translatable to the nascent needs of global manufacturing networks and then to participate and take advantage of these deep resources that are located in their location, resources, histories, intuitions, and ultimately in the people that make place.

Edward Casey (1997) asserts that it is people who make a space into a place, giving it vitality by gathering people and things together:

> By "gathering" I do not mean merely amassing. To gather placewise is to have a peculiar hold on what is presented (as well as represented) in a given place.
>
> (Casey, 1997, pp. 24–25)

Casey describes a place as a space of gathering, bringing topography together with things and people, keeping them in relationship through time at one persistent confluence of location and population:

> ...intrinsic to the holding operation of place is keeping. What is kept in place primarily are experiencing bodies regarded as privileged residents rather than as orchestrating forces (much less as mere registrants).
>
> (ibid)

People, artifacts, geography, and topography act together to make places enduring and durable. Places are also spaces where "thoughts and memories" remain, persistent and active in the imaginations and actions of the people in that place. It is perhaps an optimistic and ambitious vision, but I await other more sophisticated offerings, particularly if the only two alternatives are a neo-modernism and return to the previous epochal dehumanization, or a future of pure and reactive cynicism where purity of thought demands adherence to values of an age now gone.

This study illustrates what it means to write in the postindustrial age. Marshaling a variety of information sources, like the International Standards Organization's standards on energy management (ISO 5001), government reports like the Environmental Protection Agency's future of coal-generated electricity and the European Union's clean-energy reporting, technical and speculative reports on thorium-fuel nuclear energy production, and university-industry technology transfer partnerships designed to redefine the land-grant mission, each chapter has sought to articulate emerging sites where engagement from techno-rhetors has the potential to both improve efficiency and define new kinds and sites of TPC work in the postindustrial age. The skills and processes the discipline has developed, from usability through information design and experience architecture, iterative design, deep re-cycling and network analysis, as well as recontextualized rhetorical concepts like technê, kairos, and mêtis, apply equally to emergent practices in postindustrial manufacturing, industrial-agricultural hybrids, next-generation materials, and technology transfer once these emergent practices are recognized as the high-technology workplaces they already are.

The TPC in the postindustrial context cannot rely on documenting emergent digital technologies to provide a steady wage. All businesses are high technology, and no one sector promises the stability or identity formation that personal and business computing provided in the late 20th century. Instead, the TPC is charged with articulating how her or his expertise is translatable in each regional cluster, in each context. To force a definition of commonality is to leave too many opportunities unpursued and to relinquish the power of the technical rhetor, defined as a trickster nimbly anticipating change, deftly working not to define the terms at play nor finally to solve wicked problems but to meaningfully engage stakeholders. Interests in public understanding of science and technology, of the workings of institutions and the people who animate them, of cultural attunements, and the limits as much as the potential means of persuasion, all these elements are necessary components in a responsible engagement with postindustrial places in order to meaningfully write amid change.

Bibliography

Abizaid, Alexandre, and J. Ribamar Costa. 2010. "New Drug-Eluting Stents." *Circulation: Cardiovascular Interventions* 3 (4): 384–93. doi:10.1161/CIRCINTERVENTIONS.109.891192.

Agboka, Godwin Y. 2013. "Participatory Localization: A Social Justice Approach to Navigating Unenfranchised/Disenfranchised Cultural Sites." *Technical Communication Quarterly* 22 (1): 28–49. doi:10.1080/10572252.2013.730966.

Alexander, Christopher. 2012. *The Battle for the Life and Beauty of the Earth: A Struggle between Two World-Systems*. OUP USA.

Alexander, Christopher, Sara Ishikawa, and Murray Silverstein. 1977. *A Pattern Language: Towns, Buildings, Construction*. OUP USA.

Andersen, Rebekka. 2013. "Rhetorical Work in the Age of Content Management: Implications for the Field of Technical Communication." *Journal of Business and Technical Communication*, December, doi:10.1177/1050651913513904.

Anderson, Chris. 2009. *Free: How Today's Smartest Businesses Profit by Giving Something for Nothing*. New York: Hyperion.

Anderson, Patricia. 1984. *Course of Empire: The Erie Canal and the New York Landscape, 1825–1875*. Seattle, WA: University of Washington Press.

Ansley, Arthur C. 1957. *Manufacturing Methods and Processes*. Philadelphia: Chilton Co. http://catalog.hathitrust.org/Record/001044710.

Ariely, Dan. 2010. *Predictably Irrational: The Hidden Forces That Shape Our Decisions*. Rev. and expanded ed., 1st Harper Perennial ed. New York: Harper Perennial.

Baird, N. P., and Dilger, B. 2017. "How Students Perceive Transitions: Dispositions and Transfer in Internships." *College Composition and Communication* 68 (4): 684–712.

Barabasi, Albert-Laszlo. 2003. *Linked: How Everything Is Connected to Everything Else and What It Means for Business, Science, and Everyday Life*. 60387th ed. New York: Plume.

———. 2011. *Bursts: The Hidden Patterns Behind Everything We Do, from Your E-Mail to Bloody Crusades*. Reprint ed. New York: Plume.

Bazerman, Charles, Joseph Little, and Teri Chavkin. 2003. "The Production of Information for Genred Activity Spaces Informational Motives and Consequences of the Environmental Impact Statement." *Written Communication* 20 (4): 455–77. doi:10.1177/0741088303260375.

Bazerman, Charles, and Paul Prior. 2003. *What Writing Does and How It Does It: An Introduction to Analyzing Texts and Textual Practices.* New York: Routledge.

Bell, Daniel. 1973, 1999. *The Coming of Post-Industrial Society: A Venture in Social Forecasting.* Special anniversary ed. New York: Basic Books.

Benkler, Yochai. 2006. *The Wealth of Networks: How Social Production Transforms Markets and Freedom.* New Haven, CT: Yale University Press.

Berlin, James A. 1984. *Writing Instruction in Nineteenth-Century American Colleges.* 1st ed. Carbondale: Southern Illinois University Press.

Bernstein, Peter L. 2006. *Wedding of the Waters: The Erie Canal and the Making of a Great Nation.* 1st ed. New York: Norton.

Bienvenu, Ryan. 2012. *Method of Forming a Drug-Eluting Medical Device.* US8333801 B2, filed September 17, 2010, and issued December 18, 2012. www.google.com/patents/US8333801.

BINE. 2016. "Compressed Air Energy Storage Power Plants." www.bine.info/en/publications/publikation/druckluftspeicher-kraftwerke/.

Blakesley, D. 2002. *The Elements of Dramatism.* New York: Longman.

Bliese, John R. E. 1994. "Rhetoric Goes to War: The Doctrine of Ancient and Medieval Military Manuals." *Rhetoric Society Quarterly* 24 (3/4): 105–30.

Brenner, Joël Glenn. 1999. *The Emperors of Chocolate: Inside the Secret World of Hershey and Mars.* New York: Random House.

Brown, John Seely, and Paul Duguid. 2000. *The Social Life of Information.* Boston: Harvard Business School Press.

Brunes, Bente Taraldsten. 2009. *Increasing Power Output from Francis Turbines: Effektøkning I Vannkraftverk Med Francis Turbiner.* Institutt for energi-ogprosessteknikk.www.diva-portal.org/smash/record.jsf?pid=diva2%3A426934&dswid=-264.

Buber, Martin. 2010. *I and Thou.* Translated by Ronald Gregor Smith. Mansfield Centre: Martino Publishing.

Burbank, William, Scott Luke, and Dean Hoornaert. 2010. *Electro-mechanical Interfaces to Mount Robotic Surgical Arms.* US7762825 B2, issued July 27, 2010. www.google.com/patents/US7762825.

Burke, Kenneth. 1941. "Four Master Tropes." *The Kenyon Review* 3 (4): 421–38.

Caniëls, Marjolein C. J., and Henny A. Romijn. 2003. "Firm-level Knowledge Accumulation and Regional Dynamics." *Industrial and Corporate Change* 12 (6): 1253–78. doi:10.1093/icc/12.6.1253.

Cappelli, Peter. 2012. *Why Good People Can't Get Jobs: The Skills Gap and What Companies Can Do About It.* New York: Wharton Digital Press. http://public.eblib.com/choice/publicfullrecord.aspx?p=909613.

Casey, Edward S. 1997. "How to Get from Space to Place in a Fairly Short Stretch of Time: Phenomenological Prolegomena." In *Senses of Place*, edited by Steven Feld and Keith II. Basso. Santa Fe, NM: School of American Research Press.

Cash, David W. 2001. "'In Order to Aid in Diffusing Useful and Practical Information': Agricultural Extension and Boundary Organizations." *Science, Technology & Human Values* 26 (4): 431–53. doi:10.1177/016224390102600403.

Cassano, Erik. 2011. "How Bill Ford Jr. Led Ford Motor Co. through the Recession." *Smart Business Magazine*. Accessed April 28, 2016. www.sbnonline.com/ article/bill-ford-jr-on-the-future-of-his-brand-the-business/.

Charoensiriwath, C. 2009. "Analyzing Intellectual Capital Cluster Index in Thailand's Hard Disk Drive Cluster." In *PICMET '09–2009 Portland International Conference on Management of Engineering Technology*, 200–204. doi:10.1109/PICMET.2009.5262228.

Childress, James F., Eric M. Meslin, and Harold T. Shapiro. 2005. *Belmont Revisited: Ethical Principles for Research with Human Subjects*. Washington, DC: Georgetown University Press.

Clancy, Paula, Eoin O'Malley, Larry O'Connell, and Chris Van Egeraat. 2001. "Industry Clusters in Ireland: An Application of Porter's Model of National Competitive Advantage to Three Sectors." *European Planning Studies* 9 (1): 7–28. doi:10.1080/09654310124159.

Clark, David. 2010, 1981. *Post-Industrial America: A Geographical Perspective*. London: Routledge.

Clemens, Paul. 2011. *Punching Out: One Year in a Closing Auto Plant*. Doubleday.

Colasanti, K., W. Wright, and B. Reau. 2009. "Extension, the Land-Grant Mission, and Civic Agriculture: Cultivating Change." *Journal of Extension* 47 (4): 4FEA1.

Communication, Committee on Scientific and Technical. 1969. *Scientific and Technical Communication, a Pressing National Problem and Recommendations for Its Solution: A Report*. Washington, DC: National Academies.

Connors, Robert J. 1982. "The Rise of Technical Writing Instruction in America." *Journal of Technical Writing and Communication* 12 (4): 329–52.

Cooper, Marilyn M. 1986. "The Ecology of Writing." *College English* 48 (4): 364–75. doi:10.2307/377264.

Cooper, Thomas G., Stephen J. Blumenkranz, Gary S. Guthart, and David J. Rosa. 2010. *Modular Manipulator Support for Robotic Surgery*. US7763015 B2, issued July 27, 2010. www.google.com/patents/US7763015.

Crow, James F. 1948. "Alternative Hypotheses of Hybrid Vigor." *Genetics* 33 (5): 477–87.

Culligan, Patrick J., Charbel Salamon, Jennifer L. Priestley, and Amir Shariati. 2013. "Porcine Dermis Compared With Polypropylene Mesh for Laparoscopic Sacrocolpopexy: A Randomized Controlled Trial." *Obstetrics & Gynecology* 121 (1): 143–51. doi:10.1097/AOG.0b013e31827558dc.

Cushman, J. 2014. "Our Unstable Artistry: Donald Schon's Counterprofessional Practice of Problem Setting." *Journal of Business and Technical Communication* 28 (3): 327–51. doi:10.1177/1050651914524778.

Cutcher-Gershenfeld, Joel, Dan Brooks, and Martin Mulloy. 2015. *Inside the Ford-UAW Transformation: Pivotal Events in Valuing Work and Delivering Results*. 1 ed. Cambridge, MA: MIT Press.

Darouiche, Rabih O., Issam I. Raad, Stephen O. Heard, John I. Thornby, Olivier C. Wenker, Andrea Gabrielli, Johannes Berg, et al. 1999. "A Comparison of Two Antimicrobial-Impregnated Central Venous Catheters." *New England Journal of Medicine* 340 (1): 1–8. doi:10.1056/NEJM199901073400101.

Davis, Joel J., Emily Cross, and John Crowley. 2007. "Pharmaceutical Websites and the Communication of Risk Information." *Journal of Health Communication* 12 (1): 29–39. doi:10.1080/10810730601091326.

De Botton, Alain. 2010. *A Week at the Airport*. New York: Vintage International.

Dellinger, Jade, and David Giffels. 2008. *Are We Not Men?: We Are Devo!* London: SAF.

Devo. 1997. *Working in the Coal Mine*. Vol. The New Traditionalists, remastered. Infinite Zero Archive. https://en.wikipedia.org/wiki/New_Traditionalists.

Diamond, Jared. 2005. *Guns, Germs, and Steel: The Fates of Human Societies*. Revised ed. New York: W. W. Norton & Company.

Doheny-Farina, Stephen. 1992. *Rhetoric, Innovation, Technology: Case Studies of Technical Communication in Technology Transfers*. Cambridge, MA: MIT Press.

Dolmage, Jay Timothy. 2016. *Disability Rhetoric*. Reprint ed. Syracuse, NY: Syracuse University Press.

Du Gay, Paul. 2013. *Doing Cultural Studies: The Story of the Sony Walkman*. 2nd ed. Thousand Oaks: Sage Publications.

Easterbrook, Catherine, and Guy Maddern. 2008. "Porcine and Bovine Surgical Products: Jewish, Muslim, and Hindu Perspectives." *Archives of Surgery* 143 (4): 366–70. doi:10.1001/archsurg.143.4.366.

Edbauer, Jenny. 2005. "Unframing Models of Public Distribution: From Rhetorical Situation to Rhetorical Ecologies." *Rhetoric Society Quarterly* 35 (4): 5–24. doi:10.1080/02773940509391320.

Eichenwald, Kurt. 2001. *The Informant: A True Story*. 1st ed. New York: Broadway Books.

Faber, Brenton D. 2001. "Gen/Ethics? Organizational Ethics and Student and Instructor Conflicts in Workplace Training." *Technical Communication Quarterly* 10 (3): 291–318. doi:10.1207/s15427625tcq1003_4.

———. 2002. *Community Action and Organizational Change: Image, Narrative, Identity*. Carbondale: Southern Illinois University Press.

———. 2006. "Popularizing Nanoscience: The Public Rhetoric of Nanotechnology, 1986–1999." *Technical Communication Quarterly* 15 (2): 141–69. doi:10.1207/s15427625tcq1502_2.

———. 2007. *Discourse, Technology, and Change*. London; New York: Continuum.

Faigley, Lester. 1995. *Fragments of Rationality: Postmodernity and the Subject of Composition*. Pittsburgh: University of Pittsburgh Press.

Feenberg, Andrew. 1995. *Alternative Modernity: The Technical Turn in Philosophy and Social Theory*. Revised ed. Berkeley: University of California Press.

———. 1999. *Questioning Technology*. London; New York: Routledge.

———. 2002. *Transforming Technology: A Critical Theory Revisited*. 2nd ed. New York: Oxford University Press.

Feld, Steven, and Keith H. Basso, eds. 1996. *Senses of Place*. Santa Fe, NM: Seattle: School for Advanced Research Press.

Fellman, Michael. 1990. *Inside War: The Guerrilla Conflict in Missouri During the American Civil War*. Oxford, UK: Oxford University Press.

Fellner, Christien, and Hutson, Nick. 2010. "Available and Emerging Technologies for Reducing Greenhouse Gas Emissions from Coal-Fired Electric Generating Units." Environmental Protection Agency. https://www.epa.gov/sites/production/files/2015-12/documents/electricgeneration.pdf.

Ferrera, David A., Daniel R. Kurz, Lok A. Lei, and Julia A. Larsen. 2003. *Vasooclusive Device for Treatment of Aneurysms*. US6616617 B1, filed December 4, 1998, and issued September 9, 2003. www.google.com/patents/US6616617.

Flyvbjerg, Bent, Nils Bruzelius, and Werner Rothengatter. 2003. *Megaprojects and Risk: An Anatomy of Ambition.* United Kingdom; New York: Cambridge University Press.

Franklin, Benjamin, J. A. Leo Lemay, and Paul M. Zall. 1986. *Benjamin Franklin's Autobiography: An Authoritative Text, Backgrounds, Criticism.* 1st ed. A Norton Critical Edition. New York: Norton.

Freeberg, Ernest. 2014. *The Age of Edison: Electric Light and the Invention of Modern America.* New York: Penguin Books.

Gertner, Jon. 2012. *The Idea Factory: Bell Labs and the Great Age of American Innovation.* New York: Penguin Press.

Göde, E. 2009. "Performance Upgrading of Hydraulic Machinery with the Help of CFD." In *100 Volumes of "Notes on Numerical Fluid Mechanics,"* edited by Ernst Heinrich Hirschel and Egon Krause, 299–310. Notes on Numerical Fluid Mechanics and Multidisciplinary Design 100. Berlin, Heidelberg: Springer. http://link.springer.com/chapter/10.1007/978-3-540-70805-6_23.

Google. 2016. "Google Data Centers: Hamina, Finland." Accessed November 12. www.google.com/about/datacenters/inside/locations/hamina/.

Goyal, Deepak, Anjali Goyal, and Mats Brittberg. 2013. "Consideration of Religious Sentiments While Selecting a Biological Product for Knee Arthroscopy." *Knee Surgery, Sports Traumatology, Arthroscopy* 21 (7): 1577–86. doi:10.1007/s00167–012–2292-z.

Grabill, Jeffrey T. 2001. *Community Literacy Programs and the Politics of Change.* Albany: State University of New York Press.

———. 2007. *Writing Community Change: Designing Technologies for Citizen Action.* New Dimensions in Computers and Composition. Cresskill, NJ: Hampton Press.

Graham, Laurie. 1995. *On the Line at Subaru-Isuzu: The Japanese Model and the American Worker.* 1st ed. Ithaca, NY: ILR Press.

Graham, S. Scott. 2015. *The Politics of Pain Medicine: A Rhetorical-Ontological Inquiry.* Chicago, IL: University of Chicago Press.

Guesalaga, Rodrigo, and Pablo Marshall. 2008. "Purchasing Power at the Bottom of the Pyramid: Differences across Geographic Regions and Income Tiers." *Journal of Consumer Marketing* 25 (7): 413–18. doi:10.1108/07363760810915626.

Haldeman, Samuel Stehman. 1872. *Pennsylvania Dutch: A Dialect of South German with an Infusion of English.* Philadelphia, PA: Reformed Church Publication Board.

Haraway, Donna Jeanne, Lawrence Grossberg, Cary Nelson, and Paula A Treichler. 1992. *The Promises of Monsters: A Regenerative Politics for Inappropriate/d Others.*

Haraway, Donna Jeanne. 1997. *Modest_Witness@Second_Millennium. FemaleMan_Meets_OncoMouse: Feminism and Technoscience.* New York: Routledge.

Hård, Mikael, and Andrew Jamison. 2005. *Hubris and Hybrids: A Cultural History of Technology and Science.* New York: Routledge.

Hart-Davidson, William. 2001. "On Writing, Technical Communication, and Information Technology: The Core Competencies of Technical Communication." *Technical Communication* 48 (2): 145–55.

Hawk, Byron. 2004. "Toward a Post-technê-Or, Inventing Pedagogies for Professional Writing." *Technical Communication Quarterly* 13 (4): 371–92. doi:10.1207/s15427625tcq1304_2.

Heitmann, John. 2009. *The Automobile and American Life*. Jefferson, NC: McFarland.

Henwood, Doug. 2005. *After the New Economy*. New York: New Press.

Herndl, Carl. 1996. *Green Culture: Environmental Rhetoric in Contemporary America*. Madison, WI: University of Wisconsin Press.

Hohn, Donovan. 2011. *Moby-Duck: The True Story of 28,800 Bath Toys Lost at Sea and of the Beachcombers, Oceanographers, Environmentalists, and Fools, Including the Author, Who Went in Search of Them*. New York: Viking.

Hornik, Robert C. 1988. *Development Communication: Information, Agriculture, and Nutrition in the Third World*. Communications/the Annenberg School of Communications, University of Pennsylvania, Philadelphia. New York: Longman.

Huff, Irving Geis Darrell. 1954. *How to Lie with Statistics*. 1st ed. New York: Norton.

Imai, M. 1997. *Gemba Kaizen: A Commonsense, Low-Cost Approach to Management*. New York: McGraw-Hill.

Ishikawa, Karoru, and Kaoru Ishikawa. 1988. *What Is Total Quality Control? The Japanese Way*. Translated by David J. Lu. 1st ed. Englewood Cliffs, NJ: Prentice Hall.

Issenberg, Sasha. 2014. *The Sushi Economy: Globalization and the Making of a Modern Delicacy*. New York: Gotham Books.

Jackson, Matthew O. 2010. *Social and Economic Networks*. Princeton, NJ: Princeton University Press. http://public.eblib.com/choice/publicfullrecord. aspx?p=664598.

Jacob, Heinrich Eduard. 2015. *Coffee: The Epic of a Commodity*. Reissue ed. New York: Skyhorse Publishing.

Johnson, Carol Siri. 2009. *The Language of Work: Technical Communication at Lukens Steel, 1810 to 1925*. Amityville, NY: Baywood Publishing.

Johnson, Eldon L. 1981. "Misconceptions About the Early Land-Grant Colleges." *Journal of Higher Education* 52 (4): 333–51. doi:10.2307/1981282.

Johnson, Robert R. 1998. *User-Centered Technology: A Rhetorical Theory for Computers and Other Mundane Artifacts*. Albany: State University of New York Press.

———. 2010. "The Ubiquity Paradox: Further Thinking on the Concept of User Centeredness." *Technical Communication Quarterly* 19 (4): 335–51. doi: 10.1080/10572252.2010.502510.

Johnson, Robert R., Michael J. Salvo, and Meredith W. Zoetewey. 2007. "User-Centered Technology in Participatory Culture: Two Decades Beyond a Narrow Conception of Usability Testing." *IEEE Transactions on Professional Communication* 50 (4): 320–32. doi:10.1109/TPC.2007.908730.

Johnson, Spencer, and Kenneth Blanchard. 1998. *Who Moved My Cheese?: An Amazing Way to Deal with Change in Your Work and in Your Life*. 1st ed. New York: G. P. Putnam's Sons.

Johnson-Eilola, Johndan. 2005. *Datacloud: Toward a New Theory of Online Work*. New Dimensions in Computers and Composition. Cresskill, NJ: Hampton Press.

Johnson-Eilola, Johndan, and Stuart A. Selber, eds. 2013. *Solving Problems in Technical Communication*. Chicago, IL: University of Chicago Press.

Jonnes, Jill. 2003. *Empires of Light: Edison, Tesla, Westinghouse, and the Race to Electrify the World*. 1st ed. New York: Random House.

Jordan, Nicholas, and Keith Douglass Warner. 2010. "Enhancing the Multi-functionality of US Agriculture." *BioScience* 60 (1): 60–66. doi:10.1525/bio.2010.60.1.10.

Joy Damousi, Birgit Lang, and Katie Sutton eds. 2015. *Case Studies and the Dissemination of Knowledge*. New York: Routledge Studies in Cultural History; Abingdon, Oxon: Routledge.

Judd, Dennis R. 2006. "Commentary: Tracing the Commodity Chain of Global Tourism." *Tourism Geographies* 8 (4): 323–36. doi:10.1080/14616680600921932.

Karlovsky, Matthew E., Atul A. Thakre, Ardeshir Rastinehad, Leslie Kushner, and Gopal H. Badlani. 2005. "Biomaterials for Pelvic Floor Reconstruction." *Urology* 66 (3): 469–75. doi:10.1016/j.urology.2005.03.006.

Katz, Evie, Fiona Solomon, Wendy Mee, and Roy Lovel. 2009. "Evolving Scientific Research Governance in Australia: A Case Study of Engaging Interested Publics in Nanotechnology Research." *Public Understanding of Science* 18 (5): 531–45. doi:10.1177/0963662507082016.

Katz, Steven B. 1992. "The Ethic of Expediency: Classical Rhetoric, Technology, and the Holocaust." *College English* 54 (3): 255–75. doi:10.2307/378062.

Kaufer, David S., and Brian S. Butler. 1996. *Rhetoric and the Arts of Design*. 1st ed. Mahwah, NJ: Routledge.

Kawabata, Yasunari. 1996. *The Master of Go*. Translated by Edward G. Seidensticker. New York: Vintage.

Khodorowsky, Katherine. 2001. *The Little Book of Chocolate*. Paris; London: Flammarion; Thames & Hudson.

Kidder, Tracy. 2000. *The Soul of a New Machine*. 1st paperback ed. Boston: Little, Brown.

Kimball, Miles A. 2006. "Cars, Culture, and Tactical Technical Communication." *Technical Communication Quarterly* 15 (1): 67–86. doi:10.1207/s15427625tcq1501_6.

———. 2016. "The Golden Age of Technical Communication." *Journal of Technical Writing and Communication*. doi:10.1177/0047281616641927.

Kinneavy, James L. 1986. "Kairos: A Neglected Concept in Classical Rhetoric." In *Rhetoric and Praxis: The Contribution of Classical Rhetoric to Practical Reasoning*, edited by Jean Dietz Moss. Washington, DC: Catholic University of America Press.

Klein, Dan. 2016. "News 18 Investigates: Traffic Light Timing Part 2." *Wlfi.com*. May 19. http://wlfi.com/2016/05/18/news-18-investigates-traffic-light-timing-part-2/.

Kotter, John, Holger Rathgeber, and Spencer Johnson. 2006. *Our Iceberg Is Melting*. 1st ed. New York: St. Martin's Press.

Krug, Steve. 2010. *Rocket Surgery Made Easy: The Do-It-Yourself Guide to Finding and Fixing Usability Problems*. Voices That Matter. Berkeley, CA: New Riders.

Kurlansky, Mark. 1998. *Cod: A Biography of the Fish That Changed the World*. New York: Penguin Books.

———. 2002. *Salt: A World History.* 1st ed. New York: Walker Books.

Kynell-Hunt, Teresa, and Gerald J. Savage, eds. 2003. *Power and Legitimacy in Technical Communication.* Baywood's Technical Communications Series. Amityville, NY: Baywood Publishing.

Kynell-Hunt, Teresa, and Gerald J Savage. 2004. *Power and Legitimacy in Technical Communication Volume II.* Amityville, NY: Baywood Publishing. http://public.eblib.com/choice/publicfullrecord.aspx?p=3117822.

Kyoto Protocol to the United Nations Framework Convention on Climate Change. 1997. United Nations. https://treaties.un.org/Pages/DB.aspx?path=DB/MTDSGStatus/pageIntro_en.xml.

Lanham, Richard A. 2006. *The Economics of Attention: Style and Substance in the Age of Information.* 1st ed. Chicago, IL: University of Chicago Press.

Lather, Patricia. 2007. *Getting Lost: Feminist Efforts toward a Double(d) Science.* SUNY Series, Second Thoughts. Albany: State University of New York Press.

Latour, Bruno. 1988. *The Pasteurization of France.* Translated by Alan Sheridan and John Law. Cambridge, MA: Harvard University Press.

———. 1992. "Where Are the Missing Masses? The Sociology of a Few Mundane Artifacts." In *Shaping Technology-Building Society. Studies in Sociotechnical Change,* edited by Wiebe Bijker and John Law, 225–59. MIT Press. www.bruno-latour.fr/node/258.

———. 1993. *We Have Never Been Modern.* Translated by Catherine Porter. Cambridge, MA: Harvard University Press.

———. 1996. *Aramis, or the Love of Technology.* Cambridge, MA: Harvard University Press.

———. 2003. *Science in Action: How to Follow Scientists and Engineers through Society.* 11th printing. Cambridge, MA: Harvard Univ. Press.

———. 2004. "Why Has Critique Run out of Steam? From Matters of Fact to Matters of Concern." *Critical Inquiry* 30 (2): 225–48. doi:10.1086/421123.

Law, John. 1991. *A Sociology of Monsters: Essays on Power, Technology, and Domination.* New York: Routledge.

Ledford, Heidi. 2015. "The Printed Organs Coming to a Body near You." *Nature News* 520 (7547): 273. doi:10.1038/520273a.

Lee, Martha F., and Brad Mehlenbacher. 2000. "Technical Writer/Subject-Matter Expert Interaction: The Writer's Perspective, the Organizational Challenge." *Technical Communication* 47 (4): 544–52.

Li, Yuan-Guang, Ling Xu, Ying-Ming Huang, Feng Wang, Chen Guo, and Chun-Zhao Liu. 2011. "Microalgal Biodiesel in China: Opportunities and Challenges." Applied Energy, Special Issue of Energy from algae: Current status and future trends, 88 (10): 3432–37. doi:10.1016/j.apenergy.2010.12.067.

Liker, Jeffrey. 2004. *The Toyota Way: 14 Management Principles from the World's Greatest Manufacturer.* 1st ed. New York: McGraw-Hill Education.

Longo, Bernadette. 1998. "An Approach for Applying Cultural Study Theory to Technical Writing Research." *Technical Communication Quarterly* 7 (1): 53–73. doi:10.1080/10572259809364617.

———. 2000. *Spurious Coin: A History of Science, Management, and Technical Writing.* Albany: State University of New York Press.

Lundin, Stephen C., John Christensen, and Harry Paul. 2003. *Fish! Sticks: A Remarkable Way to Adapt to Changing Times and Keep Your Work Fresh.* 1st ed. New York: Hachette Books.

Luo, Xing, and Jihong Wang. 2013. *Overview of Current Development on Compressed Air Energy Storage Technical Report*. www.eera-set.eu/wp-content/uploads/Overview-of-Current-Development-on-Compressed-Air-Energy-Storage_EERA-report-2013.pdf.

Luo, Xing, Jihong Wang, Mark Dooner, Jonathan Clarke, and Christopher Krupke. 2014. "Overview of Current Development in Compressed Air Energy Storage Technology." *Energy Procedia* 62: 603–11. doi:10.1016/j.egypro.2014.12.423.

Makhijani, Arjun, and Michele Boyd. 2016. "Thorium Fuel-No Panacea for Nuclear Power-Institute for Energy and Environmental Research." Accessed May 5. http://ieer.org/resource/factsheets/thorium-fuel-panacea-nuclear-power/.

Mallett, Alexandra, and David G. Ockwell. 2016. "Low-Carbon Technology Transfer: David G. Ockwell, Alexandra Mallett-Book2Look." Accessed May 9. http://book2look.co.uk/book/M9nQoT2Kmo.

Manaugh, Geoff. 2016. "Hoover Dam Is a Super-Gadget That Keeps the Lights in Vegas Burning." *Gizmodo*. Accessed November 13. http://gizmodo.com/hoover-dam-is-a-super-gadget-that-keeps-the-lights-in-v-1496815769.

Mangera, Altaf, Anthony J. Bullock, Sabiniano Roman, Christopher R. Chapple, and Sheila MacNeil. 2013. "Comparison of Candidate Scaffolds for Tissue Engineering for Stress Urinary Incontinence and Pelvic Organ Prolapse Repair." *BJU International* 112 (5): 674–85. doi:10.1111/bju.12186.

Mantle, Jonathan. 1995. *Car Wars: Automobile Manufacturers and the Quest for Freedom and Power*. 1st ed. London: Macmillan.

Marsh, Peter. 2012. *The New Industrial Revolution: Consumers, Globalization and the End of Mass Production*. New Haven, CT: Yale University Press.

Martin, Richard. 2009. "Uranium Is So Last Century—Enter Thorium, the New Green Nuke | WIRED." Magazine (archive). *Wired*. December 21. www.wired.com/2009/12/ff_new_nukes/all/.

Mathison, Maureen A., Natalie Stillman-Webb, and Sarah A. Bell. 2014. "Framing Sustainability Business Students Writing About the Environment." *Journal of Business and Technical Communication* 28 (1): 58–82. doi:10.1177/1050651913502488.

Maylath, Bruce, Sonia Vandepitte, Patricia Minacori, Suvi Isohella, Birthe Mousten, and John Humbley. 2013. "Managing Complexity: A Technical Communication Translation Case Study in Multilateral International Collaboration." *Technical Communication Quarterly* 22 (1): 67–84. doi:10.1080/10572252.2013.730967.

McDowell, George R. 2001. *Land-Grant Universities and Extension into the 21st Century*. New York: Wiley.

McGonigal, Jane. 2011. *Reality Is Broken: Why Games Make Us Better and How They Can Change the World*. Reprint ed. New York: Penguin Books.

Meadows, Donella H., and Diana Wright. 2008. *Thinking in Systems: A Primer*. White River Junction, VT: Chelsea Green Publishing.

Morato, Carlos, Krishnanand N. Kaipa, Boxuan Zhao, and Satyandra K. Gupta. 2014. "Toward Safe Human Robot Collaboration by Using Multiple Kinects Based Real-Time Human Tracking." *Journal of Computing and Information Science in Engineering* 14 (1): 011006–011006. doi:10.1115/1.4025810.

Moretti, Enrico. 2012. *The New Geography of Jobs*. Boston, MA: Houghton Mifflin Harcourt.

Morville, Peter. 2014. *Intertwingled: Information Changes Everything*. Ann Arbor, MI: Semantic Studios.

Moss, Ed Jean Dietz. 1986. *Rhetoric and Praxis: The Contribution of Classical Rhetoric to Practical Reasoni.* Washington, DC: Catholic University of America Press.

Negroponte, Nicholas. 1995. *Being Digital.* 1st ed. New York: Knopf.

Neil Hamilton. 1994. "Agriculture without Farmers? Is Industrialization Restructuring American Food Production and Threatening the Future of Sustainable Agriculture?" *Northern Illinois University Law Review*, Summer 1994.

Neumann, Tracy. 2016. *Remaking the Rust Belt: The Postindustrial Transformation of North America.* Philadelphia, U Pennsylvania Press.

Norman, Donald A. 1990. *The Design of Everyday Things.* 1st Doubleday/Currency ed. New York: Doubleday.

———. 2013. *The Design of Everyday Things.* Revised and expanded edition. New York: Basic Books. 3rd ed. www.books24x7.com/marc.asp?bookid= 59487.

Ockwell, David G., and Alexandra Mallett, eds. 2012. *Low-Carbon Technology Transfer: From Rhetoric to Reality.* London; New York: Routledge.

Odell, Lee, and Dixie Goswami. 1985. *Writing in Nonacademic Settings.* New York: Guilford Press.

Off, Carol. 2006. *Bitter Chocolate: Investigating the Dark Side of the World's Most Seductive Sweet.* Toronto: Random House Canada.

Ohno, Taiichi. 2012. *Taiichi Ohnos Workplace Management: Special 100th Birthday Edition.* 1st ed. New York: McGraw-Hill Education.

Oldenziel, Ruth. 2004. *Making Technology Masculine: Men, Women, and Modern Machines in America, 1870–1945.* 1st ed. Amsterdam: Amsterdam University Press.

Ong, Walter J. 1991. *Orality and Literacy: The Technologizing of the Word.* New Accents. London; New York: Routledge.

Ong, Walter J., and Adrian Johns. 2005. *Ramus, Method, and the Decay of Dialogue: From the Art of Discourse to the Art of Reason.* Chicago, IL: University of Chicago Press.

Ong, Walter J., and John Hartley. 2012. *Orality and Literacy: The Technologizing of the Word.* 30th anniversary ed.; 3rd ed. Orality and Literary. London; New York: Routledge.

"OOH FAQs: Occupational Outlook Handbook:: U.S. Bureau of Labor Statistics." 2016. Accessed April 21. www.bls.gov/ooh/about/ooh-faqs.htm# info4.

Osborne, Roger. 2013. *Iron, Steam & Money: The Making of the Industrial Revolution.* New York: Vintage Digital.

Pender, Kelly. 2011. *Technê, from Neoclassicism to Postmodernism: Understanding Writing as a Useful, Teachable Art.* Anderson, SC: Parlor Press.

Peterson, Paul S. 2011. *The Story of Ludington: Born of Logs, Nurtured by Carferries, Forged by Resilience.* Ludington, MI: Heritage Publishers. www.heritagepublishers.com/books/city-of-ludington/.

Pflugfelder, Ehren Helmut. 2016. *Communicating Mobility and Technology A Material Rhetoric for Persuasive Transportation.* New York: Routledge.

———. n.d. "Communicating Technology and Mobility: Advancing a Kinaesthetic Rhetoric." PhD, Associate Professor Stuart Selber. 2004. *Multiliteracies for a Digital Age.* 1st ed. Carbondale: Southern Illinois University Press.

Plato. 2003. *Plato : Phaedrus: A Translation With Notes, Glossary, Appendices, Interpretive Essay and Introduction.* Edited by Albert Keith Whitaker. Translated by Stephen Scully. 1st ed. Newburyport, MA: Focus. http://classics.mit.edu/Plato/phaedrus.html.

Pope-Ruark, Rebecca. 2014. "A Case for Metic Intelligence in Technical and Professional Communication Programs." *Technical Communication Quarterly* 23 (4): 323–40. doi:10.1080/10572252.2014.942469.

———. 2015. "Introducing Agile Project Management Strategies in Technical and Professional Communication Courses." *Journal of Business and Technical Communication* 29 (1): 112–33. doi:10.1177/1050651914548456.

Porter, James E., Patricia Sullivan, Stuart Blythe, Jeffrey T. Grabill, and Libby Miles. 2000. "Institutional Critique: A Rhetorical Methodology for Change." *College Composition and Communication* 51 (4): 610–42. doi:10.2307/358914.

"Promoting Hershey: The Chocolate Bar, The Chocolate Town, The Chocolate King-ProQuest." 2016. Accessed August 26. http://search.proquest.com/openview/076a0b629b4480f8b7ba63b65ed2ab96/1?pq-origsite=gscholar.

Pullin, Graham. 2011. *Design Meets Disability.* Cambridge, MA: MIT Press.

Ragheb, Anthony O., Brian L. Bates, Neal E. Fearnot, Thomas A. Osborne, Thomas G. Kozma, Joseph W. Roberts, and William D. Voorhees III. 1999. Silver Implantable Medical Device. US5873904 A, filed February 24, 1997, and issued February 23, 1999. www.google.com/patents/US5873904.

Ramussen, Wayne D. 2002. *Taking the University to the People: Seventy-Five Years of Cooperative Extension.* West Lafayette, IN: Purdue University Press.

Ratcliffe, Krista. 2006. *Rhetorical Listening: Identification, Gender, Whiteness.* 1st ed. Carbondale: Southern Illinois University Press.

Rice, Jeff. 2012. *Digital Detroit: Rhetoric and Space in the Age of the Network.* Carbondale: Southern Illinois University Press.

———. 2016. "Professional Purity Revolutionary Writing in the Craft Beer Industry." *Journal of Business and Technical Communication* 30 (2): 236–61. doi:10.1177/1050651915620234.

Rice, Jenny. 2012. *Distant Publics: Development Rhetoric and the Subject of Crisis.* University of Pittsburgh Press.

Rickert, Thomas. 2013. *Ambient Rhetoric: The Attunements of Rhetorical Being.* 1st ed. Pittsburgh, PA: University of Pittsburgh Press.

Rifkin, Jeremy. 2004. *The European Dream: How Europe's Vision of the Future Is Quietly Eclipsing the American Dream.* Cambridge, UK: Polity.

———. 2011. *The Third Industrial Revolution: How Lateral Power Is Transforming Energy, the Economy, and the World.* New York: St. Martin's Griffin.

Rittel, Horst W. J., and Melvin M. Webber. 1973. "Dilemmas in a General Theory of Planning." *Policy Sciences* 4 (2): 155–69. doi:10.1007/BF01405730.

Rivers, Nathaniel A., and Ryan P. Weber. 2011. "Ecological, Pedagogical, Public Rhetoric." *College Composition and Communication* 63 (2): 187–218.

Rodgers, Peter. 1998. "Universities and Industry Work towards Prosperity as Peace Beckons." *Physics World* 11 (5): 10. doi:10.1088/2058-7058/11/5/12.

Rohrer, G. A., L. J. Alexander, Z. Hu, T. P. Smith, J. W. Keele, and C. W. Beattie. 1996. "A Comprehensive Map of the Porcine Genome." *Genome Research* 6 (5): 371–91.

Rorty, Richard. 1989. *Contingency, Irony, and Solidarity*. Cambridge; New York: Cambridge University Press.

———. 1999. *Philosophy and Social Hope*. New York: Penguin Books.

Ross, Derek, ed. 2017. *Topic-Driven Environmental Rhetoric*. Routledge/ Taylor & Francis in Their Studies in Technical Communication, Rhetoric, and Culture. London: Routledge/Taylor and Francis.

Rude, Carolyn D. 2015. "Building Identity and Community through Research." *Journal of Technical Writing and Communication* 45 (4): 366–80. doi:10.1177/ 0047281615585753.

Russell, Inge, and Graham Stewart. 2014. *Whisky: Technology, Production and Marketing*. New York: Elsevier.

Salvo, Michael J. 2014. "What's in a Name?: Experience Architecture Rearticu- lates the Humanities." *Communication Design Quarterly Review* 2 (3): 6–9. doi:10.1145/2644448.2644450.

Salvo, Michael J., Ehren Helmut Pflugfelder, and Joshua Prenosil. 2010. "The Children of Aramis." *Journal of Technical Writing and Communication* 40 (3): 245–63. doi:10.2190/TW.40.3.b.

Salvo, Michael, Meredith W. Zoetewey, and Kate Agena. 2007. "A Case of Exhaustive Documentation: Re-Centering System-Oriented Organizations around User Need." *Technical Communication* 54 (1): 46–57.

Sánchez, Fernando. 2016. "The Roles of Technical Communication Researchers in Design Scholarship." *Journal of Technical Writing and Communication*. doi:10.1177/0047281616641929.

Sauer, Beverly A. 2002. *The Rhetoric of Risk: Technical Documentation in Hazardous Environments*. Mahwah, NJ: Routledge.

Schook, Lawrence B., and Mike E. Tumbleson. 2013. *Advances in Swine in Biomedical Research*. New York: Springer Science & Business Media.

Scott, John Blake. 2014. *Risky Rhetoric: AIDS and the Cultural Practices of HIV Testing*. 1st ed. Carbondale: Southern Illinois University Press.

Scott, John Blake, Bernadette Longo, and Katherine Wills, eds. 2007. *Critical Power Tools: Technical Communication and Cultural Studies*. Albany: SUNY Press.

Scott, Raymond. 1937. Powerhouse. 78 rpm record. Master Records, Bruns- wick, Columbia. https://en.wikipedia.org/wiki/Powerhouse (instrumental).

Sector Policies and Programs Division Office of Air Quality Planning and Standards. 2010. "Available and Emerging Technologies for Reducing Greenhouse Gas Emissions from Coal-Fired Electric Generating Units." Environmental Protection Agency. www.epa.gov/sites/production/files/2015-12/documents/ electricgeneration.pdf.

Selzer, Jack. 1983. "The Composing Processes of an Engineer." *College Com- position and Communication* 34 (2): 178–87. doi:10.2307/357405.

Semina, O. V., A. G. Konopliannikov, and A. M. Poverennyĭ. 1976. "[Effect of polyinosinic-polycytidylic acid on the colony-forming ability of hematopoietic stem cells in conditions of allogeneic inhibition]." *Biulleten' Eksperimental'noi Biologii I Meditsiny* 81 (4): 450–52.

Shelton, Frederick E. IV, and Jerome R. Morgan. 2016. Robotic Surgical System with Removable Motor Housing. US9271799 B2, filed June 25, 2014, and issued March 1, 2016. www.google.com/patents/US9271799.

Shepard, Mark, ed. 2011. *Sentient City: Ubiquitous Computing, Architecture, and the Future of Urban Space*. New York City: Cambridge: Architectural League of New York; MIT Press.

Shirky, Clay. 2011. *Cognitive Surplus: How Technology Makes Consumers into Collaborators*. Reprint ed. New York: Penguin Books.

Silver, Nate. 2012. *The Signal and the Noise: Why So Many Predictions Fail-But Some Don't*. 1st ed. New York: Penguin Press.

Simmons, Michele W. 2008. *Participation and Power: Civic Discourse in Environmental Policy Decisions*. Albany: State University of New York Press.

Simmons, Michele W., and Jeffrey T. Grabill. 2007. "Toward a Civic Rhetoric for Technologically and Scientifically Complex Places: Invention, Performance, and Participation." *College Composition and Communication* 58 (3): 419–48.

Simmons, Michele W., and Meredith W. Zoetewey. 2012. "Productive Usability: Fostering Civic Engagement and Creating More Useful Online Spaces for Public Deliberation." *Technical Communication Quarterly* 21 (3): 251–76. doi:10.1080/10572252.2012.673953.

Sinha, Kunal. 2014. "Connecting with the Chinese Consumer." In *Luxury Brands in Emerging Markets*, edited by Glyn Atwal and Douglas Bryson, 135–47. Basingstoke: Palgrave Macmillan. http://link.springer.com/chapter/10.1057/9781137330536_13.

Slack, Jennifer Daryl, David James Miller, and Jeffrey Doak. 1993. "The Technical Communicator as Author Meaning, Power, Authority." Journal of Business and Technical Communication 7 (1): 12–36. doi:10.1177/1050651993007001002.

Snavely, Joseph Richard. 1957. *An Intimate Story of Milton S. Hershey*. Hershey, Pennsylvania.

Snow, Charles P. 2012. *The Two Cultures*. Reissue ed. Cambridge; New York: Cambridge University Press.

Snow, Charles Percy. 1959. *The Two Cultures*. London: Cambridge University Press. ISBN 0-521-45730-0.

Snow, Charles P., and Stefan Collini. 2012. *The Two Cultures*. Reissue ed. Cambridge; New York: Cambridge University Press.

Soderbergh, Steven. 2010. *The Informant!* Warner Home Video.

Solnit, Rebecca. 2016. "Easy Chair: The Habits of Highly Cynical People." *Harper's Magazine*, May.

Spash, Clive L. 1999. "The Development of Environmental Thinking in Economics." *Environmental Values* 8 (4): 413–35.

———. 2015. "Bulldozing Biodiversity: The Economics of Offsets and Trading-in Nature." *Biological Conservation* 192 (December): 541–51. doi:10.1016/j.biocon.2015.07.037.

Spinuzzi, Clay. 2003. *Tracing Genres through Organizations*. Cambridge, MA: MIT Press.

———. 2005. "Lost in the Translation: Shifting Claims in the Migration of a Research Technique." *Technical Communication Quarterly* 14 (4): 411–46. doi:10.1207/s15427625tcq1404_3.

———. 2008. *Network: Theorizing Knowledge Work in Telecommunications*. Cambridge; New York: Cambridge University Press.

———. 2015. *All Edge: Inside the New Workplace Networks*. Chicago, IL; London: University of Chicago Press.

St. Amant, Kirk, and Lisa Meloncon. 2016. "Addressing the Incommensurable A Research-Based Perspective for Considering Issues of Power and Legitimacy in the Field." *Journal of Technical Writing and Communication*. doi:10.1177/0047281616639476.

Star, Susan Leigh. 2010. "This Is Not a Boundary Object: Reflections on the Origin of a Concept." *Science, Technology & Human Values* 35 (5): 601–17. doi:10.1177/0162243910377624.

Starosielski, Nicole. 2015. *The Undersea Network*. Sign, Storage, Transmission. Durham, NC: Duke University Press.Subaru of America. 2016. "Subaru of America, INC. Appoints Denise Coogan as Environmental Partnerships Manager."

Sullivan, Patricia, and James E. Porter. 1997. *Opening Spaces: Writing Technologies and Critical Research Practices*. Santa Barbara, CA: Greenwood Publishing.

Sun, Huatong. 2012. *Cross-Cultural Technology Design: Creating Culture-Sensitive Technology for Local Users*. 1st ed. Oxford; New York: Oxford University Press.

Swarts, Jason. 2008. *Together with Technology: Writing Review, Enculturation, and Technological Mediation*. Baywood's Technical Communications Series. Amityville, NY: Baywood Publishing.

Syverson, Margaret A. 1999. *The Wealth of Reality: An Ecology of Composition*. Carbondale: Southern Illinois University Press.

Taleb, Nassim Nicholas. 2014. *Antifragile: Things That Gain from Disorder*. Reprint ed. New York: Random House Trade Paperbacks.

The Hall of Giants. 1947. The Corporation.

Tomlin, Rita C. 2008. "Online FDA Regulations: Implications for Medical Writers." *Technical Communication Quarterly* 17 (3): 289–310. doi:10.1080/10572250802100410.

Turner, Fred. 2006. *From Counterculture to Cyberculture: Stewart Brand, the Whole Earth Network, and the Rise of Digital Utopianism*. 1st ed. Chicago, IL: University of Chicago Press.

Vanderbilt, Tom. 2009. *Traffic: Why We Drive the Way We Do*. 1st reprint ed. New York: Vintage.

Vickers, Jonathan S., and Franck Renand. 2003. "The Marketing of Luxury Goods: An Exploratory Study – Three Conceptual Dimensions." *The Marketing Review* 3 (4): 459–78. doi:10.1362/146934703771910071.

Vitanza, Victor J. 1997. *Negation, Subjectivity, and the History of Rhetoric*. New York: SUNY Press.

Wang, Cheng Lu, and Xiaohua Lin. 2009. "Migration of Chinese Consumption Values: Traditions, Modernization, and Cultural Renaissance." *Journal of Business Ethics* 88 (3): 399–409. doi:10.1007/s10551–009–0308–5.

Ward, David. 1981. *Cities and Immigrants*. 8th printing. A Geography of Change in Nineteenth-Century America. London: Oxford University Press.

Ware, Norman. 1990. *The Industrial Worker, 1840–1860: The Reaction of American Industrial Society to the Advance of the Industrial Revolution*. Chicago, IL: Ivan R. Dee.

Whatley, Christopher A. 1987. *The Scottish Salt Industry, 1570–1850: An Economic and Social History*. 1st ed. Aberdeen: Aberdeen University Press.

Williams, Miriam F. 2010. *From Black Codes to Recodification: Removing the Veil from Regulatory Writing*. Amityville, NY: Baywood Publishing.

Wu, Rui. 2012. "Aspects of Chinese Consumer Behavior in Buying Foreign Branded Products: A Case Study of Dove Chocolate, at CR Vanguard Hypermarkets in Xi'an City, Shaanxi Province, China." *AU-GSB E-JOURNAL* 5 (1). http://its-3.au.edu/open_journal/index.php/AU-GSB/article/view/489.

Yates, JoAnne. 1993. *Control through Communication: The Rise of System in American Management.* Baltimore, MD: Johns Hopkins University Press.

Zingales, Luigi. 2012. *A Capitalism for the People: Recapturing the Lost Genius of American Prosperity.* New York: Basic Books.

Index

For Product Safety Concerns and Information please contact our EU
representative GPSR@taylorandfrancis.com
Taylor & Francis Verlag GmbH, Kaufingerstraße 24, 80331 München, Germany